Reading Mark

A Literary and Theological Commentary
on the Second Gospel

Reading the New Testament Series

Available

Reading Matthew
by David E. Garland

Reading Mark
by Sharyn E. Dowd

Reading John
by Charles H. Talbert

Reading Acts
by Charles H. Talbert

Reading Romans
by Luke Timothy Johnson

Reading Colossians, Ephesians, and 2 Thessalonians
by Bonnie Thurston

Reading 1 Peter, Jude, and 2 Peter
by Earl Richard

Forthcoming

Reading Luke (revised)
by Charles H. Talbert

Reading 1 and 2 Corinthians (revised)
by Charles H. Talbert

Reading Galatians, Philippians, and 1 Thessalonians
by Charles B. Cousar

Reading 1 and 2 Timothy, Titus, and Philemon
by Marion L. Soards

Reading Hebrews and James
by Marie Isaacs

Reading Revelation
by Joseph Trafton

Reading Mark

A Literary and Theological Commentary on the Second Gospel

Sharyn Dowd

SMYTH&HELWYS
PUBLISHING INCORPORATED · MACON. GEORGIA
WWW.HELWYS.COM

Smyth & Helwys Publishing, Inc.
6316 Peake Road
Macon, Georgia 31210-3960
1-800-747-3016
© 2000 by Smyth & Helwys Publishing
All rights reserved.
Printed in the United States of America.

Sharyn E. Dowd

The paper used in this publication meets the minimum
requirements of American National Standard for Information
Sciences—Permanence of Paper for Printed Library Materials.
ANSI Z39.48–1984   (alk. paper)

Library of Congress Cataloging-in-Publication Data

Reading Mark: a literary and theological commentary/Sharyn E. Dowd.
p.   cm. (Reading the New Testament series)
Includes bibliographical references.
1. Bible. N.T. Mark—Commentaries. I. Title. II. Series.
BS2585.3 .D68 2000
222.3'07—dc 21   00-041024

Contents

Editor's Foreword

"Reading the New Testament" is a commentary series that aims to present cutting-edge research in popular form that is accessible to upper-level undergraduates, seminarians, seminary educated pastors, and educated laypersons, as well as to graduate students and professors. The volumes in this series do not follow the word-by-word, phrase-by-phrase, verse-by-verse method of traditional commentaries. Rather, they are concerned to understand large thought units and their relationship to an author's thought as a whole. The focus is on a close reading of the final form of the text. The aim is to make one feel at home in the biblical text itself. The approach of these volumes involves a concern both for how an author communicates and what the religious point of the text is. Care is taken to relate both the how and the what of the text to its milieu: Christian (NT and noncanonical), Jewish (scriptural and postbiblical), and Greco-Roman. This enables both the communication strategies and the religious message of the text to be clarified over against a range of historical and cultural possibilities. Moreover, a section of commentary on a large thought unit will often contain a brief excursus on some topic raised by the material in the unit, sometimes sketching OT, postbiblical Jewish, Greco-Roman, NT, and noncanonical Christian views on the subject. Throughout, the basic concern is to treat the NT texts as religious documents whose religious message needs to be set forth with compelling clarity. All other concerns are subordinated to this. It is the hope of all participants in this project that our efforts at exposition will enable the NT to be understood better and communicated more competently.

—Charles H. Talbert
General Editor

Author's Preface

This volume is the result of a long-standing fascination with the Gospel of Mark that began during my graduate studies at Emory University and was nurtured by ten years of teaching at Lexington Theological Seminary and in congregational and other ecclesial settings. I have learned much from all my students, but two in particular have made specific contributions to insights reflected in this commentary. I am indebted to Betty J. Grimes for a significant influence on my reading of Mark 7:24-30 and to Kristen Plinke Bentley for insights reflected in the commentary on Mark 8:34–9:1. Kristen read the results of our joint effort at the southeastern regional meeting of the Society of Biblical Literature in March, 1996, in a paper titled, "Self-Denial in the Gospel of Mark: A Response to Rita Nakashima Brock."

Appreciation is also due to my colleagues in the New Testament Section of the SBL/SE, who have listened patiently to many of my interpretations of Mark and offered helpful criticism, particularly to Elizabeth Struthers Malbon of Virginia Polytechnic Institute and State University, and to the members of the Rhetoric and the New Testament section of the national SBL, particularly to Vernon Robbins of Emory University. I was directed to valuable sources relevant to the interpretation of Mark 14:3-9 by papers read in a 1992 session of the Rhetoric and the New Testament section by Marianne Sawicki ("Making the Best of Jesus") and Emily Cheney ("Honor and Shame: From Whose Point of View?").

The faculty of Lexington Theological Seminary also offered encouragement and critique, particularly Michael Kinnamon and Jerry Sumney, who read and responded to several sections and caught numerous errors. I am indebted to the Seminary for the sabbatical year 1992–1993 in which the writing of this volume began. The Jesuit School of Theology at Berkeley, California, extended generous hospitality to me for that period, particularly in the person of John R. Donahue, S.J., from whom I have learned more about Mark than even I am aware. My thinking about the Gospel was also enhanced by the invitation of the National Association of Baptist Professors of Religion to write for *The Mercer Commentary on the Bible* (Macon GA: Mercer University Press, 1995).

I owe much to the encouragement and patience of Charles Talbert, editor of this series, as well as to the prayers of the Christian community, specifically the congregations of Greater Faith Baptist Church, Berkeley, California, and of Trinity Baptist Church and St. Agnes House chapel, Lexington, Kentucky. As always, my family has supported me in prayer. My spiritual director, Betty W. Talbert of Truett Theological Seminary, Waco, Texas, has repeatedly prayed me out of the "slough of despond"; without her support this work would not have seen the light of day.

Works Cited

Translations of Primary Sources

In addition to my own translations of passages from the Gospel of Mark and from the Septuagint (LXX), the reader will find abbreviated references to the Revised Standard Version (RSV), the New Revised Standard Version (NRSV), and the Scholars Version (SV), translated by Daryl D. Schmidt and available with the Greek text as *The Gospel of Mark* (Sonoma CA: Polebridge Press, 1990). An occasional translation is taken from W. Bauer, *A Greek-English Lexicon of the New Testament and Other Early Christian Literature*, trans. W. F. Arndt and F. W. Gingrich, 4th ed. (Chicago: University of Chicago Press, 1957), abbreviated BAG.

Translations of passages from the Pseudepigrapha are taken from James Charlesworth, ed., *The Old Testament Pseudepigrapha*, 2 vols. (Garden City NY: Doubleday, 1983, 1985), abbreviated OTP. An occasional quotation from the Mishnah comes from Jacob Neusner, *The Mishnah* (New Haven/ London: Yale University Press, 1988). For the Babylonian Talmud I have used the edition edited by Isidore Epstein and published in London by the Soncino Press, 1948.

Translations from Greek and Latin authors usually come from the Loeb Classical Library edition (LCL) and translations from patristic sources from A. Roberts and J. Donaldson, eds. *The Ante-Nicene Fathers*, 10 vols. (Buffalo /New York: Christian Literature Publishing Company, 1886–1897). I have also used the following: James R. Butts, "The 'Progymnasmata' of Theon: A New Text with Translation and Commentary" (Ph.D. diss., Claremont Graduate School, 1987); Robert Graves, trans. *Lucan: Pharsalia* (Baltimore: Penguin Books, 1957); Lynn R. LiDonnici, *The Epidaurian Miracle Inscriptions: Text, Translation and Commentary* (SBLTT 36; Atlanta: Scholars Press, 1995); Thomas Taylor, trans. *Iamblichus' Life of Pythagoras* (London: A. J. Valpy, 1818); Owsei Temkin, trans., *Soranus' Gynecology* (Baltimore: Johns Hopkins Press, 1956).

Secondary Sources

Note: *ABD* abbreviates David Noel Freedmon et al., eds., *The Anchor Bible Dictionary*, 6 vols. (New York: Doubleday, 1992). Other abbreviations follow the conventions of the *Journal of Biblical Literature*.

Anderson, Janice Capel
    1992   "Feminist Criticism: The Dancing Daughter." In *Mark and Method*, ed. J. C. Anderson and S. D. Moore, 103-134. Minneapolis: Fortress Press.

Baltzer, Klaus
    1975   *Die Biographie Der Propheten*. Neukirchen-Vluyn: Neukirchener Verlag.

Bascom, Robert A.
    1988   "Preparing the Way: Midrash in the Bible." In *Issues in Bible Translation*, ed. P. C. Stine, UBSMS 3. London: UBS.

Basser, H. W.
    1994   "Jesus and the Pharisees." Unpublished paper for Rhetoric and the New Testament Section, Society of Biblical Literature, Chicago.

Beardslee, William A.
    1979   "Saving One's Life by Losing It." *JAAR* 47 (March): 57-72.

Beasley-Murray, G. R.
    1990   "Baptism." In W. E. Mills, et al. eds., *The Mercer Dictionary of the Bible*. Macon GA: Mercer University Press.

Beavis, Mary Ann
    1989   *Mark's Audience*. JSNTSup 33. Sheffield: JSOT.

Becatti, Giovanni
    1967   *The Art of Ancient Greece and Rome*, trans. J. Ross. Englewood Cliffs NJ: Prentice-Hall.

Beker, J. Christiaan
    1982   *Paul's Apocalyptic Gospel*. Philadelphia: Fortress, 1982.

Best, Ernest
    1978   "Mark's Use of the Twelve." *ZNW* 69:11-35.

Boring, M. E., K. Berger, and C. Colpe
    1995   *Hellenistic Commentary to the New Testament*. Nashville: Abingdon Press.

Brock, Rita Nakashima
    1988   *Journeys by Heart*. New York: Crossroad.

Brown, Raymond E.
  1988   "The Burial of Jesus (Mark 15:42-47)." *CBQ* 50 (April): 233-45.
Burridge, R. A.
  1992   *What Are the Gospels? A Comparison with Graeco-Roman Biography.* SNTSMS 70. Cambridge: Cambridge UP.
Camery-Hoggatt, J.
  1992   *Irony in Mark's Gospel.* SNTSMS 72. Cambridge: Cambridge University Press.
Chance, J. Bradley
  1991   "Fiction in Ancient Biography: An Approach to a Sensitive Issue in Gospel Interpretation." *PRS* 18 (Summer): 125-42.
Collins, Adela Yarbro
  1992   *The Beginning of the Gospel: Probings of Mark in Context.* Minneapolis: Fortress.
Conrad, Edgar W.
  1992   *Reading Isaiah.* Minneapolis: Fortress Press.
Cox, Steven L.
  1993   *A History and Critique of Scholarship Concerning the Markan Endings.* Lewiston: Mellen.
Coxon, A. H.
  1970   "Pythagoras" (1). In *The Oxford Classical Dictionary*, ed. N. G. L. Hammond and H. H. Scullard, 903-904. 2d edition. Oxford: Clarendon.
Crossan, J. D.
  1973   *In Parables.* New York: Harper & Row.
Crowder, Stephanie B.
  1997   "Simon of Cyrene: A Case of Roman Conscription." Unpublished paper for Synoptic Gospels Section, Society of Biblical Literature, San Francisco.
Day, John
  1992   "Dragon and Sea, God's Conflict with." *ABD* 2:228-31.
Derrett, J. D. M.
  1974   "Contributions to the Study of the Gerasene Demoniac." *JSNT* 3 (April): 2-17.
Dewey, Joanna
  1980   *Markan Public Debate: Literary Technique, Concentric Structure and Theology in Mark 2:1-3:6.* SBLDS 48. Chico CA: Scholars Press.

1989   "Oral Methods of Structuring Narrative in Mark." *Interp*
              43 (January): 32-44.
1991   "Mark as Interwoven Tapestry: Forecasts and Echoes for a
              Listening Audience." *CBQ* 53 (April): 221-36.
Donahue, John R.
1982   "A Neglected Factor in the Theology of Mark." *JBL* 101
              (December): 563-94.
1988   *The Gospel in Parable*. Philadelphia: Fortress.
1992a   "The Quest for the Community of Mark's Gospel." In *The
              Four Gospels 1992: Festschrift Frans Neirynck*, ed. F. Van
              Segbroeck et al., 817-38. Leuven: Peeters.
1992b   "Tax Collector." *ABD* 6:337-38.
Dowd, Sharyn
1988   *Prayer, Power and the Problem of Suffering: Mark 11:22-25
              in the Context of Markan Theology*. SBLDS 105. Atlanta:
              Scholars Press.
1995   "Reading Mark, Reading Isaiah." *Lexington Theological
              Quarterly* 30 (Fall): 133-43.
Droge, Arthur J.
1983   "Call Stories in Greek Biography and the Gospels." In
              Society of Biblical Literature 1983 Seminar Papers, ed. Kent
              H. Richards, 245-57. Chico CA: Scholars Press.
Fiorenza, Elizabeth Schuessler
1983   *In Memory of Her: A Feminist Theological Reconstruction of
              Christian Origins*. New York: Crossroad.
Fowler, Robert M.
1981   *Loaves and Fishes: The Function of the Feeding Stories in the
              Gospel of Mark*. SBLDS 54. Chico CA: Scholars Press.
1991   *Let the Reader Understand: Reader-Response Criticism and
              the Gospel of Mark*. Minneapolis: Fortress Press.
Freyne, Sean
1992   "Galilee, Sea of." *ABD* 2:899-901.
Funk, R. W., et al.
1988   *The Parables of Jesus: Red Letter Edition. A Report of the Jesus
              Seminar*. Sonoma: Polebridge.
Garland, David
1993   *Reading Matthew*. New York: Crossroad.
Goncalves, Francolino
1992   "Isaiah Scroll, The." *ABD* 3:470-72.

Guelich, Robert A.
1989   *Mark 1-8:26*. WBC 34A. Dallas: Word Books.
Gundry, Robert H.
1993   *Mark: A Commentary on His Apology for the Cross*. Grand Rapids: Eerdmans.
Hadas, Moses
1959   *Hellenistic Culture*. Morningside Heights NY: Columbia UP.
Heinemann, Joseph
1977   *Prayer in the Talmud*. Berlin: de Gruyter.
Hock, Ronald F.
1992   "Chreia." *ABD* 1:912-14.
Hock, R. F. and E. N. O'Neill
1986   *The Chreia in Ancient Rhetoric*. Vol. 1. *The Progymnasmata*. SBLTT 27. Atlanta: Scholars Press.
Juel, Donald H.
1994   *A Master of Surprise: Mark Interpreted*. Minneapolis: Fortress.
Kealy, Sean P.
1982   *Mark's Gospel: A History of Its Interpretation*. New York: Paulist.
Kee, Howard Clark
1977   *Community of the New Age: Studies in Mark's Gospel*. Philadelphia: Westminster Press.
Keener, Craig S.
1991   *. . . And Marries Another: Divorce and Remarriage in the Teaching of the New Testament*.Peabody MA: Hendrickson.
Kelber, Werner H.
1974   *The Kingdom in Mark: A New Place and a New Time*. Philadelphia: Fortress Press.
Keuls, Eva C.
1985   *The Reign of the Phallus: Sexual Politics in Ancient Athens*. New York: Harper and Row.
Lang, F. G.
1976   "Sola Gratia im Markusevangelium: Die Soteriologie des Markus nach 9,14-29 und 10,17-31." In *Rechtfertigung: Festschrift Ernst Kaesemann*, ed. J. Friedrich, W. Poehlmann, and P. Stuhlmacher, 321-37. Tuebingen: Mohr.

Lefkowitz, Mary R. and Maureen B. Fant
   1992   *Women's Life and Greece and Rome: A Source Book in Translation*. 2d ed. Baltimore: Johns Hopkins University Press.
Lewis, T. J.
   1992   "Beelzebul." *ABD* 1:638-40.
Lohmeyer, E.
   1965   *"Our Father": An Introduction to the Lord's Prayer*. Translated by John Bowden. New York: Harper and Row.
Longman, Tremper and D. G. Reid
   1995   *God Is a Warrior*. Grand Rapids: Zondervan.
Mack, Burton L.
   1988   *A Myth of Innocence: Mark and Christian Origins*. Philadelphia: Fortress Press.
   1989a   "Elaboration of the Chreia in the Hellenistic School." In *Patterns of Persuasion in the Gospels*, by B. L. Mack and V. K. Robbins, 31-67. Sonoma CA: Polebridge Press.
   1989b   "Teaching in Parables: Elaboration in Mark 4:1-34." In *Patterns of Persuasion in the Gospels*, by B. L. Mack and V. K. Robbins, 143-60. Sonoma, CA Polebridge Press.
   1990   *Rhetoric in the New Testament*. Minneapolis: Fortress Press.
Magness, J. Lee
   1986   *Sense and Absence*. Semeia Studies. Atlanta: Scholars.
Malbon, Elizabeth Struthers
   1984   "The Jesus of Mark and the Sea of Galilee." *JBL* 103 (September): 363-77.
   1986a   "Disciples/Crowds/Whoever: Markan Characters and Readers." *NovT* 28 (April): 104-130.
   1986b   *Narrative Space and Mythic Meaning in Mark*. San Francisco: Harper and Row.
   1991   "The Poor Widow in Mark and Her Poor Rich Readers." *CBQ* 53 (October): 589-604.
   1992   "Narrative Criticism: How Does the Story Mean?" In *Mark and Method: New Approaches in Biblical Studies*, ed. J. C. Anderson and S. D. Moore, 23-49. Minneapolis: Fortress, 1992.
   1993   "Echoes and Foreshadowings in Mark 4-8: Reading and Rereading." *JBL* 112 (Summer): 211-30.

Marcus, Joel
  1986   *The Mystery of the Kingdom of God*. SBLDS 90. Atlanta: Scholars.
  1992a   "The Jewish War and the *Sitz im Leben* of Mark." *JBL* 111 (Fall): 441-62
  1992b   *The Way of the Lord: Christological Exegesis of the Old Testament in the Gospel of Mark*. Louisville: W/JKP.
Marlatt, Earl
  1995   " 'Are Ye Able' Said the Master." In *Chalice Hymnal*, ed. S. L. Adams, et al., 621. St. Louis: Chalice Press.
Marshall, C. D.
  1989   *Faith as a Theme in Mark's Narrative*. SNTSMS 64. Cambridge: Cambridge UP.
Matera, F. J.
  1993   " 'He Saved Others, He Cannot Save Himself': A Literary-Critical Perspective on the Markan Miracles." *Interp* 47 (January): 14-26.
Metzger, B. M.
  1994   *A Textual Commentary on the Greek New Testament*. 2d ed. Stuttgart: Deutsche Bibelgesellschaft.
Meye, R. P.
  1968   *Jesus and the Twelve*. Grand Rapids: Eerdmans.
Meyer, M. W., ed.
  1987   *The Ancient Mysteries: A Sourcebook*. New York: HarperCollins.
Muddiman, John
  1992   "Fast, Fasting." *ABD* 2:773-76.
Myers, Ched
  1988   *Binding the Strong Man: A Political Reading of Mark's Story of Jesus*. Maryknoll: Orbis.
Parker, Robert
  1983   *Miasma: Pollution and Purification in Early Greek Religion*. Oxford: Clarendon.
Patten, Priscilla
  1983   "The Form and Function of Parable in Select Apocalyptic Literature and Their Significance for Parables in the Gospel of Mark." *NTS* 29: 246-58.
Payne, Humphrey
  1931   *Neocorinthia: A Study of Corinthian Art in the Archaic Period*. Oxford: Clarendon.

Pettazzoni, Raffaele
    1937   "Confession of Sins and the Classics." *HTR* 30 (January): 1-14.

Pomeroy, Sarah B.
    1975   *Goddesses, Whores, Wives, and Slaves: Women in Classical Antiquity.* New York: Schocken Books.

Reiser, Marius
    1984   "Der Alexanderroman und das Markusevangelium." In *Marcus-Philologie*, ed. H. Cancik, 131-63. Tuebingen: Mohr (Siebeck).

Robbins, V. K.
    1987   "The Woman Who Touched Jesus' Garment: Socio-Rhetorical Analysis of the Synoptic Accounts." *NTS* 33: 502-515.

    1989a   *Plucking Grain on the Sabbath. In Patterns of Persuasion in the Gospels*, by B. L. Mack and V. K. Robbins, 107-141. Sonoma: Polebridge.

    1989b   "Rhetorical Composition and the Beelzebul Controversy." In *Patterns of Persuasion in the Gospels*, by B. L. Mack and V. K. Robbins, 161-93.Sonoma: Polebridge.

    1992a   *Jesus the Teacher: A Socio-Rhetorical Interpretation of Mark. With a New Introduction.* Minneapolis: Fortress.

    1992b   "The Reversed Contextualization of Psalm 22 in the Markan Crucifixion: A Socio-Rhetorical Analysis." In *The Four Gospels 1992: Festschrift Frans Neirynck*, ed. F. Van Segbroeck et al., 1161-83. Leuven: Peeters.

    1994   "Jewish and Greco-Roman Modes of Argumentation in Mark 7:1-23." Unpublished paper for Rhetoric and the New Testament Section, Society of Biblical Literature, Chicago.

Rousseau, J. J and R. Arav
    1995   *Jesus and His World: An Archaeological and Cultural Dictionary.* Minneapolis: Fortress.

Schmidt, T. E.
    1995   "Mark 15.16-32: The Crucifixion Narrative and the Roman Triumphal Procession." *NTS* 41: 1-18.

Seeley, David
    1993   "Rulership and Service in Mark 10:41-45." *NovT* 35 (July): 234-50.

Selvidge, Marla J.
  1990   *Woman, Cult, and Miracle Recital.* Lewisburg: Bucknell UP.
Smith, Morton
  1978   *Jesus the Magician.* New York: Harper and Row.
Stock, Augustine
  1985   "Hinge Transitions in Mark's Gospel." *BTB* 15 (January):
              27-31.
  1989   *The Method and Message of Mark.* Wilmington: Michael
              Glazier.
Sundberg, A. C.
  1959   "On Testimonies." *NovT* 3: 268-81.
Swetnam, James
  1984   "On the Identity of Jesus." *Bib* 65: 412-16.
Talbert, C. H.
  1977   *What Is a Gospel?: The Genre of the Canonical Gospels.*
              Philadelphia: Fortress.
  1982   *Reading Luke.* New York: Crossroad.
  1992   *Reading John.* New York: Crossroad.
Tannehill, R. C.
  1977   "The Disciples in Mark: The Function of a Narrative
              Role." *JR* 57 (October): 386-405.
  1979   "The Gospel of Mark as Narrative Christology." *Semeia* 16:
              57-95.
  1980   "Tension in Synoptic Sayings and Stories." *Interp* 34
              (April): 138-150.
Tarn, W. W.
  1961   *Hellenistic Civilization.* 3d ed. Cleveland/New York: World.
Theissen, Gerd
  1983   *The Miracle Stories of the Early Christian Tradition.* Trans.
              Francis McDonagh. Ed. John Riches. Philadelphia:
              Fortress.
Tolbert, Mary Ann
  1979   *Perspectives on the Parables.* Philadelphia: Fortress.
  1989   *Sowing the Gospel: Mark's World in Literary-Historical
              Perspective.* Minneapolis: Fortress.
Ulansey, David
  1991   "The Heavenly Veil Torn: Mark's Cosmic Inclusio." *JBL*
              110 (Spring): 123-25.
Vancil, J. W.
  1992   "Sheep, Shepherd." *ABD* 5:1187-90.

van Iersel, Bas
    1988   *Reading Mark*. Translated by W. H. Bisscheroux. Collegeville: Liturgical Press.

Vermaseren, M. J.
    1963   *Mithras, The Secret God*. Translated by T. and V. Megaw. New York: Barnes and Noble.

Via, Dan O.
    1985   *The Ethics of Mark's Gospel: In the Middle of Time*. Philadelphia: Fortress.

Waetjen, H. C.
    1989   *A Reordering of Power: A Sociopolitical Reading of Mark's Gospel*. Minneapolis: Fortress.

alzer, R.
    1949   *Galen on Jews and Christians*. London: Oxford UP.

Wiedemann, Thomas
    1989   *Adults and Children in the Roman Empire*. New Haven: Yale UP.

Wilkins, Michael J.
    1992   "Barabbas." *ABD* 1:607.

Wright, D. P. and H. Huebner
    1992   "Unclean and Clean." *ABD* 6:729-45.

Wright, D.P. and R. N. Jones
    1992   "Leprosy." *ABD* 4:277-82.

Wright, A. G.
    1982   "The Widow's Mites: Praise or Lament?—A Matter of Context." *CBQ* 44 (April):256-65.

Wuellner, Wilhelm
    1967   *The Meaning of "Fishers of Men."* Philadelphia: Westminster.

Introduction

The Gospel of Mark stands second in the New Testament canon, though it is widely regarded as the first of the four canonical Gospels to have been written. The title, "The Gospel According to Mark," did not come from the hand of the author, but was added to a manuscript copy dated no earlier than the end of the first century CE and perhaps as late as the second. Thus, the name and gender of the author, the date and place of composition, and the identity of the intended audience are all unknown, and therefore can provide no assistance with the interpretation of the text. Such introductory questions are much debated by scholars; the best recent summary is John R. Donahue, "The Quest for the Community of Mark's Gospel," (1992a), which should be supplemented by Joel Marcus, "The Jewish War and the *Sitz im Leben* of Mark," (1992a).

The neo–orthodox consensus that "Gospel" was a completely new genre invented by the author of Mark has been abandoned by most scholars, but no new consensus has arisen to take its place. It is likely that an ancient reader encountering this text for the first time would have regarded it as a "life," or biography of Jesus of Nazareth (Talbert 1977, Burridge 1992). This does not mean that "the work has significance primarily for the ethics and piety of the individual" (Collins 1992, 2). On the contrary, ancient biographies of founders of religious and philosophical communities were documents of formation for those communities (see, e.g., Robbins 1992a 126-28, 167). Since the author of Mark understands Jesus as the catalyst for the inbreaking of the reign of God in history, this biography looks backward to the past of God's relationship with Israel and forward to the final consummation of all human history when the Son of Man will come as liberator and judge. Thus, though the Gospel has a concern for "history in an eschatological or apocalyptic sense" (Collins 1992, 37), its subject is Jesus—who he was and how he inaugurated God's reign in history.

But Mark is not the literature of the cultured elite like much history and biography in Greco-Roman antiquity. Its style is popular and novelistic (Tolbert 1989, 59-78), characterized by episodic narration, a journey motif, parataxis, asyndeton, the use of the historical present, pleonasm, repetition, and frequent use of direct discourse and dramatic dialogue (Reiser 1984). In fact, the distinction between biography and novel was not nearly as clear in antiquity as it is today (Chance 1991, 141). Many of these characteristics also suggest that the Gospel was written to be read aloud to a listening audience rather than to be read privately by one person (Dewey 1989). An early Christian congregation made up of gentiles and Jews would have been both entertained and instructed by hearing the Gospel read aloud.

This strongly oral approach to the composition of Mark makes it difficult to outline for today's individual silent reader, and for that reason, scholars have been unable to agree on an outline for the Gospel. The Gospel does not consist of discrete sections connected end to end, but of threads woven into a narrative "tapestry"—of themes and motifs that resound and "echo" again and again, of "foreshadowings" and flashbacks that keep the audience on track as to where the story has been and where it is going (Dewey 1991; Malbon 1993). These characteristics account for the unusual character of the outline developed for this commentary. The reader will notice that the sections in the outline overlap; for example, the prologue consists of 1:1-15, but the first section of Jesus' ministry in Galilee and gentile territory begins at 1:14. There are many sections of Mark that appear in more than one place in the outline and therefore receive treatment twice in the commentary. These are "hinge transitions" characteristic of compositions that are meant to be read aloud and heard by an audience (Stock 1985).

Although the exact identity of the intended audience of Mark is unknown, the text itself gives some clues. First and most obviously, since the Gospel was composed in Greek, the entire audience must have understood spoken Greek. Not only did they understand Greek, but also they were familiar enough with Hellenistic modes of argumentation to find persuasive the various kinds of rhetorical devices that the author of Mark employs. Part of the audience understood no Aramaic, one of the languages spoken in Palestine during the time of Jesus; we know this because the semitic words and phrases in the Gospel are immediately translated into Greek for the benefit of the listeners (3:17; 5:41; 10:46; 14:36).

The audience cannot have been made up entirely of Jews, because some Jewish practices require explanation (7:3-4, 11). On the other hand, the author of Mark expected that the listeners were already familiar with the basics of Jesus' story; he simply informs them in 15:1 that the council handed Jesus over to Pilate and goes right on with the story, never having to explain what position Pilate held or why he was the primary Roman authority in Jerusalem. This is a formation narrative for a Christian community, not an evangelistic tract for people who have never heard of Jesus.

Not only are the members of the Markan audience familiar with Jesus' story, at least some of them are also familiar with the Scriptures of Judaism, though in their Greek translation, the Septuagint (LXX). The Gospel is full of allusions to the story of Israel in the wilderness and echoes of the Psalms and other Old Testament writings. In fact, the author of Mark has interpreted the story of Jesus through the theology of the materials collectively known as "the prophet Isaiah" (1:2).

Until recently the tendency in Markan studies has been to agree with A. C. Sundberg's pronouncement that "Daniel is the most important book to Mark" (Sundberg 1959, 274). It is, of course, the case that Daniel figures prominently in the Markan apocalypse and is the source of the mysterious "abomination of desolation," about which the hapless reader is exhorted to "understand" (13:14). But although the Markan outlook is thoroughly apocalyptic, Daniel is actually quoted only twice in Mark 13 and only once elsewhere in the Gospel. That one instance (in 14:62) repeats a prediction from 13:26 to the effect that the Son of Man will come in (or with) the clouds. A number of the Markan phrases for which the marginal notes in Nestle-Aland[26] suggest a reference to Daniel are merely the common stock of apocalyptic imagery and do not require dependence on the text of Daniel.

Mary Ann Beavis has called attention to the fact that "Isaiah is the only prophet named in Mark (1.1; 7.6) . . . and the prophet quoted most often in Mark . . ." (Beavis 1989, 110). In fact, the evangelist quotes Isaiah more often than any other biblical document. As indicated below, Isaiah is quoted directly eight times in Mark:

Mark 1:2-3	Isa 40:3
Mark 4:12	Isa 6:9-10
Mark 7:6-7	Isa 29:13
Mark 9:48	Isa 66:24
Mark 11:17	Isa 56:7
Mark 12:32	Isa 45:21
Mark 13:24	Isa 13:10
Mark 13:25	Isa 34:4

Isaiah is quoted directly in the Markan apocalypse as often as Daniel is— twice. When the investigation is widened to include not only direct quotations, but also allusions and motives, the impression is strengthened that from the evangelist's point of view, the good news began "just as it was written in Isaiah the prophet" (1:2a). In fact, Joel Marcus used the phrase, "The Gospel According to Isaiah," as the title of his treatment of Mark 1:2-3 (Marcus 1992b, 12-47). The influence of Isaiah on the structure and theology of the Gospel has been further demonstrated by Rikki Watts, whose Isaiah's *New Exodus and Mark* (WUNT 2/88; Tuebingen: Mohr Siebeck, 1997) came into my hands too late to be taken into account by this commentary.

It is likely that the author of Mark read Isaiah as a literary and theological unity, rather than dividing it into two or three compositions from different periods as scholars do today. The evidence of 1QIsa establishes that the book of Isaiah was in its present form by the late second century BC, long before Mark was written (Goncalves 1992, 471). It is also likely that the author of Mark read Isaiah in Greek and anticipated that his audience's knowledge of Isaiah was based primarily on a Greek translation.

Although there is no consensus on the question of the language or languages in which the author of Mark read Isaiah, two claims can be made with some confidence. First, since he wrote Greek, he also read Greek. We can thus be certain of his ability to use the LXX. In fact, studies have shown almost certain dependence on the LXX at some points. We cannot have a similar level of certainty about his ability to read Hebrew or Aramaic despite occasional similarities between the wording of his quotations and the MT or the Targumim. Second, the departures from the LXX in Markan quotations of scripture can be accounted for without positing the evangelist's knowledge of Hebrew or Aramaic texts of Isaiah. Since the translators of the LXX, 1QIsa, and the Targumim felt free to make alterations in the wording of the text for theological reasons, it is likely that the author of Mark would have had few compunctions about making his own alterations. In fact, we have hard evidence of Markan alteration of scripture in the treatment of Zech 13:7 in Mark 14:27b.

Edgar Conrad (1992) has argued that the present form of Isaiah is addressed to a community of survivors who experience themselves as a minority among the exiled Jews. It feels threatened by corrupt leaders, who are blamed for the suffering of the "servant" (themselves as the faithful minority). The present situation of the audience is reflected in chapters 1–5 and 40–66, which form the context for the rereading of the vision of Isaiah, chapters 6–39. This vision is a word out of the past in which a future was predicted. Part of that future is now the community's present, but part is still unfulfilled. "The implied present community hears about its own future in the past vision of Isaiah. Hearing about the future helps the community to make sense of its present" (Conrad 1992, 158).

The pattern of promise and fulfillment in Isaiah is as follows: Judah is threatened by the Syro-Ephraimite alliance (7:1-2). Ahaz is promised deliverance (7:3-9). Ahaz is warned about a future threat from Assyria (7:10-25). The deliverance from Syria and Israel is not narrated, but taken for granted. Judah is then told not to fear the Assyrians (10:24-27). Judah is threatened by Assyria (36:1–37:20). Hezekiah, whose birth was predicted in 7:14 and celebrated in 9:2-7, is promised deliverance (37:5-7, 21-35). Judah is delivered from the threat of Assyria (37:36-38). Hezekiah is warned about a future threat from Babylon (39:5-8). About the defeat of Judah by Babylon the audience needs no narration; they are all too aware of the reason for their present plight.

But Isaiah has good news for the exiles. They are told not to fear, and promised deliverance from Babylon (41:8-13, 14-16; 43:1-4, 5-6; 44:1-5). They are also promised eschatological salvation: a time of peace, abundance and wholeness and the conversion of the gentile nations to the one true God of Israel (2:1-4, 24-27, 35; 49:6, 60-61). These things are promised, but not fulfilled within the book itself. The audience is still waiting for those promises to be fulfilled, but they can have confidence that God will do what God has promised, because of the pattern of the past. "Just as the Hezekiah narrative mirrors the same sequence of motifs as the Ahaz narrative, so the narrative still to be determined will mirror a similar sequence of motifs" (Conrad 1991, 51).

By the time Mark was written, Isaiah's promise of a new exodus from bondage in Babylon and a return to the land of promise had been fulfilled. But new oppressors have come and gone in the land and in Mark's present Rome appears to be the new Babylon, ruling over the entire world. Just as the exiles were invited to read the prophecies of Isaiah to see God's faithfulness in the past and God's promise for the future, the audience of Mark is invited to see how the past of Jesus of Nazareth fits into God's plan and begins the fulfillment of the final promises of eschatological deliverance, not only from temporal powers but also from the spiritual forces that stand behind those powers—Satan and the demons.

The author of Mark writes a story about Jesus ("he will save") who, like Isaiah ("Yahweh gives salvation"), was not understood at the time he brought his message. Like Isaiah, he identifies with the sin of his people. Like Isaiah's, his message results not in understanding and repentance, but in blindness, deafness, and hardness of heart. But his actions restoring sight to the blind and hearing to the deaf recall Isaiah's promised eschatological deliverance—

the part of Isaiah that was not fulfilled even by the return from exile. Jesus announces the nearness of the reign of God, performs the restorative miracles Isaiah associated with the eschatological age, and then dies, like the suffering servant, at the hands of corrupt religious and civic leaders, after replacing their program of purity and exclusivism with a program of inclusivism and forgiveness.

Before he dies, the Markan Jesus promises the restoration of the faithless disciples in the immediate future and warns about the persecutions that will precede the coming of the Son of Man in glory to usher in the eschatological age, when he will again drink wine at the banquet, as Isaiah had promised. The story ends with the report of the resurrection and the report that Jesus has gone ahead of the disciples to Galilee, where they will see him, as he promised. The meeting is not narrated. The audience, knowing that the meeting did in fact take place and that the preaching of the gospel to the gentiles has begun (13:10), is confident of the final fulfillment of the promise of eschatological salvation. The story is still open-ended, but another chapter has been written. Like Isaiah's audience, the Markan audience is called to faithfulness and transformation as they wait for God's final promises to be fulfilled.

Since those final promises involve the destruction of all that stands in opposition to God's reign and the restoration of creation and human community to God's original ideal, Mark's popular biography of Jesus is set within an apocalyptic worldview that makes it unlike any other Greco-Roman biography. Its apocalyptic outlook and its portrayal of Jesus as the human embodiment of the Divine Warrior raise obstacles for some of today's readers who find apocalypticism appalling.

Ever since the nineteenth century, interpreters of the Gospels have been attempting to rescue Jesus from this embarrassingly premodern and violent perspective. Recently, Burton Mack has advanced the thesis that Jesus himself was a wandering Cynic philosopher who taught no apocalyptic ideas. Rather, it was the Markan community, frustrated by its failure to reform the synagogue along Christian lines, that created the fiction that Jesus died as an innocent sufferer at the behest of the Jewish leaders and projected an apocalyptic scenario in which all their enemies would be destroyed and they would come out on top. This, Mack argues, has become the controlling worldview of Christian trimphalism, so that the author of the Gospel of Mark is ultimately responsible for the paranoia of Reagan's "Star Wars" program. Such a worldview should never have been canonized, according to Mack (1988).

This commentary is an interpretation of the text of Mark and therefore will not participate in the discussion about the "authentic" teachings of the "historical" Jesus. It is appropriate at this point, however, to engage the issue of the theological appropriation of the apocalyptic worldview, since the one thing about which Mack is correct is the observation that the Gospel assumes an apocalyptic interpretation of history and of the ministry of Jesus.

What can be made of this notion that the world will end, not with a bang or a whimper, but (so Mark claims) exactly as it began: with an act of God? Is this a form of cosmic paranoia that needs to be rejected in the name of more central gospel values? Is apocalyptic the husk to be peeled away from the kernel of Jesus' ethical teachings—an outmoded mythology to be translated into an existential stance toward being, self, and others?

The following observations are indebted to the work of J. Christiaan Beker (1982). Although Beker's work deals with the positive appropriation of Paul's apocalyptic, his major emphases are applicable to any Christian text with an apocalyptic worldview.

• Apocalyptic Christianity regards the triumph of God's reign and God's will as a certainty in which the church participates with joy and anticipation. Nonapocalyptic Christianity turns God's reign into an assignment to be carried out against impossible odds with inadequate resources.

• Therefore, apocalyptic Christianity has the character of celebration and freedom, whereas nonapocalyptic Christianity has the character of moralizing bondage.

• Apocalyptic Christianity "compels ethical seriousness" (110) because the apocalyptic community believes that Christ will require an accounting of their faithfulness "in establishing signs and beachheads" of God's coming reign. Nonapocalyptic Christianity, having abandoned all notion of ultimate sanctions, is left with no power to compel ethical seriousness except to the extent that the unhealthy can be manipulated by sentimentality, blaming, and shaming.

• Because apocalyptic Christianity expects the final triumph of the will of God the Creator, it provides the church with a sense of solidarity with all people and with all of creation. Beker writes, "In the light of God's coming glory and vindication all the creatures of God's world are our neighbors because we share with them not only the suffering of the power of death in this world but also the hope in our communal salvation (109)." Nonapocalyptic Christianity becomes either spiritualized individualism or secular politics with a thin theological veneer.

This telling of the story of Jesus through the lenses Isaiah provides was meant to create in its original audience a confidence that, despite all appearances to the contrary, God's reign of wholeness and freedom has already begun to impinge upon the present and will soon break through in fullness. Meanwhile, the extraordinary community created by the resurrection of Jesus lives out the implications of the eschatological age in its conflicted present and waits with joyful certainty for the promise that is sure to come.

Note to Reader

No one can know what is in the mind of another human being, much less one long dead. Nevertheless, the reader will find many comments about what "the author of Mark" or "the Gospel writer" or "the evangelist" meant or thought or wanted his audience to do. Such statements are shorthand for, "the author implied by this text seems to" mean or think or want this or that. Similar statements about the audience of the Gospel are not based on any preconception about who, where, or when the historical audience was, but on observations about the audience that seems to be implied by the text. That this is my reading of Mark, and not some purely objective interpretation made from a nonexistent neutral vantage point, is a fact for which I make no apology. I try to reserve the word "Mark" for the text itself, rather than for the unknown author.

Translations of Mark within the commentary are my own unless otherwise specified. The sources of other translations of primary texts are specified in the parenthetical notes and bibliography.

The commentary is not intended as a substitute for the Gospel of Mark. Therefore, it is deliberately written in such a way that it will make little sense unless the reader has an open Bible beside the commentary.

Prologue
The Good News Begins

(Mark 1:1-13)

The first literary unit in the life of Jesus is held together by an inclusion in 1:1-3 and 1:14-15: the word "good news" (*euangelion*)followed by an ambiguous genitive (good news of/about Jesus Christ, 1:1; good news of/about God, 1:14). The evangelist explicitly connects the beginning of the good news about Jesus Christ with the Scriptures as he knows them in the LXX; for him, the good news about Jesus begins with the prophecy of Isaiah. And in fact, the summary of Jesus' proclamation of good news in 1:14-15 is derived from the theology of Isaiah, as will be shown below.

Within this framework there are three smaller units, each of which emphasizes the activity of the Spirit in connection with the ministry of Jesus: 1:4-8 (the "stronger one" will baptize with the Holy Spirit, 1:8); 1:9-11 (the Spirit comes upon/into Jesus at his baptism, 1:10); and 1:12-13 (the Spirit drives Jesus out into the wilderness, 1:12).

The framework and the three inner sections are knit together by repeated words and phrases: "messenger(s)"—1:2, 13; "in the wilderness"— 1:3, 4, 12; "baptize/baptizer/baptism"—1:4, 5, 8, 9; "Jordan"—1:5, 9; "son"—1:1, 11; "proclaim"—1:7, 14; "repentance/repent"—1:4, 15.

The heavy reliance of this narrative on the interpretation of Scripture is introduced right away by the unusual construction with *kathōs* in the first (verbless) sentence. The beginning of the good news happened just as it stands written in the prophet Isaiah (construing the grammar with Guelich 1989, 6-12, and Marcus 1992b, 17-18). Here is no Marcionite chasm between the good news and the "old" news. Rather, this story will unfold as an interpretation of the gospel according to Isaiah: the one God who reigns over all the nations has anointed a warrior-king to lead God's captive people, both Jews and gentiles, out of bondage into freedom.

Many explanations have been offered for the fact that Mark attributes to Isaiah a quotation that is in fact a combination of Exodus 23:20, Malachi 3:1, and Isaiah 40:3. The early church leader Jerome complained in a sermon, "O Apostle Peter, your son Mark, son in the Spirit, not in the flesh, expert in spiritual matters, has made a mistake here." (Translated in Kealy 1982, 12; see Bascom 1988, 231-32). The appeal to Isaiah as the scriptural authority for the interpretation of the good news of Jesus Christ is important, however, because it prepares those members of the audience who would have been familiar with the Septuagint for the allusions to the motifs of light, blindness, sight, deafness, hearing, and alienation of heart that pervade both the book of Isaiah and the Gospel of Mark. The voice cries out, but many who have ears fail to hear. (On the textual problem in 1:1 and the background of *euangelion*, "good news," see Guelich's discussion).

The first and longest of the three sub-units in the introduction, 1:4-8, introduces John as the promised Elijah-figure who prepares for the coming of the Lord. It is apparent that this document is intended for people who already know the basic elements of the story. They do not have to be told who John is or what baptism is and apparently would have had no trouble imagining how someone could set up a baptizing ministry in a desert; the Jordan river is not mentioned until 1:5.

The portrayal of John is based on the model of the prophet Elijah. The description of his clothing is taken almost word-for-word from the Septuagint translation of 2 Kings 1:8, where Elijah is recognized by his clothing. John is portrayed as the promised Elijah, who was identified in Malachi 4:5 as the "messenger" of Malachi 3:1—the one who would be sent to prepare the way for God's coming in judgment. The setting of John's ministry in the desert also conforms to the Septuagint of the Isaiah quotation, where the wilderness is understood as the location of the crying voice: "A voice cries in the wilderness, 'Prepare the way of the Lord . . .' " The Hebrew original reads, "A voice cries, 'In the wilderness prepare the way of the Lord . . .' "

John's mission seems to be succeeding; in Mark "all the Jerusalemites" and everyone in the entire region were flocking to him, being baptized in the Jordan River, and confessing their sins. However, like Elijah's temporary victory over the prophets of Baal on Mount Carmel, John's success will be only temporary; before the story is over, his headless body will be buried by his followers (6:29), and the Jerusalem crowd will be howling for Jesus' death (15:12-14). It may be significant that although John proclaimed "a baptism of reversal of mindset (*metanoia*) for the forgiveness of sins" (1:4), Mark does not say that the people adopted a new mindset. He says only that they "were baptized, confessing their sins" (1:5). Their baptism and confession do not effect their death to human ways of thinking and acting (8:33); the baptism with which Jesus is baptized is a costlier matter, as he will warn James and John (10:38-39) (Waetjen 1989, 68).

In fact, the Markan account of John's preaching makes it clear that no mere confessing and washing ritual will be effective. Rather, John prepares the way for some one more powerful than he who will administer the transforming baptism in the Holy Spirit. It is this baptism, promised but not narrated in the story itself, that will go beyond confessions and good intentions to produce real *metanoia*, selfless service (9:35; 10:43-44), and fearless witness (13:11).

In the second sub-unit, 1:9-11, the one who is to baptize in the Spirit is first baptized in the Spirit himself. Jesus comes from "Nazareth of Galilee," a very prosaic origin after the extravagant claims made for the "coming one" in John's preaching. Like the rest of the crowd, Jesus is baptized by John in the Jordan. It does not occur to Mark, as it does to Matthew, that the parallel with the other baptisms requires the explanation that Jesus had no sins to confess. This is important, because the Markan portrait places Jesus firmly within the tradition of the prophet who identifies with the sin of the people even as he accepts his call to the prophetic vocation (Isa 6:5). In addition, Jesus' baptism prefigures his passion: "He was counted among the lawless" (LXX Isa 53:12).

The author of Mark uses the baptism tradition as the basis for the legitimation of Jesus' role as prophet, son, and servant. In the "lives of the prophets" embedded in the biblical tradition, the installation scene is an important component (Baltzer 1975, 185). This is the scene in which the prophet experiences God's commissioning for the prophetic task. The baptism in Mark is such a scene, and again the influence of Isaiah is heavy: God's spirit "rests upon" or is "put upon" the prophet (61:1), the servant (42:1), and the ideal Davidic ruler (11:1-3). It is a spirit of strength (*ischuos*, 11:2; cf. Mark 1:7) and is interpreted as an anointing (*echrisen me*,) 61:1; cf. Mark 1:1, Jesus Christ [anointed one]). In Mark, Jesus sees the heavens ripped apart and the spirit, like a dove, descending both upon and into him (1:10). Even those members of the audience who would not have been familiar enough with the LXX to recognize the biblical allusions would nevertheless have understood the sign of divine approval. Any ancient Mediterranean hearer would have known that the appearance of a dove at the legitimation scene in a biography could be taken as an omen of divine blessing (Talbert 1982, 40).

What Jesus sees is then reinforced by what Jesus hears. The voice from heaven speaks only twice in Mark: here and at the transfiguration scene. The heavenly voice quotes a combination of Psalm 2:7 ("You are my son"— God's word to the Davidic ruler) and Isaiah 42:1b ("my chosen, in whom my soul delights"). But there is another, more disturbing element. Neither the Psalm nor the Isaiah passage contains the word "beloved," which appears in Mark. The "beloved son" betrays the influence of Genesis 22:2, an ominous note, given the fact that Abraham's "beloved son" barely escaped death. For Jesus, there will be no last-minute substitution, no ram in the thicket (Swetnam 1984, 412-16).

Members of the audience familiar with the biblical traditions would have recognized these allusions and would surely have taken note of the fact that not only the narrator, but also even the voice from heaven is quoting scripture. There can be no doubt of the continuity between the good news and the old, old story, if even God does not have original lines.

It is important to notice, however, that the heavenly voice speaks only to Jesus, not to the crowd (as in Matthew) and not to John (as in the Fourth Gospel), which means that only Jesus and the audience know about his commission from God. The characters within the story itself will discuss and misconstrue Jesus' identity and mission throughout the entire Gospel, but the audience, informed by the omniscient narrator, always knows more than any character except Jesus. Within the story any onlookers to Jesus' baptism would have seen and heard nothing except one more small-town tourist from up country joining in the frenzy of baptism and confession along with the Jerusalem crowds.

Already the evangelist is reserving the right to define what it means for Jesus to be the anointed son of God. So far the definition embraces royalty and back-country anonymity, endowment with God's spirit and a life in jeopardy like Isaac's. These are the kinds of tensions from which the evangelist will weave this story.

The third and shortest sub-unit of this section, 1:12-13, introduces the conflict that will drive the plot: the cosmic conflict between Jesus—God's agent—and Satan—leader of the resistance to God's reign. The first act of the Spirit after entering the Markan Jesus is to drive him out into the desert. Since he was already in the desert, because that was where John was baptizing (1:4), the repeated reference to *erēmos* cannot be a change of scene, but must have symbolic significance. Indeed this is the case; for Jesus, as for Israel after the exodus, the desert is the place of testing (*peirazomenos*).

The content of the testing is not specified, but the agent is indicated. Satan is introduced here briefly; later, Satan is identified with Beelzebul, the chief of the demons, whose dominion opposes God's and with whose minions Jesus does battle in the exorcisms (3:22-27). The author of Mark does not at this point reveal the outcome of Jesus' testing experience; it is not until the exorcisms begin that a first-time hearer is assured that Jesus has defeated his opponent. However, the presence of the angels recalls God's provident care for Elijah in similar circumstances, when, as in this story, the food provided strength enough for forty days (2 Kgs 19:4-8).

The notice that Jesus remains unharmed in the presence of "wild animals" signals to the audience that he stands under the special protection of deity. Like Romulus and Remus, he has nothing to fear from animals that are the nemesis of ordinary human beings. In ancient thought, criminals who escaped human justice would be punished by natural forces; conversely, those who went unharmed by dangerous animals were clearly the recipients of divine favor and were usually thought of as unusually wise or virtuous. Thus, Romulus, the founder of Rome, is nurtured by a wolf and the philosopher Pythagoras tames a wild beast (a story later told about St. Francis of Assisi).

In the Israelite wisdom traditions it was the righteous sage who was protected against wild animals; in Psalm 91:11-13 God assigns angels to guard the righteous, who will be able to trample unharmed on lions and poisonous snakes. In the eschatological age, according to Isaiah, all humanity will be at peace with the animals (11:6-9). This will happen when "a shoot shall come out from the stump of Jesse" upon whom "the spirit of the Lord shall rest (11:1-2). Anyone in the Markan audience would know that Jesus was under unusual divine protection; after the quotation from Psalm 2:7 at the baptism and the allusion in the temptation scene to the Spirit-anointed Davidic ruler who ushers in peace and reconciliation with the animal world, some hearers would expect an announcement that the long-awaited reign of God was about to begin. They would not be disappointed.

The imminent inbreaking of God's reign is just what the Markan Jesus announces in the programmatic summary of his preaching that closes the frame on this introductory section of the narrative. Jesus, having come from Galilee in 1:9, returns to Galilee in 1:14 with a message much like Isaiah's message to the exiles in Babylon: God's timing has come full circle, and God's reign is about to begin. Isaiah says that the time of humiliation is filled up (*eplēsthe*, Isa 40:1), the time of God's favor has arrived (*kairō dektō*, Isa 49:8), and God reigns (*basileusei sou ho theos*, Isa 52:7, where to announce God's reign is to "bring good news" [*euangelizomai*] Robbins 1992a, 79). The author of Mark writes, "The time is fulfilled (*peplērōtai ho kairos*), and the reign of God (*basileia tou theo*u) has come near" (1:15). To prepare for participation in the reign of God means a complete reversal of mindset *meta-noeite* is usually translated "Repent!" but this is much more all-encompassing than mere regret or admission of fault). This reversal of mindset amounts to putting unreserved trust in the good news from God and about God that will unfold in the course of the narrative. That is all the Markan Jesus asks—a complete reversal of humanity's values, priorities, and ground of security.

The notice that Jesus' preaching begins after John has been handed over is more than a chronological marker. Being handed over (*paradidomi*) is what happens to the one who first preached repentance, and it will happen to Jesus (3:19; 9:31; 10:33; 14:10, 11, 18, 21, 41, 42, 44; 15:1, 10, 15) and to those who follow him (13:9, 11, 12). The composite Scripture quotation in 1:2-3 had introduced John as the promised messenger who would prepare the way (*hodon*) for Jesus, whose way is at the same time the way of "the Lord." It will become clear as the story unfolds that in the Markan interpretation of Isaiah's theology, the "way" of the new exodus leads first to the cross.

Ministry in Galilee and in Gentile Territory

(Mark 1:14-8:30)

The first major section of the Gospel is an interpretation of how God's reign has been inaugurated by Jesus' ministry of teaching, exorcism, healing, and reconciliation. It extends from the calling of the first disciples in 1:16-20 through the discussion of Jesus' identity in 8:27-30. The section is unified by repeated references to "the sea," settings near the Sea of Galilee, and accounts of travel across the sea. In this section Jesus is portrayed in a way that combines the Old Testament prophetic tradition with the Hellenistic concept of a traveling teacher with his band of disciple/followers. This major section is made up of three overlapping subsections:

(1:14–3:12)	an account of Jesus' ministry in Capernaum and environs that is paradigmatic of the entire Galilean ministry
(3:7–6:13, 30)	an account of the extension of Jesus' ministry and the intensification of his conflict with the religious authorities
(6:14–8:30)	an account of Jesus' removing the barriers between Jews and Gentiles

Paradigmatic Beginning of Jesus' Ministry

(1:14–3:12)

Mark 1:14–3:12 begins with a story in which Jesus calls four disciples by the Sea of Galilee. The call story is followed by two panels of narrative, each arranged chiastically: 1:21-45 and 2:1–3:6. Although each panel has its own inner unity, they are also carefully bound together by literary clamps. The first story, 1:21-27 is an exorcism that takes place in a synagogue on the sabbath. The final story, 3:1-6, is a healing that takes place in a synagogue on the sabbath. At the joint between the two panels of narrative, the last story of panel one (1:41-45) is carefully joined to the first story of panel two (2:1-12) by a chiastic repetition of words and phrases: *logon, hōste mēketi, eiselthein* (1:45); *eiselthōn, hōste mēketi, logon* (2:1-2) (Marshall 1989, 82).

Taken together, the two panels demonstrate Jesus' power over illness and demonic oppression and his authority to teach, to forgive sins, and to reinterpret scripture. Throughout, a negative comparison is made with the priests, scribes, and Pharisees, whose religious leadership the author of Mark rejects as inadequate for the coming reign of God. God's reign clearly does not involve religious business as usual, only on a grander scale. The continuity that Mark sees between God's dealings with the people of the covenant and God's activity in Jesus' ministry is not a smooth transition from present practice to new developments. There is continuity, but it is continuity between the eschatological vision of Isaiah and the one whose way was prepared by the voice crying in the wilderness.

Summary of Jesus' Message (1:14-15)

Mark 1:14-15, although it closes the frame on the introduction to the Gospel, also serves as a transition into the narrative about Jesus' authority and power. It provides the change of scene that gets Jesus out of the desert and into Galilee, where all the action in 1:16–4:34 takes place. It gives the audience a summary of Jesus' preaching and serves notice that all that follows should be understood as manifestations of the nearness of God's reign, announced by Jesus in 1:15.

Calling of the First Disciples (1:16-20)

The summary of Jesus' message is followed by the narrative of the calling of Peter, Andrew, James, and John. These are the only four disciples in the Gospel who have speaking parts, and they are treated by the author as a kind of inner circle. These four hear the apocalyptic discourse in Mark 13, and Peter, James, and John are the only disciples allowed to accompany Jesus to the raising of Jairus' daughter (5:37) and to the transfiguration (9:2). These three are also the ones whom Jesus chooses to watch with him in Gethsemane (14:33). As evidenced by the parallels in the call of Levi in 2:14, this call narrative is meant to be understood as typical of the practice of the Markan Jesus.

In 1:16-20 the Markan Jesus uses one of the disciple recruitment methods attributed to philosophical teachers in Mediterranean antiquity: the direct call that demands a response from the one recruited. Jewish rabbis are not generally portrayed as seeking out disciples, but rather as being sought by those eager to learn. Similarly, respectable philosophers did not often recruit disciples lest they be characterized as sophists or charlatans (Plato,

Apology 19E, Aristophanes, *The Clouds*). However, according to Diogenes Laertius, Socrates' call of his disciple Xenophon followed this pattern:

> The story goes that Socrates met him in a narrow passage, and that he stretched out his stick to bar the way, while he inquired where every kind of food was sold. Upon receiving a reply, he put another question. "And where do men become good and honorable? Xenophon was fairly puzzled; "Then follow me," said Socrates, "and learn." From that time onward he was a pupil of Socrates. (*Lives of Eminent Philosophers* 2.48; see Talbert 1992, 83-84).

The choice of this more direct method of call and response has its parallel in the self-understanding of the covenant people that was familiar to the author of Mark from his Bible. Abram did not go shopping for an appropriate god and finally settle on Yahweh; rather, God called Abram out of his familiar religion and lifestyle into a relationship of response: "Now the Lord said to Abram, 'Go . . . So Abram went . . .' " (Gen 12:1, 4). Similarly, Isaiah understands the covenant people as called by God for a purpose; the verb used in the LXX for this calling is the same verb Mark uses to describe Jesus' summoning of disciples (*ekalesa*, Isa 42:6, cf. 49:1; *ekalesen*, Mark 1:20).

The pattern of a summons to leave one's work and family to accompany and become the successor to a man of God is found in the call of Elisha, 1 Kgs 19:19-21. Elisha responds by following Elijah (v. 21). So when the author of Mark portrays Jesus' calling of fishermen (1:16-20), a tax collector (2:14), sinners (2:17), a rich man (10:21), and a blind beggar (10:46-52) who respond either by following or by turning away, he skillfully combines a call story pattern from Hellenistic culture with the basic biblical notion of God's sovereign call of the least likely into covenant relationship.

In his call the Markan Jesus promises to make the four fishermen into "fishers of people." The notion of fishing for humans was common in both Greek and Jewish culture (The following discussion is based on Wuellner 1967, passim). To be caught in the nets of the gods was a symbol of salvation. Since evil spirits were also believed to be fishing for people, it was important to put oneself in a position to be caught by the benevolent spiritual powers. According to Greek tradition, the way to avoid the nets of the evil spirits was to travel on the road of Zeus (*Dios hodos*). In the prophetic tradition Yahweh may appoint others to be fishers. In particular, the enemies of Israel are understood as Yahweh's fishers, gathering Israel for judgment (Ezek 17:19-21; Jer 16:16). But this judgment is designed to lead to Israel's return to covenant faithfulness; it is a kind of discipline, designed to correct, not to destroy. Israelite and Hellenistic traditions merge in the novella *Joseph and Aseneth*, where Aseneth, the Egyptian princess, speaks about her conversion to the one true God by the witness of Joseph: ". . . by his wisdom he grasped me like a fish on a hook, and by his spirit, as by bait of life, he ensnared me" (*JosAsen* 21:21).

This element of correction and restoration is also present in the use of the fishing metaphor in Greek *paideia* and Israelite wisdom traditions. To be educated is to be lured by the bait of the teacher's ideas and thus to be saved from a wasted life and saved for a life of meaningful responsibility. To be sure, there were hazards, just as in literal fishing. Diogenes Laertius tells of an incident in which the lawmaker Solon was trying to persuade someone to his point of view, but was spat upon for his trouble. Solon is supposed to have said, "Fishermen endure being sprayed by the sea when catching fish; why shouldn't I when catching a man?"

The paradigmatic call narratives in Mark 1:16-20 portray Jesus as a disciple-gathering teacher who fishes for those whom he will train as fishers of others. Like Yahweh and some of the philosophers (e.g., Socrates), the Markan Jesus issues a call to specifically chosen people that demands a response. In this, their introduction to the Markan audience, the disciples who will make up the inner circle in the story respond correctly: "Immediately, they left . . . and followed him" (1:18, 20).

Healings and Exorcisms (1:21-45)

The narrative panel of Mark 1:21-45 establishes Jesus' authority as a teacher, exorcist, and healer and introduces the challenge to the religious status quo that his ministry represents. At the same time the prayer scene in 1:35 makes it clear that Jesus is not acting on his own authority or by his own power; rather, his power and authority come from God. Again, the series of scenes is meant to be paradigmatic; 1:21-34 is an example of a typical day in the ministry of Jesus, and 1:35 is supposed to represent Jesus' regular prayer practice. The concentric arrangement may be outlined as follows:

A—Jesus makes a demon "go out from" a man. Jesus contrasted with the scribes(1:21-27)
    B—Jesus' reputation goes from a synagogue into "all Galilee"(1:28)
        C—Simon's mother-in-law is healed by Jesus (1:29-31)
            D—Summary: healings, exorcisms, Jesus' identity (1:32-34)
        C'—Simon interrupts Jesus' prayer (1:35-38)
    B'—Jesus goes into synagogues in "all Galilee" (1:39)
A'—Jesus makes leprosy "go off of" a man. Jesus contrasted with the priests (1:40-45)

The parallel elements will be considered together.

1:21-27 (A) and 1:40-45 (A'). Jesus' ministry in this panel begins in a synagogue and ends in a desert place. Throughout the Gospel the Markan Jesus will repeat this move from traditionally sacred space to secular space. Eventually, all sacred spaces will be replaced by "the house," which is a place of healing, table fellowship, and instruction of disciples. Like most first-century Christians, Mark's audience would have met in homes for worship, study, and common meals (For a full discussion of this topic, see Malbon 1986b, 131-36).

The author of Mark makes it clear that Jesus' primary activity is that of teaching. It is the first thing he does after calling his disciples, and in the Gospel the most common way of addressing Jesus is "Teacher." Jesus thus shares the activity of the servant of Yahweh (Isa 50:4), and like the servant songs, Mark puts more emphasis on what the teacher does than on what the teacher teaches. Unlike the other Gospels, Mark does not contain several large blocks of teaching material. Jesus' teaching is given in some detail in chapters 4 and 13, but little teaching material appears elsewhere. The evangelist wants it understood, however, that all that Jesus does is also teaching; when Jesus casts out an unclean spirit in the Capernaum synagogue, the people respond, "What is this! A new teaching with authority! He commands even the unclean spirits and they obey him!" (1:27).

Jesus' authority over the unclean spirits also extends to the most unclean of diseases—the various skin maladies lumped together in the biblical material under the name "leprosy." (See Wright and Jones 1992, 277-82). At one stage in the transmission of the final story in this panel the leprosy afflicting the man whom Jesus heals may have been thought of as a demon. In its present form the account has elements that are more typical of exorcisms than of healing stories: Jesus' anger in 1:41 (the more difficult reading) and 1:43, the verb *exebalen* (to cast out, 1:43). H. C. Kee explains, "What is 'thrown out' (v. 43) is not the leper but the demon" (Kee 1977, 35). The report of the result of Jesus' action in 1:42, "and immediately the leprosy went away from him" (*apēlthen ap' autou*), resembles the parallel report in the exorcism story in 1:26, "and . . . it went out of him" (*exēlthen ex autou*).

This healing makes three points that are very important aspects of Markan theology. First, the healing of a leper was believed to be something that only God could do (2 Kgs 5:7). All the priests could do was certify that a leper had been healed and perform the necessary rituals to effect his cultic cleansing (Lev 14:2-32). Jesus' ability to heal the leper demonstrates that God is acting through him.

Second, this story introduces the tension between divine power and human suffering that pervades all religious discourse, including the Gospel of Mark. The early Christian theologian Lactantius summarizes the problem in a quote he attributes to the pre-Christian philosopher Epicurus: "God either wills to take away evils and is not able, or God is able and does not will to do so, or God is neither willing nor able, or God is both willing and able" (*De Ira Dei* 13.19). The Epicurean statement goes on to argue that to deny either omnipotence or benevolence is to be left with a deity who is not really divine, but to affirm both, "which alone is suitable for God," is to be unable to account for either the origin or the continued existence of evil in the world. Any biography of a crucified miracle worker would have to take account of this religious and philosophical problem, which was widely debated in antiquity. The author of Mark will develop his own approach to the problem as the story unfolds; at this point he merely establishes the non-negotiable premise. When the leper approaches Jesus, he says, "If you *will*, you *are able* to make me clean." In Markan theology, what has to be discerned in any situation of suffering is what God's *will* may be. That God is *able* to act is never in question.

Third, the story of the leper, like the synagogue exorcism it parallels, sets Jesus over against established religious authorities. In the Capernaum synagogue the people had remarked on Jesus' authority, which was "not like their scribes." Here, Jesus sends the leper to offer sacrifice for his cleansing in the presence of the priests, "as a witness against them" (1:44; cf. 6:11, 13:9). The hostility toward Jesus that becomes explicit in the next panel is prepared for in these two stories. It is not without reason that the religious leaders will try to destroy Jesus; long before he overturns any tables in the temple he overturns the established lines of authority to teach and the code of ritual purity upon which much of the sacrificial system was based. The rule is that the one who comes in contact with an unclean person or object contracts uncleanness (Wright and Huebner 1992, 729-45). But when an unclean leper comes in contact with Jesus, Jesus is not polluted, and the leper is cleansed. The reign of God, which turns everything upside down, has come near in the ministry of Jesus.

1:28 (B) and 1:39 (B'). Immediately after the exorcism in the Capernaum synagogue, which concludes with the response of the onlookers in 1:27, the audience learns that "the report about Jesus immediately went out everywhere, into the whole region of Galilee." Since Jesus himself will stay in Capernaum until 1:35, this notice that his reputation was spreading prepares for his actual ministry tour of "all Galilee" in 1:39. On this tour Jesus "proclaims" (1:39; cf. 1:14, which specifies the content of the proclamation), and "casts out demons" (1:39; cf. 1:21-27, 34).

1:29-31 (C) and 1:35-38 (C'). These two episodes, which differ in content, are linked by the name "Simon" (1:29, 36), the first named of the four disciples called in 1:16-20. In 1:29-31 the Markan Jesus moves from the synagogue to the house of Simon and Andrew, where he heals Simon's mother-in-law of a fever. Her response to her healing is to "serve" (*diakonei autois*). There is a double message here. On the surface of the story, her ability to carry out her domestic responsibilities functions as proof of her healing. However, when James and John request places of privilege and glory as reward for their association with Jesus, they learn that the sign of authenticity for Jesus and for his disciples is not domination, but service (10:45, *ouk elthen diakonēthēnai alla diakonēsai*). This woman, known to the tradition not by name, but only by her relationship to a male disciple, demonstrates immediately the proper response to the healing presence of Jesus: she serves.

In the parallel passage, 1:35-38, the source of one's power for service is made explicit. While others sleep, Jesus rises, goes out to a deserted place (not to a sacred building) and prays. The use of the imperfect (*prosēucheto*) suggests an activity extended over time. This was not a quickly recited formula to begin the day. In fact, the way Mark tells the story Jesus is gone so long that "Simon and those with him" hunt him down and remind him of his humanitarian responsibility. Why is Jesus wasting time praying when there are hurting people back in Capernaum? The response of the Markan Jesus implies that through prayer he learns which of several worthy activities should claim his time; although everyone in Capernaum is looking for him, he begins a tour of the other villages, having been reminded of his purpose, which is the proclamation of God's reign (1:38). This brief scene also reminds the audience of what they learned at the baptism scene—that Jesus' power comes from God, not from within himself. The disciples, who had been so quick to follow Jesus, are already seen as lacking an understanding of what he is about and of the importance of prayer (cf. 9:29).

1:32-34 (D). This central member of the chiastic structure sums up the healing and exorcistic activity of Jesus, which the individual stories in this panel are intended to illustrate. Jesus attracts large numbers of the sick and demon-possessed; he cures the sick and drives out the demons. Here for the first time the author of Mark introduces a theme that will become increasingly problematic as the story progresses: the issue of Jesus' identity. The evangelist writes, "He would not permit the demons to speak because they knew him" (1:34).

This echoes the claim of the demon in the Capernaum synagogue: "I know who you are—the Holy One of God!" (1:24). One of the ironies threaded through the Markan narrative is the fact that although the demons recognize Jesus immediately and acknowledge his unique relationship to God, Jesus' own disciples puzzle over his identity and fail to understand him despite their close association and private instruction. It is not by accident that the last sentence spoken by a disciple in Mark is Peter's denial: "I don't know the person of whom you are speaking" (14:71). Since the audience of the Gospel has the advantage of having heard 1:1, the disciples' failure to grasp Jesus' identity and Jesus' puzzling commands to silence create a tension and expectation that contribute to the movement of the narrative.

To sum up: In panel one the author of Mark has arranged a series of stories and summaries that epitomize Jesus' authoritative ministry in word and deed and introduce the important issues of christology, theodicy, and discipleship that will appear throughout the Gospel.

Controversies (2:1–3:6)

The second narrative panel (2:1–3:6) of Mark 1:16–3:6 consists of a series of controversy stories in which Jesus responds to objections to his behavior or the behavior of his disciples. These objections are raised by the religious leadership: the scribes and Pharisees. Panel two begins exactly as panel one began; Jesus enters Capernaum (*eisporeuontai eis Kapharnaoum*, 1:21; *eiselthōn palin eis Kapharnaoum*, 2:1). Whereas the movement in panel one was from the synagogue to the house to outdoor settings, panel two moves from the house to outdoor settings to the synagogue, with the result that the setting of 3:1-6 matches the setting of 1:21-27: in the synagogue, on the sabbath. Thus the author indicates the completion of a literary unit.

Joanna Dewey's interpretation of the concentric structure of 2:1–3:6 remains the most convincing, except that the call of Levi appears to be more of a brief digression than an integral part of the second controversy (Dewey 1980). The outline is:

A—(2:1-12) Healing of paralytic
    Indoor scene: house (2:1)
    Controversy apophthegm imbedded in healing miracle
    "rise" (2:9), "rise" (2:11), "he rose" (2:12)
    Positive response: "They were all ecstatic and glorified God, saying,
    'We never saw anything like this before!' " (2:12)
    Link word to next story: sins

[Call of Levi echoes 1:16-20 and prepares for 2:15-17]

B—(2:15-17) Controversy over eating
    Indoor scene: house (2:15a)
    Jesus and his disciples eat with the wrong people. (2:15b)
    Proverb: "The strong don't need a doctor, but the sick do." (2:17a)
    Christological saying: "I didn't come to call the righteous, but sinners." (2:17b)
    Link word to previous story: sinners

C—(2:18-22) Controversy over fasting
    Controversy apophthegm about fasting (2:18-19)
    Oblique reference to crucifixion: bridegroom taken away (2:20)
    Two sayings on new vs. old (2:21-22)

B'—(2:23-28) Controversy over eating
    Outdoor scene (2:23a)
    Disciples "harvest" food on sabbath;
    David and his followers eat the "wrong" bread. (2:23-26)
    Proverb: "The sabbath was made for *anthrōpon*, not *anthrōpos* for the sabbath" (2:27)
    Christological saying: "The *huios tou anthrōpou* is Lord even of the sabbath." (2:28).
    Link word to next story: sabbath

A'—(3:1-6) Healing of withered hand
    Indoor scene: synagogue (3:1)
    Controversy apophthegm imbedded in a healing miracle
    "rise up to the midst" (3:3)
    Negative response: "The Pharisees went out and immediately conspired with the Herodians against him, how to destroy him." (3:6)
    Link word to previous story: sabbath

Dewey points out that there is a "linear development of hostility" through the five controversies. In the first story the scribes question in their hearts, but do not criticize Jesus publicly. In the second story the scribes of the Pharisees question the disciples about Jesus' behavior. In the third story "they" question Jesus directly about his disciples' failure to fast. In the fourth story the Pharisees themselves question Jesus about his disciples' "unlawful" behavior; they have not only failed to do good, but also they have broken the law. In the fifth story "they" watch Jesus, and Jesus is said to be angry. This final story, and the entire panel, ends with a conspiracy between religious and political leaders to do away with Jesus.

Here the audience begins to get a sense for what is at stake in the proclamation and activity of Jesus. The reign of God will not be welcomed by everyone. If the reign of God has drawn near, that means that all other regnant structures are radically relativized and soon to be eliminated. Isaiah had portrayed Yahweh declaring historical war on all the nations in order to establish the eschatological reign of Yahweh in universal peace (Isa 13–27;

see Conrad 1992). Mark portrays Jesus' conflicts with power structures in history as signs that the promised reign of God has indeed drawn near. In Isaiah, God's own people are not exempt from judgment; judgment falls on Jerusalem as surely as on Assyria and Babylon. In order for God to reign, all other powers must abdicate or be defeated, even the powers that claim to represent God. In Mark, not only Rome, but also the Jewish leaders stand to lose when Jesus announces God's reign, so they oppose Jesus. This is not Christian anti-semitism; it is typical of Israelite prophetic rhetoric.

2:1-12 (A) and 3:1-6 (A'). The two controversy stories that include healing miracles foreshadow the two trials of the Markan Jesus (Dewey 1978, 189). The healing of the paralytic foreshadows the trial before the Sanhedrin, where Jesus publically claims his status as Son of God. For this he is accused of blasphemy (14:64). But this is not a new charge. Jesus is also accused of blasphemy in 2:7 because he assumes the divine prerogative to forgive sins (Isa 43:25). Jesus speaks of himself as the Son of Man for the first time in 2:10, and for the last time in 14:62. These are the only Son of Man sayings that are preceded by verbs addressed to Jesus' opponents ("that you may know," 2:10; "you will see," 14:62). The healing of the withered hand establishes Jesus' innocence of any wrongdoing, which is also an important function of the trial before Pilate. Both scenes rely on rhetorical questions, the obvious answer to which establishes Jesus' innocence: 15:14, "What evil has he done?" (Answer: He has done no evil); 3:4, "Is it appropriate on the sabbath to do good or to do evil—to make a life whole, or to kill?" (Answer: It is appropriate to do good. Implication: Since Jesus makes a life whole, rather than killing, Jesus does good, not evil).

Both these stories are heavily ironic. In 2:7 the scribes are correct when they note that no one can forgive sins except God. LXX Isaiah 43:25 connects the divine *ego eimi* with forgiveness: "I, I am the one who blots out your transgressions and will not remember them." But the scribes draw the wrong conclusion. Instead of recognizing Jesus' divine authority to forgive, and instead of recognizing the inbreaking of God's reign in his healing of the lame (Isa 35:6), they accuse him of blasphemy, thus condemning themselves. In 3:1-6 the Markan Jesus is innocent of violating the sabbath; it is not illegal to command a person to stand up in the synagogue or to command him to stretch out his hand. Jesus does not do anything that might be construed as "work" on the sabbath. However, as Jesus points out, it is not legal to do evil or to kill on any day of the week, let alone the sabbath. The Pharisees and Herodians violate this law by plotting on the sabbath to commit murder (Camery-Hoggatt 1992, 118).

Jesus is the one who makes whole, or saves, life (*psuchēn sōsai*, 3:4). The repetition of the verb "to rise" (*eigerō*) in these two healing stories points ahead to Jesus' own resurrection (16:6). The religious leaders plot the death of the life-bringer, whose resurrection will put an end to death forever.

2:13-14. This brief return to the sea (2:13) and the call of Levi (2:14) suggests that the gathering of disciples is an ongoing project of the Markan Jesus. Levi is called in language that echoes the call of the four fishermen, but he is not named in the list of the twelve in 3:16-19. This makes it clear that, from the evangelist's point of view, the group of disciples—those who respond to the call to follow Jesus—is much larger than the traditional twelve. Indeed, in 2:15 we hear about *many* tax collectors and sinners who follow Jesus.

The inclusion of Levi is extremely important for Markan theology. Levi, although he bears the priestly name, is a tax collector who profits from Roman oppression (Donahue 1992b, 337-8). In the language of today's liberation movements, Levi is a collaborator. A true freedom-fighter would have nothing to do with such a weasel, except perhaps to murder him as an enemy of the revolution. Jesus calls the likes of Levi and eats with them.

2:15-17 (B) and 2:23-28 (B'). The call of Levi prepares for the scene in 2:15. Jesus shares table fellowship with tax collectors and sinners. This offense to the Pharisaic sense of purity by means of separation is beaten into the hearer's mind by repetition:

> . . . and many tax collectors and sinners were at table with Jesus and his disciples . . . and the scribes and the Pharisees, seeing that he ate with sinners and tax collectors, said to his disciples, "Why does he eat with tax collectors and sinners?" (2:15-16)

The Markan Jesus responds with an analogy that was common in philosophical circles in antiquity; he compares himself with a medical doctor. Diogenes Laertius records two such comparisons in the *Lives of the Eminent Philosophers*:

> One day when [Antisthenes] was censured for keeping company with evil men, the reply he made was, "Physicians attend to their patients without getting the fever themselves" (6.6). In answer to one who remarked that he always saw philosophers at rich men's doors, [Aristippus] said, "So, too, physicians are in attendance on those who are sick, but no one for that reason would prefer being sick to being a physician." (2.70)

In his Eighth Discourse, Dio Chrysostom remarks upon the choice of Diogenes the Cynic to live in Corinth:

> . . . just as the good physician should go and offer his services where the sick are most numerous, so, said he, the man of wisdom should take up his abode where fools are thickest in order to convict them of their folly and reprove them. (8.5-10)

Similarly, those whom Jesus came to call are not the strong and healthy (*ischuontes*), but the sick—not the righteous, but sinners. Not only does this overturn the value of purity-by-separation, which is the etymological basis for the designation "Pharisee" (the separated ones), but also it presents a significant challenge to Mark's audience.

Those who consider themselves as among the ones Jesus came to call have to be willing to put themselves in the category of "sinners," because if they see themselves as "righteous," they are not included. Specifically, those who want to be insiders in Jesus' group must envision themselves reclining next to people whose politics and behavior they find disgusting, and eating out of the same dish with them (14:20). In Christian communities in which the Jewish food laws had long been abandoned (7:19), those who were despised might well have been the Jewish Christians who clung to tradition and who were known in the Roman church as "the weak" (Rom 14:1–15:13). Lest "the strong" find themselves in the position of the Pharisees, the evangelist would have wanted to remind them that Jesus came to call the ones who needed healing. "If you don't consider yourself to be in that category," the Gospel writer says, "so much the worse for you."

The fourth controversy story, 2:23-28 (B'), is also about eating, but this time the disciples provide themselves with food by breaking the sabbath law against reaping (2:23). This particular story is an excellent example of technique of ancient rhetoric known as the elaborated chreia.

The chreia is explained by the rhetorician Theon of Alexandria as "a concise statement or action which is attributed with aptness to some specified character or to something analogous to a character" *Progymnasmata* 3.2-3). At the most basic level of Hellenistic education (up to age 14), children learned to write by copying and then elaborating chreiai (Mack 1990, 30; see also Hock 1992, 912-14, and Hock and O'Neill 1986). The elaboration could take a number of forms; in 2:23-28 a chreia about the sabbath is elaborated according to the canons of judicial rhetoric, that is, in order to establish whether or not an action was illegal. Mack suggests that the chreia was developed as follows (Mack 1990, 52-53):

Narrative:	Plucking grain on the Sabbath. (2:23)
Issue:	It is not lawful. (2:24)
Rebuttal:	Citation of an authority or precedent:
	What David did in the Scriptures (2:25-26)
	[David's action is cited as an example, and an analogy is implicitly made to the disciples' situation: Just as David and his men were hungry while on an important mission, so Jesus' disciples were hungry while on an important mission. In the precedent case the need was more important than the law that was broken; so in this case it is appropriate to break a law to meet a need.]
Maxim:	Sabbath made for *anthrōpon*, not *anthrōpos* for sabbath. (2:27)
Conclusion:	The Son of Man *huios tou anthrōpou* is lord even of the sabbath. (2:28)

The maxim is related to the conclusion as the major premise in a syllogism is related to its conclusion:

Major premise:	The sabbath was made by God for man.
Minor premise:	The Son of Man came to serve man with what God created for man.
Conclusion:	Therefore the Son of Man is lord even of the sabbath [and has authority to use it to serve human need].

When one of the premises of a syllogism is implied, rather than stated, as in this example, the construction is called an enthymeme (For more detail, see Robbins 1989a).

The reason for setting the argument up in this way is to undercut the authority of the Pharisees with Jesus' authority. Thus, the evangelist argues that the relaxation of sabbath law among Christians is not evidence against their claims to continuity with scripture. Rather, scripture supports the principle by which the sabbath was subordinated to human need. Jesus and his followers, not the Pharisees, stand in continuity with the real meaning of the sabbath as God intended it. Although the author of Mark is using the principles and techniques of Greek rhetoric, the use of scripture against the interpreters of scripture was already a favorite technique of the Israelite prophets. Against those who appealed to the laws prescribing sacrifice and public worship, Isaiah appealed to the laws prescribing faithfulness to Yahweh and just treatment of others (Isa 1:10-17). Like Isaiah before him, the author of Mark establishes the principle that Scripture is not set aside arbitrarily because it is no longer convenient; rather, what may appear to others to be radical departures from scripture are in fact grounded in even more basic principles of scripture as interpreted by Jesus.

2:18-22 (C). Bracketed by two pronouncement stories about eating, the central member of the chiasm is a controversy over not eating. Jesus is asked why, when the disciples of John and the disciples of the Pharisees fast, his own disciples do not fast. The Markan Jesus' reply is an oblique reference to his crucifixion and exaltation; it is not appropriate for the wedding guests to fast in the midst of the party; but when the bridegroom (Jesus) is taken away, they will fast. The same early Christian theologian who regards the food laws and sabbath observance as dispensable nevertheless takes fasting seriously as appropriate Christian practice after Jesus' departure (See Muddiman 1992, 776-78).

The two examples that follow (new patch on old garment, new wine in old wineskins) suggest that the very character of the community that follows Jesus is fermentation and disruption. The new does not fit smoothly into old patterns. New structures will be required. It is clear that for the Markan community the break with the synagogue is in the past. It is better to put the new wine into new leather bottles than to burst the old ones and lose both the wine and the bottles.

By the end of the two panels, 1:21-45 and 2:1–3:6, the evangelist has established Jesus' authority to teach, heal, cast out demons and reinterpret both scripture and the boundaries of table fellowship. It is not, however, a cheap victory. It will cost Jesus his life (3:6). To side with Jesus will mean for the audience of the Gospel the loss of any claim to righteousness, the loss of the prerogative of avoiding unpleasant people, and the loss of absolute certainty about biblical interpretation. But before they have had time to mourn their losses, the audience finds themselves hustling to keep up with Jesus and the disciples, who are on the move again.

Conclusion (3:7-12)

The material in Mark 3:7-12 provides a conclusion to the paradigmatic beginning of Jesus' Galilean ministry. Jesus and his disciples return to the sea, where the first disciples were called (1:16). Jesus again heals people and conquers demons. The list of place names emphasizes Jesus' popularity (cf. 1:32, 14; 2:2). The audience is reminded of Jesus' identity as "Son of God" (1:1, 11), an identity known by the demons (1:33; cf 1:24), but one that Jesus is not yet willing to have made public (1:34). This short conclusion indicates that aspects of Jesus' activity now familiar to the audience will continue, and that new themes will begin to emerge.

Extension of Ministry; Intensification of Conflict

(3:7–6:13, 30)

Introduction (3:7-12)

In addition to providing the conclusion to 1:14–3:12, Mark 3:7-12 also pre-
views the second major subsection of the ministry. It falls into two parts:
verses 7-8 emphasize the scope of Jesus' popularity, and verses 9-12 sound
the major themes that will continue and some that will be introduced in the
subsequent development of the story of Jesus' life. After a change of scene, an
inclusio sets off the list of places from which people came to Jesus: "a great
many (*polu plēthos)* followed him from Galilee and from Judaea and from
Jerusalem and from Idumea and beyond the Jordan [river] and [the region]
around Tyre and Sidon a great many (*plēthos polu)* hearing what he was
doing came to him."

Like all Greek manuscripts, the earliest copies of Mark have no punctu-
ation. This fact exacerbates the ambiguity in sentences like this one. The subject, "a great many," is repeated, and there are two finite verbs: "followed"
and "came." Does the author mean that Jesus had followers from all these
places, who came to him after hearing about his activity, or that he had followers from Galilee and that people from the other places came to him out
of curiosity, but were not followers? The textual variants demonstrate
considerable scribal confusion over this issue. They also show that the early
copyists of the Gospel recognized the importance of the word "follow" in
Markan theology and knew that to speak of gentiles from Tyre and Sidon as
"following" Jesus would have been theologically significant. The use of the
verb and the presence and activity of the disciples in this preview reminds
the audience that this is the life of a disciple-gathering teacher, not of an
itinerant magician.

However the sentence is understood, there can be no doubt that the list
is intended to inform the audience that Jesus' following is large and that it
includes people from places where Jesus has not yet preached or performed
any healings or exorcisms. Judea and Jerusalem had been the territory of
John's baptizing activity (1:5), and Jesus will pass through Judea and the
other side of the Jordan (10:1) on his way to Jerusalem, the future scene of
his suffering and death. Idumea would have been recognized by some hearers as Herod's family's place of origin its mention here may foreshadow 6:14-
29. The area around Tyre and Sidon will become the setting of an important
conversation and exorcism in 7:24-30. That people from these areas have
"heard what Jesus was doing" is information that makes sense of the

narrator's later claims that people expected miracles from Jesus on the basis of having heard about him (5:27; 7:25).

In 3:9 the boat that will become the instrument for bridging the gulf between Jews and gentiles and the scene of teaching, miracles and misunderstanding in chapters 4–8 is introduced. There also may be some humor here at the expense of the disciples. The fishermen who had abruptly left their boat in 1:20, and who claim to have left "everything" in 10:28, seem to have no trouble procuring a boat at a moment's notice; if they had no property, they at least had plenty of connections, the narrator suggests.

The healings and exorcisms that began Jesus' ministry in 1:21-45 continue to be central to his activity and the thing that draws people to him. The story of the hemorrhaging woman in 5:25-34 is prepared for by the notice that people were pressing upon Jesus in order to touch him (3:10). Whereas the spirit cast out in the Capernaum synagogue merely shouted at Jesus, the unclean spirits in this summary fall down in front of him, as will the Gerasene demoniac in 5:6.

The introduction is followed by a chiastic arrangement of material that may be outlined as follows:

A—Disciples appointed (3:13-19)
    B—Misinterpretation by family and religious leaders (3:20-35)
        C—Jesus' words and deeds heard and seen but not understood (4:1–5:43)
        Words (4:1-34)
        Deeds (4:35–5:43)
    B'—Misinterpretation by associates in home town (6:1-6)
A'—Disciples sent out (6:7-13, 30)

Appointment of Disciples (3:13-19)

At the beginning of this second subunit the theme of discipleship is reiterated, recalling 1:16-20 and 2:14. The original call from Jesus was abrupt ("Follow me"), and the purpose was stated metaphorically ("I will make you fish for people"). This second focus on discipleship is more explicit, both in the Old Testament linkages and in the definition of the purpose of discipleship according to Mark.

The scene in which twelve disciples are appointed and named takes place on a mountain (3:13). For the ancients, the mountain was the place of encounter with deity; the Greek pantheon was thought to dwell on Mount Olympus, and Israel's God was believed to be present in a special way in the temple on Mount Zion. In Israel's story of origin, Moses first encountered God on Mount Sinai (Exod 3) and then led the people back there to enter into covenant with God (Exod 19). The setting of this scene on a mountain and the tradition of there having been twelve disciples appointed by Jesus reflect the early Christian conviction that in Jesus' life, death, and resurrection God had redefined the covenant and the covenant people, though Mark does not develop the symbolic significance of "twelve" as much as Matthew does (For a discussion of "the mountain" in Mark, see Malbon 1986b, 84-89).

The vocabulary of calling (*proskaleitai*, 3:13) echoes not only 1:20, but also the many instances in the biblical tradition in which God calls the chosen people (e.g., Isa 42:6; Hos 11:1-2).

Although it is missing from some manuscripts, the phrase "whom he also called missionaries (*apostolos*)" may very well have stood in the original text of Mark, where it served the dual function of forming an inclusio with 6:30 and of emphasizing the missionary character of the new people of God as those who are "sent out." Another disputed reading should be regarded as original: the repetition of the clause "he appointed twelve" in 3:14 and 3:16, which appeared redundant to some scribes, actually frames the important material in 3:14b-15 in which the character of discipleship is outlined.

The description of the disciples' assignment falls into two parts, with the second part also having two aspects:

and he appointed twelve (whom he also named missionaries)
   in order that they might be with him
      and
   in order that he might send them out
      to proclaim
         and
      to have authority to cast out the demons
and he appointed the twelve (3:14-16)

According to Mark, being with Jesus is the aspect of discipleship that is both chronologically and theologically prior to everything else. This emphasis is consistent with ancient notions of discipleship, which stressed the importance of the disciples' spending time with the teacher and accompanying him on his travels in order to observe and learn to imitate his life (Xenophon, *Memorabilia* 4.3.18, Philostratus, *Life of Apollonius* 1.19, 6.3, 6.12). It is impossible to overestimate the importance for Christian formation of community life that is centered on the presence of Jesus. To counteract today's individualistic and activist construals of discipleship, Christocentric community life is essential, though extraordinarily hard to find.

After being with Jesus, the disciples are sent out by Jesus to do two things. They are to proclaim, as Jesus does, the good news (1:14-15), and they are given Jesus' authority in spiritual warfare against the demonic forces that oppose God's rule and oppress and distort God's creation. In other words, their mission, like that of Jesus, is to include both proclamation and action. Neither is optional, and one may not be substituted for the other. It should also be noticed that they are given no "apostolic" authority over other followers of Jesus (Best 1978, 33). They may give orders to demons, but not to people (10:43-44).

The names of "the twelve" in 3:16-19 are the same as those in Matthew 10:2-4, but the author of the First Gospel puts them in a different order and designates Matthew as a tax collector. In Mark, Levi is the tax collector, and is not among the twelve, although he is singled out and called by Jesus. The lists in Luke 6:14-16 and Acts 1:13b omit Thaddaeus and include a second Judas, who is called "the son of James." The Fourth Gospel refers to "the twelve," but does not list them. Much effort has been expended in attempts to harmonize the lists in the synoptic tradition, and those who find harmonization appropriate are satisfied with the results. Nevertheless, it appears obvious that there was neither clarity nor agreement in the earliest traditions about this list. This may suggest that the number twelve was important for symbolic reasons, but that the exact identification of these people was not so important.

Furthermore, Mark does not portray "the twelve" as occupying an especially privileged position by contrast with the larger group of disciples/ followers of Jesus. The passage that seems to bestow the greatest privilege on a group of insiders is 4:11 in which Jesus says, "To you has been given the mystery of the reign of God." However, this is said to "those who were around him along with the twelve" (4:10), and this group of more than "the twelve" is called "disciples" in 4:33-34 (Tannehill 1977, 388 n. 8, *contra* Meye 1968, 228). This Markan expansion of the notion of discipleship may be the reason for the otherwise enigmatic presence of "other boats" in 4:36, since a typical boat would have been able to carry only fifteen to seventeen adults across the lake (Rousseau and Arav 1995, 26).

Malbon has demonstrated the importance of private teaching to Jesus' disciples in the setting of "the house," but in no case is it "the twelve" who are alone in the house with Jesus; the text always specifies this "house church" group as Jesus' "disciples." The group in 3:34 that replaces the biological family of Jesus is not "the twelve," but "those who sat around him," and this group is immediately enlarged in the saying of 3:35 to include "whoever does the will of God" (see Malbon 1986a). To be sure, the author

of Mark places Peter, James, and John (5:37; 9:2; 14:33) with Jesus at important times in the narrative, but there is no attempt to establish "the twelve" as
an inner circle with more privileged access to Jesus than "the disciples" (Best
1978, 35). Even the attendance at the last supper is expanded by the evangelist to at least fifteen, since Jesus sends "two of his disciples" ahead to prepare
(14:13) and later arrives "with the twelve" (14:17).

A much larger group including Mary Magdalene, Mary the mother of
James and Joses, Salome (15:40), Bartimaeus (10:52), Levi (2:14), "many"
tax collectors and sinners (2:15), and the Gethsemane streaker (14:51) are
spoken of as "following" Jesus, just as the first four fishermen did when Jesus
called them. It would seem, then, that the references in Mark to "his
disciples" should be conceived of as referring to a group that includes "the
twelve," but is not limited to them.

It would appear that the vagueness in the text as to the numerical limits
of "the disciples" of Jesus or "those following" him has the effect of opening
the possibility of the audience's finding themselves in these scenes, for better
or worse (Malbon 1986a, 110). The audience of Mark cannot escape the
responsibilities of discipleship by historicizing, that is, by assuming that the
Markan Jesus called only twelve Jewish males in the past. Rather, the audience is called to examine whether they as disciples are faithful in spending
time together in the presence of Jesus and in going out to proclaim the
gospel and to expel the demons from their own cultural context.

Misinterpretation by
Family and Religious Authorities (3:20-35)

This unit consists of controversial material framed by the misunderstanding
of Jesus by his family of origin and their replacement by "those who do the
will of God." Since the controversy involves two charges by opponents, to
which Jesus responds in reverse order, the result is a chiastic structure
(Robbins 1989b, 172, n. 27):

A—Those akin to him come to seize him (vv. 20-21).
    B—Accusation 1: He has Beelzebul (v. 22a).
        C—Accusation 2: By the prince of demons he casts out demons (22b).
        C'—Refutation 2: Satan would not cast out demons (vv. 23-27).
    B'—Refutation 1: Saying Jesus has an unclean spirit is blasphemy (vv. 28-30).
A'—Jesus' kin are those who do the will of God (vv. 31-35).

The aspect of this unit that has a structural role within 3:13–6:13, 30 is
the frame; therefore, 3:20-21 and 3:31-35 will be discussed first. Here the

early Christians who constituted the audience of the Gospel learn that to the extent that they are misunderstood and rejected by their families they are following a pattern characteristic of their founder.

The literary structure is the factor that determines that the somewhat vague Greek phrase *hoi par' autou* (3:21) designates the family of Jesus. In 3:21 their response to the crowds that Jesus is attracting (3:20) is to come out to seize him (*kratēsai auton*; cf. 14:1, 43, 45, 46, 49, where the verb is used for the arrest of Jesus in Gethsemane). According to his family's view of the situation, Jesus is out of his mind (*exestē*, lit. "standing outside [himself]"). However, the author of Mark makes it clear in verse 31 that it is the family members who are standing outside (*exō stēkontes*), by contrast with those who are inside with Jesus. When the Markan Jesus is informed that his mother and brothers are outside (*exō*, repeated for emphasis) seeking him, he responds with a rhetorical question that he then proceeds to answer.

"Who is my mother and [who are] my brothers?" Looking at those seated around him in a circle, he said, "Look! My mother and my brothers! For whoever may do the will of God, . . . this one is my brother and sister and mother." Jesus' kin are not those related to him by blood, but those related to him by sharing his purpose.

This redefinition of what constitutes family is an especially strong rhetorical strategy because of the importance placed upon family in the ancient world. A similar rhetorical move is attributed to the Theban general Epameinondas by the rhetorician Theon: "Epameinondas, as he was dying childless, said to his friends: 'I have left two daughters—the victory at Leuctra and the one at Mantineia' " (*Progymnasmata* 3.227-29). Here, as in the saying of the Markan Jesus, family is redefined along the lines of vocation rather than blood, and the importance of family is relativized.

The Markan emphasis is twofold: (1) Doing the will of God will look crazy to some people—often to one's own relatives; and (2) those whose relatives misunderstand their Christian commitment find a new family in the Christian community, just as Jesus did.

Another point is made that connects the frame with the charges and refutations it brackets. If Jesus' "true kin act according to the will of God . . ., this implies that he himself has his mind on the will of God. Thus, instead of being 'out of his mind,' he and his kin have their minds on God and are seeking to do his will" (Robbins 1989b, 176). And what, at this point in the narrative, would the audience understand doing the will of God to look like? The reference must be to the activity of Jesus that has drawn the crowd of 3:20 (still there in 3:32) and caused such alarm in Jesus' family: the proclamation of God's reign, accompanied by healings and exorcisms. The author has prepared the audience for this conclusion by using the language of willing in the leper story: "If you *will*, you can make me clean . . . I *will*. Be clean!" (1:40-41). Jesus wills and does what God wills, and in performing healings and exorcisms, Jesus and his true family (including the healers and exorcists in the Markan community) do the will of God.

The assertion that Jesus' miracles are the will of God is the clinching argument in the rhetoric of the controversy story that is framed by the misunderstanding of the family. That rhetoric is designed to show that Jesus and his followers are not magicians.

The controversy with "scribes who came down from Jerusalem" picks up the theme of conflict with opponents that was introduced in a panel (2:1–3:6) of the first subsection of the Galilean ministry (1:14–3:12). The identification of Jesus' opponents with Jerusalem, to be repeated in 7:1, foreshadows the passion narrative. The conflict is intensified here because the opponents make public accusations about Jesus; in 2:1–3:6 they confronted Jesus directly only about the behavior of his disciples. The accusations of 3:22 make the opponents look both desperate and ridiculous. In 2:7 they had objected that Jesus identified himself too closely with God; here they object that Jesus has identified himself with "Beelzebul," "the ruler of the demons." The opponents will continue to have trouble getting their story straight, as will be seen in the narrative of the Sanhedrin trial (14:56-59).

When the scribes accuse Jesus of having Beelzebul and of using that demon's power to perform exorcisms, the audience would have understood that the charge was that of practicing magic. Magicians were believed to have gained control of spirits that they could call upon to do their bidding (Smith 1978, 30-34, 97-100). Beelzebul, unattested in antiquity outside the synoptic tradition (Lewis 1992, 638-40), is identified by Jesus' opponents as "the ruler of the demons" and by Jesus as "Satan" (3:23). Thus, the two related accusations are that Jesus has control of the ruler of demons, whose power he uses to perform his exorcisms. The Markan Jesus responds to these charges in reverse order, using the standard tactics of Hellenistic rhetoric (Robbins, 1989b).

Responding to the charge that he uses the chief demon to cast out demons, the Markan Jesus first paraphrases the charge in the form of a mocking question: "How can Satan cast out Satan?" The defense is characterized by the author of Mark as "in parables," which in ancient rhetoric meant "using analogies." The argument from analogy draws upon comparisons with a political entity (*basileia*, 3:24) and a domestic entity (*oikos*, 3:25). Neither one, if divided against itself, is able to stand. If these two analogous situations are accepted as self-evidently accurate, then the opponents' charge is shown to be implausible. Satan would not cast out a demon, because as the ruler of demons it is in his interest to maintain unity in his domain, not to introduce destructive internal division.

This argument is followed by a second, which Theon calls the argument from falsity. Theon's example is from *Progymnasmata* 3.264-66: "Bion said untruthfully that love of money is the mother city of evil. Rather, it is intemperance." In other words, Bion's statement is false because intemperance, not the love of money, is the basic cause of evil. The analogy about the strong man makes the same point. Since Jesus is plundering Satan's property (by casting out demons), he cannot be using Satan's power to do so. Instead, he must be using a stronger power than Satan. That is, the scribes' charge is false because a contrary explanation is true. The attentive listener would remember that John had predicted the coming of Jesus as the "stronger one" (*ischuroteros*, 1:7), and would readily agree that Jesus has bound "the strong one" (*ischuron*, 3:27) and is therefore able to wreak havoc in his domain. This victory over Satan was implied by the temptation scene in 1:12-13 and demonstrated in the exorcisms that followed. The author of Mark may also be alluding to Isaiah 49:24-25, where the promise to the exiles includes the liberation of those who have fallen prey to "the strong" (*ischuontos*). The power of Jesus to break the bondage of Satan's victims must come from a source more powerful than Satan.

The refutation of the first accusation (that Jesus "has" Beelzebul) follows up on the point just made. The audience is reminded of the identity of the source of Jesus' power: the Holy Spirit (1:8, 10). This backward reference to the baptism confirms the argument from falsity and displays the gravity of the charge made by the scribes. Their false characterization of the activity of the Holy Spirit as the activity of an unclean spirit is not an innocent mistake; it is unforgivable blasphemy (For detailed analysis of the rhetoric, see Robbins, 1989b).

The clinching argument against the charge of practicing magic is the claim that Jesus and his family "do the will of God." This was a common argument made by ancient miracle workers who were accused of being magicians. The Greek magical papyri illustrate the way in which a magician would use spells and incantations to force deities to do the will of the magician or the paying client of the magician. One spell placed on the moon says, "You have to do it, whether you want to or not" (Tarn 1961, 352). According to the first-century Roman writer Lucan, witches could "make the gods subservient" and "force the reluctant gods to pay heed" (*Pharsalia* 6.438-44). So when the miracle worker Apollonius of Tyana has to stand trial before Domitian on charges of magical practice, his biographer Philostratus portrays him as one who does not "compel the gods," but rather teaches "how the gods ought to be worshiped" (*Life of Apollonius* 8.7.2). In 8.7.9, Philostratus has Apollonius argue that rather than claiming credit for his miracles, he prays to the gods and gives them credit for the wonders they perform. As an example, Apollonius explains that he was able to stop a plague at Ephesus by praying to Hercules. In the ancient world, the pious instrument of the gods distinguished herself or himself from the magician by insisting that whereas the magician forced the gods to do the magician's will, the pious miracle-worker did only the will of the gods. Thus, when the author of Mark portrays Jesus and his followers as those who "do the will of God," he is relying on commonly accepted modes of argumentation to make his point. Such a defense was a necessary component of any biography of a wonder-worker in antiquity because the person that one group claimed as a holy man would inevitably be regarded as a magician by competing groups (For a more detailed discussion, see Dowd 1988, 133-50).

To sum up: Jesus' family and opponents refuse to see God at work in one such as Jesus, so they pronounce him crazy and accuse him of alliance with Satan. Mark first shows why the opponents' accusations are false and then turns the tables on them by accusing them of blasphemy that permanently alienates from God. As for the family, they are left standing outside —replaced by those on the inside who, like Jesus himself, do the will of God. This contrast between insiders and outsiders, which seems so clear-cut in this passage, will become increasingly problematic as the story progresses.

Misunderstanding of
Jesus' Words and Deeds (4:1–5:43)

Words (4:1-34). Mark 4:1-34 is the first long speech by the Markan Jesus, and although the audience has heard much about the fact that Jesus was a teacher, this is the first teaching that takes place in the Gospel outside the context of controversy with opponents. It is followed by a panel of miracle stories, 4:35–5:43. The other long discourse, 13:1-37, is placed near the end of the Gospel and is followed by the passion narrative. Thus the evangelist demonstrates a concern to show that what Jesus teaches is consistent with his life lived according to the will of God, whether active (miracles) or passive (suffering and death).

The setting recalls 3:7-12. Jesus is beside the sea, and the crowd is so large that he retreats to a boat. "Beside the sea" is where Jesus teaches (2:13) and calls people to discipleship (1:16-20; 2:14). The dual notice of his teaching in the narrative introduction to the parables (4:1a,2) and the references to disciples (4:10, 34) maintain a pattern established earlier. The reintroduction of the boat prepares for the numerous sea crossings that are to follow in 4:35–8:25.

So much ink has been spilled in parable scholarship that it is necessary to begin a discussion of this chapter with a brief statement about the presuppositions of the discussion. Much like the various quests for the "historical" Jesus, recent parable scholarship has revealed more about the interpreters than about the texts allegedly being interpreted. Despite inflated claims that parables "subvert" and "shatter" the world of the complacent hearer, this is far more often the ambition of the scholar than the effect of the texts themselves. As Mary Ann Tolbert has observed, we do not have any evidence that actual readers or hearers of the parables have experienced the kind of existential breakdown that the parables are supposed to be capable of producing (Tolbert 1979, 42-43).

Although the Greek word *parabolē* is used in the LXX to translate the Hebrew *mashal*, and therefore designates a fairly wide range of literary forms, the author of Mark uses the term *parabolē* in a way that is consistent with the understanding of the term in the Greek rhetorical tradition. By contrast with the historical example story, the parable is understood by Aristotle to be realistic fiction—a story that might have happened, but did not happen. This distinguishes it from a fable, which could not have happened (*Rhetoric* 2.20). Aesop's fables, for example, often involve animals that talk.

Recent work on Mark's usage has been done by Burton Mack, who writes, "The term [*parabolē*] refers in general to an 'illustrative comparison' or 'analogy.' . . . The purpose of comparison was understood to be instructive —to clarify, illustrate, or demonstrate some aspect of the subject under investigation" (Mack 1989b, 147). In this commentary, *parabolē* will be understood in the rhetorical sense of a fictional analogy used for instructive purposes.

The close alliance between parable scholarship and historical Jesus studies has meant that heroic efforts have been made to recover the "authentic" parable once told by Jesus by peeling away the contributions of the later tradition and particularly the editing of the Gospel writers, who have supposedly domesticated the alleged (and conveniently modern) political radicalism of Jesus (Funk, *et al.*, 1988, 19; A refreshing exception is Donahue 1988). This commentary will focus, not on historical speculation about the original form of the parables, but on the text before us and will interpret the parables of Jesus as they contribute to the Gospel of Mark as a whole.

The parable chapter, like the apocalyptic discourse in Mark 13, is primarily about eschatology. The author of Mark uses the parables and sayings of Jesus to explain why the proclamation of God's reign is meeting with resistance and to assure the audience that despite the apparent lack of progress, God's reign will eventually burst forth in amazing fruitfulness. The secondary concern addressed in this text is also present in Mark 13. It is a warning about the possibility of apostasy, even among those who have experienced God's grace mediated through Jesus.

The author of Mark has arranged the material into a carefully constructed chiastic arrangement (Marcus 1986, 221):

A—Narrative introduction (4:1-2)
    B—Seed parable (4:3-9) (public teaching)
        C—Statement about hiddenness (4:10-12) (private teaching)
            D—Allegorical explanation of parable (4:13-20) (private teaching)
        C'—Statements about revelation (4:21-25) (private teaching)
    B'—Seed parables (4:26-29, 30-32) (public teaching)
A'—Narrative conclusion (4:33-34)

The author of Mark understands all three seed parables to be addressed to the crowd that assembles in 4:1 and is left behind in 4:36. This public teaching, then, is based primarily on agricultural images. The public teaching frames the private teaching to "those around him with the twelve" (4:10-25), and this private teaching, while it picks up the agricultural images of the parable in the allegorical explanation (4:13-20), also introduces images drawn from domestic life: lamp, basket, bed, lampstand, house, measure (4:21-25). While the shift from the public to the private setting is clear in 4:10, the shift back to the public setting in 4:26 is less clear and requires the following supporting evidence:

• The narrative conclusion (4:33-34) implies that the parables that have immediately preceded it are only two examples of the "many such" parables with which Jesus spoke "to them" and goes on to emphasize that although Jesus spoke "to them" in parables, he explained everything in private to his disciples. This means that the parables in 4:26-32 were spoken "to them," that is, to the crowd, by contrast with "his disciples/those around him with the twelve."

• The parables in 4:26-32 are explicitly said to be about the reign of God (4:26, 30). In Mark, Jesus always proclaims God's reign in public (1:15; 3:24; 10:14; 12:34), though he may give further private explanation about it to his disciples (Donahue 1988, 32).

• In 4:36 Jesus and the disciples leave the crowd to cross the sea. Clearly the
evangelist understands the final parables to have been addressed to the
same crowd described in 4:1.

It seems necessary, therefore, to assume that a shift back to public discourse
should be understood to occur at 4:26.

The narrative introduction (4:1-2) places Jesus in the boat that the disciples secured for him in 3:9 as part of the introduction to this subsection.
The boat is necessary here, as in the introduction, because of the size of the
crowd, which is now opposite Jesus on the land (4:1). The author specifies
what follows as teaching *en parabolais*, that is, by analogy.

The evangelist's choice of the agricultural parables (B—4:3-9 and B'—
4:26-32) from among the "many such" parables in the Jesus tradition available to him was a master stroke of crosscultural communication. Agricultural
teaching illustrations are found in the Old Testament, in Christian and
Jewish apocalyptic literature of the first century, and among Greek philosophers and rhetors. Thus, hearers of different cultural backgrounds would
have found points of connection with these stories.

Burton Mack has pointed out that "the image of agricultural endeavor,
especially that of sowing seed, was the standard analogy for paideia (i.e.,
teaching and culture) during this period" (Mack 1989b, 149). For example:
"The views of our teachers are as it were the seeds. Learning from childhood
is analogous to the seeds falling betimes upon the prepared ground" (Mack
1989b, 156, citing Hippocrates, III).

As in the first parable in Mark 4, undesirable plants such as thorns are
used as examples of impediments to learning: "If you wish to argue that the
mind requires cultivation, you would use a comparison drawn from the soil,
which if neglected produces thorns and thickets, but if cultivated will bear
fruit" (Quintilian, V.xi.24). Another obstacle to fruitfulness, rocky soil,
appears in an analogy in Sirach 40:15 (mid-second century BCE) "The children of the ungodly put out few branches; they are unhealthy roots on sheer
rock" (NRSV).

The apocalyptic document known as 2 Esdras (4 Ezra) (late first century
CE) employs the motif of mixed results in agriculture: "For just as the farmer
sows many seeds in the ground and plants a multitude of seedlings, and yet
not all that have been sown will come up in due season, and not all that were
planted will take root; so also those who have been sown in the world will
not all be saved" (8:41, NRSV). In the Markan parable of the different kinds
of soil (4:3-9), all the seed is presumed to be equally good; the problems
result from the kind of ground on which the seed happens to fall. This

differs from the emphasis of the parable that follows this one in Matthew, in which some seeds are good and some are bad, but they are allowed to grow together until the harvest (Matt 13:24-30).

In the parable of the soils the fruitfulness is remarkably abundant. This is clear from the rhetoric of the passage itself and does not require special knowledge about normal expectations in first-century agriculture. If his intent had been merely to report a final success by contrast with the three failures, the narrator would have had only to say that "the seeds grew into plants and produced grain." Instead, the final sentence "explodes with verbs of motion. The seeds fell (*epesen*) and brought forth (*edidou*) grain, growing up (*anabainonta*), increasing (*auxanomena*), and they yielded (*epheren*) thirtyfold, sixtyfold, and a hundredfold" (Donahue 1988, 34).

The parable of the soils mentions the yield, but not the harvest. However, the harvest as the time when the final results are evident is present in the parable of the seed that grows automatically (4:26-29). This second parable seems to emphasize that there is nothing for the farmer to do between planting and harvesting; the earth bears fruit *automatē* (literally, "automatically"). Here is a sharp contrast with most Hellenistic notions of paideia, where the emphasis is on the human effort necessary to produce the "fruit" of genuine education.

In his *Progymnasmata* (7.10–8.14) the rhetorician Hermogenes shows how to elaborate a chreia to make this point: "Isocrates said that the root of education is bitter, but the fruit is sweet. . . . Then the elaboration from analogy: For just as farmers must work with the soil before reaping its fruits, so also must those who work with words" (Mack 1989a, 51-52). Hellenistic hearers would have noticed the absence in the Markan parables of exhortations to constant tilling, weeding, and watering (Mack 1989b, 156, 158). A similar minimization of the human role is found in Paul: "I planted, Apollos watered, but God gave the growth. So neither the one who plants nor the one who waters is anything, but only God who gives the growth" (1 Cor 4:6-7). In both Mark and Paul the contrast with the Hellenistic emphasis on human effort is a result of the apocalyptic worldview in which God is the primary actor and humans respond to God's initiative.

The last line of the second seed parable echoes Joel 3:13a: "Put in the sickle, for the harvest is ripe." In the apocalyptic worldview "harvest" is a common image for the final judgment of creation at the shift of the ages (cf. Matt 13:24-30). This will occur at a time chosen by God, about which it is not the business of human beings to inquire:

Then I answered and said, "How long?" . . . He answered me and said, "Do not be in a greater hurry than the Most High. . . . Did not the souls of the righteous in their chambers ask about these matters, saying, 'How long are we to remain here? and when will the harvest of our reward come?' And the archangel Jeremiel answered and said, 'When the number of those like yourselves is completed; for he has weighed the age in the balance.' " (2 Esdras 4:33-36 NRSV; cf. 4:28-32)

A successful harvest is not something that human beings can accomplish, but it is something for which they may pray:

And this I pray: that your love may increase more and more with knowledge and all discernment so that you recognize what really matters, with the result that you may be pure and blameless at the day of Christ, filled with the fruit of righteousness *that comes through Jesus Christ*, to the glory and praise of God. (Phil 1:9-11, my translation and emphasis)

This theme of God's reign as gift, not achievement, is present in the parable of the seed that grows automatically. The farmer merely sows the seed. After that, all he does is "sleep and rise," not knowing how the seed is growing, not calculating what the result will be. This certainty of success parallels the first parable in which abundance results despite the failure of many seeds to mature. It is also reminiscent of Isaiah 55:10-11:

For as the rain and the snow come down from heaven, and do not return there until they have watered the earth, making it bring forth and sprout, giving seed to the sower and bread to the eater, so shall my word be that goes out from my mouth; it shall not return to me empty, but it shall accomplish that which I purpose, and succeed in the thing for which I sent it. (NRSV)

Although the growth is gradual and automatic in the parable, the time of the harvest comes with jolting suddenness—"immediately." The suddenness of the end will be reemphasized in the later apocalyptic discourse, Mark 13.

The parable of the mustard seed (4:30-32) plays another of the themes of the first seed parable in a different key: The final result is a remarkable contrast to the ordinary beginnings. In the parable of the soils the threefold failure was overcome by the final success. This time the smallness of the mustard seed is contrasted with the resulting "greatest of all shrubs."

The portrayal of a kingdom as a great tree with large branches that shelter the birds of the air would have been a familiar image to those members of the Markan audience who knew their Bible. It was used in Daniel 4:10-17 as a symbol for the arrogant Babylonian empire, in Ezekiel 31:3-14 for the Assyrian empire, and in Ezekiel 17:22-24 for the glorious Messianic kingdom that was expected after the humiliation of the exile. The Markan story, however, does not end with the portrayal of a mighty cedar or the cosmic tree at the center of the universe but with an almost comically humble mustard bush (Waetjen 1989, 108-109).

So the parable makes two points: (1) The large bush is quite a contrast with its tiny beginnings, and so God's reign, though it began with one Galilean teacher, will grow surprisingly large. (2) God's reign will not be a prideful domineering empire like the Babylonians, the Assyrians, or even the Messianic kingdom expected by Ezekiel. It will not be a means by which the underdogs overthrow their oppressors and replace the evil empire with one in which they are on top for a change. But when God reigns unopposed, the shelter will be large enough to include all who flock to it.

The cumulative effect of the three seed parables is encouragment to hearers who may feel that God's reign is losing more ground than it is gaining. The promise is that sowing is enough. If that one step is taken, God will do the rest. When the time of harvest comes, the yield will be surprisingly abundant. Why, it will be as great as . . . a mustard bush! Like the fox in Joel Chandler Harris' fable, the unsuspecting listener has been encouraged to expect great things, and the crafty narrator has delivered a briarpatch. But as it turns out, that is just the shelter needed by a homeless bird or a wily rabbit.

In the two units of private teaching (C—4:10-12 and C'—4:21-25) that frame the allegorical interpretation of the parable of the soils, the going becomes difficult for the audience of the Gospel. In 4:10-12 the purpose clauses indicate that the reason for parables is to conceal meaning, but in 4:21-25 the audience learns that the purpose of concealment is revelation and openness. It is clear that this constitutes a challenge to the audience, but clarity is short-lived in this chapter. The audience is well advised to "Watch out for what you hear" (4:24).

The private teaching to "those around him with the twelve" (C) begins with a request for an explanation (4:10). This pattern of dialogue, in which a teaching or parable evokes a question that leads to further explanation, is found in both Greek and Jewish literature in antiquity. In Greek narratives about or dialogues among teachers and students "the disciple is never completely able to fathom the system of thought and action taught and manifested by the teacher" (Robbins, 1992a, 168). It is this characteristic that enables the story to continue. If Theaetetus had been allowed by Plato to define knowledge correctly at the beginning of his conversation with Socrates, there would have been nowhere else to go with the composition. The student(s) must be deficient in understanding in order for the teacher to tease the readers "overhearing" the conversation into thinking about the issues.

The pattern has a slightly different function in Jewish apocalyptic literature, where parables and visions require interpretation by the seer's angelic interlocutor before they can be fully understood. For example, in 2 Esdras 4:13-18, an angel tells the parable of the forest and the sea. The forest plots to take over the sea's territory for trees, and the sea plots to expand its territory into the forest, but both plans are thwarted by nature. Ezra's response in 4:19 indicates that he understands the parable partially. The angel rebukes his inadequate perception and provides a fuller explanation in 4:20-21.

Similarly, in 1 Enoch the seer experiences "parables," which are actually combinations of prophetic speech and visions. The "first parable" is found in 1 Enoch 38:1—43:2. In 43:3 Enoch asks his angelic interlocutor, "What are these things?" and the angel provides the interpretation—which is itself somewhat enigmatic (see also 2 Baruch 22:3-8). Thus, although parables in apocalyptic literature are used to communicate important and mysterious truths to human recipients, the process of communication is not complete without additional explanation from an agent of God. Furthermore, revelation in apocalyptic literature is limited. Certain things are restricted to the seer and the few he may be instructed to tell. Ezra is told, "Some things you shall make public, and some you shall deliver in secret to the wise" (2 Esdras 14:26) (Patten 1983).

This means that the evangelist regards Jesus' teaching in parables as apocalyptic revelation that cannot be understood without further explanation by God's authorized interpreter. Those to whom the interpretation is given are often rebuked for their obtuseness, but this highlights the importance and profundity of the teaching by contrast with the inadequacy of human understanding. That "those about him with the twelve" asked about the parables and received the explanation would have indicated to the audience that they were in the standard posture of those who learn secrets from a wise teacher or an apocalyptic revealer. That they had to ask and that they received a rebuke for not understanding immediately (4:13) would not have been regarded as an indication that they were failures as disciples.

Jesus responds to the inquiring disciples that in the parable he has just told they have been given the secret of God's reign (4:11), and that if they don't understand the parable of the soils, they will not be able to understand all the parables (4:13). Not until the allegorical interpretation in 4:14-20 does the audience understand what was revealed in the parable: Despite the fact that the reign of God is opposed by Satan and that its adherents are vulnerable to persecution and apostasy, it is nevertheless taking root and will finally flourish (Marcus 1986, 49, 122, 224). The mystery is *given* in the parable, but it is *explained* in the allegory. Note that the evangelist never comments on whether or not the disciples *understood* this explanation or any of the explanations alluded to in 4:34. That the mystery of God's reign and the explanation of the parables is given to the disciples (and, courtesy of the narrator, to the audience of the Gospel) is a matter of grace. Whether or not the disciples (and the audience) really hear and appropriate what they have been given is another matter altogether.

The Markan Jesus contrasts this group to which he is about to explain the parable of the soils with "those outside," to whom "everything happens in parables." He then paraphrases Isaiah 6:9-10 to provide the reason: "So that they may indeed look, but not perceive, and may indeed listen, but not understand so that they may not turn again and be forgiven." No text of Isaiah is extant that corresponds to this wording, and many have pointed to similarities with the Aramaic targum, or posited a lost Greek version of Isaiah (Beavis 1989, 140). There is no compelling reason, however, to deny that the evangelist is responsible for the paraphrase.

The author of Mark has written the Gospel in such a way that the themes of sight and hearing pervade both story and discourse. The parable of the soils began with the double summons, "Listen! See!" (*akouete, idou*) and ended with the warning, "Let anyone with ears to hear listen!" That warning is repeated in 4:23 and followed in 4:24 by "Look at what you hear!" *(blepete ti akouete)*. It has already become clear in the narrative up to this point that interpreting correctly what they see and hear is not easy for people who encounter the Markan Jesus. Peter and his companions see in the praying Jesus a healer who is shirking his responsibilities (1:36-37). The scribes hear blasphemy in his word of forgiveness to the paralytic (2:2). The Pharisees see meeting human need as violating Torah (2:24; 3:2). Jesus' family hears about his activity and concludes that he is insane (3:21), and the scribes from Jerusalem view his exorcisms as evidence that he is demon-possessed (3:22).

At the same time, however, the audience of the Gospel has heard and seen things that give them more insight than the characters in the story. They heard 1:1 and know that Jesus is the Messiah, Son of God. Only the audience shared Jesus' experience of seeing the heavens split apart and the Spirit descending on Jesus (1:10). The voice from heaven spoke only to Jesus, but the audience was listening to the divine affirmation of him (1:11). When Jesus was alone in the desert with wild animals, Satan, and angels, the hearers of the story were his unseen companions (1:12-13). When the Pharisees and Herodians privately plotted Jesus' undoing, only the audience was privy to their scheme (3:6). Now the audience is among those around Jesus hearing that the secret of God's reign was given in the parable of the soils and waiting to learn what that secret might be. They have heard the summons to listen and look (4:3) and have also heard that just having ears is not enough; it is necessary to use ears to listen (4:9).

Before he gives the interpretation of the parable of the soils, the Markan Jesus appeals to the theology of Isaiah. From the perspective of outsiders, the entire ministry of Jesus ("all things," *panta*)happens in parables. They see, but they can't read between the lines. They hear, but the message goes in one ear and out the other. This is the way God has planned things, so that the outsiders will not change direction and be forgiven. The purpose of the parables and deeds of Jesus is to prevent insight and repentance on the part of "those outside" (*exō*, 4:11). By citing Isaiah, the evangelist points out that this strange purpose is consistent with God's purpose in the past.

Immediately after Isaiah eagerly responds to God's call in 6:8b, he learns in 6:9-10 that his job is to "make the heart of this people thick," to "stop their ears and close their eyes," so that they may not see, hear, understand, and repent. In the ministry of Jesus, according to Mark, God is again at work in history. God has again sent a messenger, and again the message makes eyes blind and ears deaf. But this time the messenger provides an explanation to a smaller group. Like the apocalyptic interpreting angel, he explains what would otherwise be inexplicable, but only to a few who inquire. But before they begin to congratulate themselves on being the privileged insiders, the disciples and the audience would do well to reflect on the fact that it was precisely God's beloved elect insiders whom Isaiah was sent to harden, deafen, and make blind. The hardness of heart that is part of the original passage in Isaiah is not mentioned here in Mark, but it would have been expected by hearers who were familiar with the scriptures. The evangelist satisfies that expectation the next time he alludes to Isaiah 6:9-10. In the final boat scene, 8:14-21, those who are blind, deaf, and hard of heart are the disciples.

It is one of the persistent scandals of biblical theology that those whose hearts are hardened by God or God's agents are nevertheless regarded as culpable for their stubborn resistance to God's word and will. The pharaoh of the Exodus narrative is perhaps the best known example of this motif. Modern readers of the Bible are not the first to find this notion offensive. The author of the Wisdom of Solomon found it necessary to engage in apologetic explanations of the Exodus story, no doubt in response to pagan objections:

> God knew in advance even their future actions: how, though they them-
> selves had permitted your people to depart . . . they would change their
> minds and pursue them . . . For the fate they deserved drew them on to
> this end, and made them forget what had happened, in order that they
> might fill up the punishment that their torments still lacked. (Wis 19:1, 4
> NRSV)

This idea that the hardening serves the purpose of keeping people unrepen-
tant until they have received appropriate discipline for their rebellion is
found in Isaiah 6:11:

> Then [in response to the commission to cause deafness, blindness and
> hardness of heart in God's people] I said, "How long, O Lord?" And he
> said, "Until cities lie waste without inhabitant and houses without people
> and the land is utterly desolate; until the Lord sends everyone far away and
> vast is the emptiness in the midst of the land." (NRSV)

Deutero-Isaiah then begins with the proclamation that this period has been
completed:

> Comfort, O comfort my people, says your God. Speak tenderly to
> Jerusalem, and cry to her that she has served her term, that her penalty is
> paid, that she has received from the Lord's hand double for all her sins. (Isa
> 40:1-2 NRSV)

Paul also found it necessary to defend God against the charge of injustice
when he employed the hardening motif in Romans 9–11. In the course of
his argument Paul appealed to Isaiah frequently, not leaving out the topic of
eyes that do not see and ears that do not hear (9:7; Isa 29:10). In Romans
11:25 Paul calls the hardening of Israel a *mysterion*, the same noun used in
Mark 4:11.

Certainly human resistance to the Sovereign of creation and history has
always been a mystery. One biblical solution is that even this resistance falls
within the purposes of God. To find this solution unsatisfying puts the interpreter in good philosophical company. However, to excise from the text of
Mark 4:10-12 its obvious meaning simply because the interpreter finds it
unsatisfying is exegetically irresponsible, if all too common. The evangelist's
way of dealing with the problem is more subtle. He balances the *hina*

purpose clauses about blindness and concealment in 4:10-12 (C) with the *hina* purpose clauses about enlightenment and openness in 4:21-25 (C') (Via 1985, 184).

The material in 4:21-25 (Section C') abandons the agricultural images for domestic ones: lamp, basket, bed, lampstand. Rhetorical questions, worded so as to evoke a negative response, ask whether a lamp is brought into a dark room for the purpose of being hidden under a basket or under a bed. Of course not! Rather, the purpose of the lamp is to be placed on a lampstand so that it can light up the room. Then, since this is teaching to insiders, an interpretation is given: "For there is nothing hidden except to be disclosed; nor is anything secret, except to come to light." The synonymous parallelism reinforces the point: The hiddenness that may appear as senseless as putting a lamp under the bed will eventually be shown to have served the purpose of openness and manifestation. What is hidden now is hidden *in order that* it may ultimately be brought to light (Marcus 1986, 147).

The private teaching ends with a summons to see and hear, followed by two cryptic warnings about measuring, having, and losing. In the apocalyptic texts found in the caves near Qumran, the image of the "measure" is used in contexts about having or not having knowledge or spiritual insight. In 1QS 8:4, community members are dealt with "according to the measure of truth" and in 1QH 14:18-19 the phrase "the greatness of his portion" is placed parallel to "his understanding" (Marcus 1986, 153). If the images in the sayings of 4:24-25 are taken as referring to the measure of understanding that one has, and the insight into the "things of God" (Mark 8:33) that one possesses, then they may be paraphrased as Marcus suggests:

> To the degree that you pay attention to what God has already revealed, to that degree will more revelation be bestowed upon you (154). "He who has" the things of God, the mystery of God's kingdom, will be further enriched by new revelations of the glory that breaks forth in the midst of darkness; but "he who does not have" the things of God, who remains enmeshed in "the things of human beings," the realm of appearances associated with the old age, will in the end lose even the superficial perception that he possesses (156).

The use of the second person plural in 4:24 again expands the address beyond the characters at the story level to include the audience of the Gospel. Knowing that they have been given the secret of God's reign should not make them complacent. They need to pay attention to the insight they have. A warning is implied both for the disciples and for the audience.

The allegorical interpretation of the parable of the soils occupies the place of emphasis at the center of the chiastic structure (D—4:13-20). The Markan Jesus tells those gathered around him that understanding this parable is critically important for understanding all the parables. Since 4:11 implied that even Jesus' actions are parabolic in the apocalyptic sense and therefore require insight, it is hard to overemphasize the importance of 4:13-20 for understanding the Gospel as a whole. The interpretation reveals that although Jesus proclaims the good news about God's coming reign everywhere, it is not received everywhere it is proclaimed. God's reign is opposed by Satan, and those who do respond are in danger of apostasy caused by persecution and the distractions of wealth and other temporal pursuits. In some people, however, the gospel will take root and thrive, producing an abundant crop.

Although the sower is not identified explicitly, the author must have intended the audience to identify the sower with Jesus. The sower sows "the word" (*logos*) on "the earth" (*gēs*). Jesus, who was portrayed in 2:2 as speaking "the word" (*logos*) to the crowd, sat in a boat in 4:1 and taught the crowd, who remained on "the land" (*gēs*). The sower casts the seed widely, onto a variety of different kinds of soil.

The failure of some seed to bear fruit is interpreted by three sets of circumstances. The seed that falls on (or beside) the path does not take root because Satan (the birds) snatches it away. The hearers learn that Satan's activity consists not only of possessing the victims that Jesus has been liberating by exorcism, but also of preventing persons from taking in the message of God's reign that Jesus is announcing. The first failure refers to those people who, although they hear the message, do not even begin as followers of Jesus.

The second and third failures are not failures of people to be converted, but failures of converts to follow through in discipleship. Although Satan is not mentioned explicitly in the interpretation of the rocky soil and the thorny soil, his activity is understood to be behind these failures as well. The evangelist has already identified Satan's "house" as the opposition to God's reign and therefore the focus of Jesus' offensive (3:23-27). The whole parable chapter is heavily apocalyptic in tone. The allegorical interpretation in particular contains vocabulary suggesting the battle between God's reign and Satan's opposition; besides the explicit name *satanas*, one finds *thlipsis*, the "tribulations" associated with the shift of the ages (4:17), and *aion*, the present evil "age" (4:19).

The plants that take root on rocky ground are unable to withstand "tribulations and persecution on account of the word" and "fall away" or, literally, "are caused to stumble" (*skandalizomai*, 4:17). Those that take root among thorns are prevented from bearing fruit because they are choked by personified evils: the concerns of this age, the "seduction which comes from wealth" (BAG trans.), and the lust for other things. The "other things" that choke the word here will later in the Gospel be specified as "human things," which stand in opposition to "the things of God." In 8:33 these are explicitly blamed on "Satan" (Marcus 1986, 62-64). Those who succumb to the seduction of wealth are not people who fail to become disciples at all (10:17-22), but disciples who fail to bear fruit because the word is choked out of them by the distractions of the present evil age.

Thus, the three failures point to (1) those who are prevented from converting (seeds along the path), (2) converts who apostasize under conditions of persecution (seeds on rocky ground), and (3) converts who apostasize under conditions of ease and complacency (seeds among thorns).

Marcus is correct in his insistence that the allegorical interpretation is not parenetic in character (60-62). Neither seeds nor soil can change their nature, and the failure of the seeds to take root, or to flourish once they have taken root, is attributed to the influence of Satan, as we have seen. The Markan Jesus is not warning the disciples to be good soil; rather, he is warning them (and the overhearing audience) that even as the reign of God takes root and flourishes in some quarters, it will provoke opposition, persecution, and seduction from the forces of evil. It is the nature of the reign of God to provoke opposition; it cannot be otherwise.

This interpretation at the focal point of the parable chapter serves a dual purpose in the Gospel. It explains why Jesus, the bringer of life and wholeness, encounters obtuseness and opposition and is finally put to death. It also explains the present situation of the Christians for whom this biography in an apocalyptic mode is addressed. Marcus points out that while the parable of the soils is narrated in the past tense (A sower went out to sow, the seed *fell*, *grew*, etc.), the interpretation is narrated in the present tense (The sower *sows* the word, they *hear*, they *receive*, they *fall away*, they *bear fruit*, etc.). Thus, "in the parable itself, the primary horizon is the time of Jesus' ministry, while in the interpretation, the primary horizon is the time of the church" (69). When Christians in the evangelist's time encounter opposition and persecution, or when they see converts lost to the seductive addictions of increased ease and affluence, they are not to be discouraged. This is all part of the ministry to which they are called, and their assignment is to keep sowing, not to calculate success by appearances.

Deeds (4:35–5:43). The unit of parables, 4:1-34, is followed by a unit of miracle stories in 4:35–5:43. Like the parables, the powerful deeds of Jesus proclaim the reign of God and are a source of misunderstanding for those who see, but do not perceive (Matera 1993, 15-26). The connection is emphasized by a chiastic pattern produced by the way in which the quotation from Isaiah 6:9 is altered in Mark 4:12. Although the LXX reads, "Listen but do not understand and look but do not perceive," the Markan version puts seeing before hearing in the quotation and then reverses the order in the narrative structure:

A—They may look, but not perceive (4:12a).
B—They may listen, but not understand (4:12b).
B'—Outsiders hear parables, but receive no explanation (4:1-34).
A'—Outsiders (and disciples!) see miracles but do not perceive (4:35-5:43).

The four miracle stories are grouped in two pairs and reproduce the pattern set in the paradigmatic 1:21-45 by combining exorcisms with healings. The first pair of stories, the conquest of the storm (4:35-41) and the conquest of the Gerasene demons (5:1-20), is set on or near the sea. Both are told as exorcism stories, and both benefit men in need of Jesus' saving power (the disciples, the demoniac). The second pair of stories is joined sandwich-style. The story of Jairus' daughter begins at 5:21, is interrupted by the story of the bleeding woman (5:25-34), and concludes in 5:35-43. Both of these are stories about women who are healed by Jesus; they also have in common "twelve years" (the age of the child and the length of the woman's illness) and the word "daughter" (5:23, 34, 35).

There is a progression through the four stories of the seriousness of the situations from which Jesus rescues people. In the first story the disciples are afraid they may die. The man in Geresa lives among the dead in a kind of living death. The bleeding woman has been experiencing her life draining out of her for twelve years; in ancient thought, "the life is in the blood" (Lev 17:11). Finally, Jairus' daughter is actually dead, but is raised by Jesus.

In this panel of miracle stories the author of Mark makes the point that through Jesus, God's power overcomes every threat to life and wholeness, even the ultimate threat of death. Moreover, Jesus extends this wholeness to men *and* women, Jews *and* gentiles, the pure *and* the polluted. No place or condition is beyond the reach of God's saving power.

To seek Jesus' help on the basis of one's confidence that God's unlimited power is at work in Jesus is called "faith" in these miracle stories. The evangelist puts them here not only to record Jesus' past activity, but also to encourage those who hear the Gospel read aloud to resist paralyzing fear (4:40; 5:36) and to maintain confidence in God's power to overcome evil and death, to heal and make whole.

The first miracle story in this panel takes place on "the sea," and we have already seen that the settings for the ministry of Jesus in Galilee (1:16–8:26) often include a reference to "the sea" (*thalassa*). Jesus calls disciples by the sea (1:16-20, 2:14) and teaches beside the sea (2:13, 4:1). Most of the action in 4:35–8:26 takes place on or near the sea, as Jesus crosses back and forth from one side to the other in the boat to which the audience was introduced in the summary 3:7-12 and from which Jesus taught the crowds in 4:1-34.

Mark 4:35–8:26 involves numerous boat trips on and across the sea. The crossings are from west (the Jewish territory in Galilee) to east (the gentile territory of Bethsaida and the Decapolis) and back again. Jesus heals, casts out demons, and feeds multitudes on both sides of the sea. In this way the evangelist makes it clear that in Jesus the boundaries between Jews and gentiles are eliminated; there is healing and (eucharistic) bread for all (Kelber 1974 and Malbon 1986b, contra Fowler 1981).

The Gospel of Mark is the first written evidence we have of the use of the name "Sea of Galilee" for the large freshwater lake in north central Palestine. It is called a "lake" (*limnē*) by Josephus (e.g., *War* 2.20.6.573; *Antiquities* 5.1.22.84; *Life* 65.349), Pliny (*Nat. Hist* 5.7.1), and the Gospel of Luke (5:1, 2; 8:22, 23, 33) (Malbon 1984, 364; Freyne 1992, 900). Ancient writers typically use *thalassa* in reference to an ocean, such as the Mediterranean.

The Markan use of *thalassa* conforms to the practice of the LXX, which translates the Hebrew *yam* with the Greek *thalassa* (cf. Num 34:11; Josh 12:3; 13:27). This enables Mark's narrator to evoke the ancient Near Eastern myth of the divine warrior who battles and finally conquers the forces of chaos represented by "the sea," or a sea-dwelling monster or dragon. The Canaanite god Baal, "rider of the clouds," defeats the sea monster and rules with the authority of the supreme god El. In the Babylonian *Enuma Elish*, Marduk defeats the sea monster and creates the world. Yahweh subdues the sea in creation and in the deliverance of Israel from the Egyptians (Ps 74:12-17; 89:9-14; 104:1-9; 77:16-20; Isa 51:9-11) and is able to save those in danger at sea (Ps 107:23-32; Jonah 1-2; Day 1992).

The defeat of the sea monsters, originally a creation motif, later became an apocalyptic image of God's final victory. In Daniel 7 "one like a son of man (human being)" comes with the clouds and receives authority from the Ancient of Days to replace the beasts from the sea as the ruler of the universe (Day 1992). The deliverance of the elect by the defeat of the sea in the original exodus story became the model for the deliverance from Babylonian bondage in Isaiah and for ultimate deliverance from the powers of evil in later apocalyptic thought (Longman and Reid 1995, 72-82). In the Gospel of Mark, Jesus is portrayed as the divine warrior marching through the wilderness at the head of his liberated people (Marcus 1992b, 40-45). Along the way he fights and defeats the demonic distorters of human wholeness, ironically winning his final victory by his death on the cross.

In Mark 4:35-41 Jesus rebukes the stormy sea that threatens the disciples with death and transforms it from a barrier separating Jewish from gentile territory into a bridge connecting them. The message of the sea crossings and the exorcisms reinforce the message of the parables: God's eschatological victory over Satan is being manifested proleptically in the ministry of Jesus. The battle with Satan has already been won at one level, but is ongoing at another.

Jesus was tempted by Satan in the wilderness (1:14), and his first act after calling four disciples was to drive a demon out of a man in the Capernaum synagogue. Before leaving the scene the demon succeeds in informing the audience that Jesus has come to destroy all such opponents of God's life-giving reign (1:24). Indeed, the demon's cry seems to be directed primarily at the overhearing audience, since the information apparently has no effect on the characters in the story (Fowler 1991, 217). The people of Capernaum notice that the unclean spirits obey Jesus, but apparently they do not grasp the eschatological implications of the arrival of the divine warrior who has come to destroy destruction forever.

Jesus continues his ministry of exorcism and gets in trouble for it (3:20-35). Here the audience learns that Jesus, the "stronger one" (1:7) has tied up "the strong man" and is in the process of robbing him of all he possesses (3:27). As the struggle continues, Satan will succeed in preventing many people from allowing the seed of Jesus' word to take root in them and bear fruit (4:13-19). Nevertheless, the final yield will more than make up for the losses.

As Jesus and his disciples leave the crowd and head east across the sea, into the darkness (1:35), the forces of chaos rise up against this intruder who is headed into battle against their legion in Gerasa. The supernatural character of the storm is made clear by the narrator. The disciples, some of whom are experienced boat fishermen, are convinced they are being destroyed (*apollumetha*; cf. Rev 9:11, where the chief angel or "king" of the abyss is called *Apolluōn*, "Destroyer"). Notice that Jesus does not rebuke the disciples' fear because he regards it as exaggerated; he does not say, "Why are you cowardly; haven't you ever been in a storm before?" Rather, he rebukes them because their fear shows that they have no confidence that Jesus' power is stronger than that of the forces of destruction: "Why are you cowardly? Don't you have faith yet?" After having seen Jesus cast out demons so many times, they should have been confident in his victory over the demonic storm.

There are other clear indications that the storm is portrayed by the narrator as demonic. Parallels with the Capernaum exorcism include the word "rebuke" (4:39; 1:25) the command to silence (4:39; 1:25), and the response to the exorcism (4:41; 1:27). The disciples' whispered question, "Who then is this?" contrasts with the shout of the Capernaum demoniac: "I know who you are, the Holy One of God!" (1:24), to be echoed by the Gerasene demoniac: "What do you want with me, Jesus, you son of the most high God?" (5:7, sv). The missing response to the question "Who then is this?" is provided by the audience who, having been given the answer by the narrator himself (1:1), the voice from heaven (1:11), and the demons, feel like shouting at the disciples, "This is the Son of God!"

Having thwarted the attempt to prevent his invasion, Jesus establishes a beachhead in gentile territory at 5:1 (On the geographical and textual problems, see Guelich 1989, 275-77). The divine warrior motif continues to build upon the traditions surrounding the exodus. Having commanded the sea (cf. Pss 104:1-9; 107:23-32; Isa 43:2), the representative of the Most High God now drowns the troops of the oppressor.

Derrett (1974, 5) has pointed out the numerous military allusions in the Gerasene exorcism story:

- *Legion* (5:9) is a loan word from Latin, meaning a military unit of about 6,000 soldiers.
- *Aposteilē* (5:10) means to order troop movements in Josephus, Herodotus 5.32, Judith 6:3, and 1 Macc 3:35.
- *Agelē*, "herd," (5:11, 13) also can be used for a group of military trainees, which may explain its use here, since pigs do not move in herds as horses, cattle, and sheep do.
- *Epitrepein* (5:13) means "permitted" in this context, but carries the secondary connotation of military command.
- *Hormēsen*, "rushed," (5:13) is the term used by Josephus (*Antiquities* 2.340, 342) and Philo (*Moses* 2.254) for the rush of Pharoah's troops to their death in the sea.

Like Deutero-Isaiah before him, the author of Mark exploits exodus imagery to proclaim God's new act to deliver from oppression (Isa 40:3;

43:2, 16-17; cf. 63:10-14). But this time God is not delivering Jews from the hands of gentiles; rather, the Son of God delivers both Jews and gentiles from the oppression of the Destroyer. Bondage that is apparent, whether political or personal, is for the author of Mark a symptom of the cosmic and spiritual oppression that, although sometimes disguised, is never beyond the reach of the power of Jesus the "stronger one" (1:7) who can bind the "strong man" (3:27).

The description of the man of Gerasa emphasizes the power of the demons that possess him: (5:3-5)

A—He had his dwelling in the tombs (cf. Isa 65:4)
    B—and *no one was able* any longer to bind him with a chain
        C—because he had been bound with many (a) leg-irons and (b) chains
        C'—and the (b') chains were wrenched apart by him and the
            (a') leg-irons broken in pieces
    B'—and *no one was strong enough* to subdue him.
A'—Night and day in the tombs and on the mountains he was howling and bruising himself with stones.

But face to face with "the Son of the Most High God," the demonic power blusters in confusion, tries to steal the exorcist's lines ("I adjure you by God") and finally whines, "Do not torment me!" It is the audience's turn to howl at the tormentor trying to pass itself off as a victim.

But Jesus has already started the exorcism before the spirit has finished its harangue (5:8). For the Markan Jesus, there are limits to inclusiveness. That which destroys the self and makes community impossible is driven out, and wholeness is restored. The good news for this tormented specimen of humanity is not that he is accepted just as he is, but that he is transformed into the person his Creator intended for him to be, no longer distorted by powers that are alien to his created self.

To no one's surprise, the unclean spirits claim an identity with the troops of the alien oppressive power (*legion*) and seek permission to enter the unclean pigs nearby (5:9-12). The pigs then become as self-destructive as the man had once been and rush (30 miles?) to the sea, where the spirits can presumably commiserate with the other demons Jesus has just defeated in the previous story.

The loss of the pork they might have sold to the Roman quartermasters does not incline the citizens of Gerasa to respond favorably to Jesus' presence. Like the disciples in the boat, they are afraid (*ephobēthēsan*—4:41; 5:15). The former demoniac, who is not likely to be very popular either, begs to go with Jesus, but instead is sent away from his dwelling in the tombs and back to his home to take up residence among the living rather than among the dead and to bear witness to "how much the Lord has done" for him. The man's response has two effects: (1) By preaching (*kerussein*, cf. 1:14, 3:14), he participates in the activity of Jesus and his disciples, becoming the one who makes the deeds of the Lord "known among the Gentiles" (Isa 12:3). (2) His proclamation equates the merciful activity of the Lord with the ministry of Jesus, thus suggesting an answer to the disciples' question, "Who then is this?" Of course, since they are with Jesus and not in the Decapolis where the proclamation takes place, the disciples do not benefit from this information. Only the audience of the Gospel does.

The final two stories in this panel take place in Jewish territory, as the narrator makes clear by having Jesus cross "to the other side" and encounter a synagogue official (Malbon 1992, 39). The emphasis shifts away from cosmic combat to healing, but the boundary-crossing character of Jesus' ministry is still apparent. Having crossed geographical boundaries to release a gentile from bondage to the Destroyer, Jesus returns to Jewish territory where his healing power crosses traditional impurity boundaries to restore life to two suffering women.

The bleeding woman plays the two roles in her story that are divided between Jairus and his daughter in their story; she is both the one who needs healing and the one who believes in Jesus' power and seeks his help. The way the stories are told emphasizes the similarities between the woman and Jairus' daughter and the differences between the woman and Jairus himself.

Both the woman and Jairus' daughter are female, and both are nameless in the narrative. Only Jairus has a name; perhaps a few hearers would have enjoyed the recognition that his name meant "he enlightens" or "he awakes" (Guelich 1989, 295). The bleeding woman has been dying as long as the child has been living—twelve years. Both are "daughters." Although it is clear that the girl has a caring father, it would appear that the woman has no one. However, Jesus calls her "daughter;" she is not alone after all.

Both women are ritually impure when Jesus encounters them. According to Torah, vaginal bleeding rendered a woman unclean (Lev 5:19-30), and all corpses were unclean (Num 19:11-21). Anyone who came in contact with a bleeding woman or a corpse, or who entered a dwelling where a corpse lay, also became unclean. A living person who was unclean was ineligible to participate in the worship of God until a specified time had passed and certain cleansing rituals had been performed. It was appropriate for Jairus to ask Jesus to touch his daughter as long as she was alive (5:23), but Jesus should have been rendered unclean by taking the dead girl by the hand (5:41) and by the woman's touch (5:27). Exactly the reverse, however, is what takes place. Jesus does not become impure; the woman becomes pure, and the dead child is restored to life. Impurity is not transmitted to Jesus; rather, both physical health and ritual purity are transmitted to the women.

This is not a polemic against Jewish purity codes (contra Selvidge 1990). Vaginal bleeding was also regarded as mysterious (Aristotle, *On Dreams*, 459b-460a), magical (Pliny, *Natural History*, 28.23) and polluting (Plutarch, Fragment 97) by non-Jews in antiquity. The story does not suggest that the bleeding woman should not have been regarded as ritually impure prior to her healing; it celebrates her restoration to purity by her healing. What Jesus does for the bleeding woman here and for the leper in 1:40-45 is to restore the right relationships symbolized by the purity codes; he restores people to the presence of God and to the human community.

Both Jairus and the bleeding woman are portrayed positively as demonstrating confidence in Jesus' healing power—Jairus, by what he says to Jesus (5:23), and the woman, by what she says to herself (5:28). The Markan Jesus names this confidence "faith" (5:34, 36), where the present imperative may be translated "keep on believing," in recognition that Jairus had believed for his daughter's healing and now must keep on believing for her resuscitation (Stock 1989, 173). But there the similarity ends.

Jairus is a leader of the synagogue—a religious and social insider. He has a right to ask for help and he does so directly, but not arrogantly. Rather than flaunting his social and religious status, he humbles himself (5:22-23), an attitude that Jesus will praise in 9:35 and 10:41-45.

The bleeding woman, by contrast, has been a religious and social outsider for twelve years, experiencing neither the worship of God nor human embrace. She has no right to be brushing up against people in the crowd and no right to jeopardize Jesus' ritual status by touching him, but like the anointing woman in Mark 14, she does what she can. She refuses to let her life be defined by what appear to be hopeless circumstances.

Mark 5:26 represents the strongest polemic against physicians found in the entire Bible; Matthew 9:20 omits the sentence, and Luke 8:43 softens it to "she could not be healed by anyone." Mark's fourfold indictment is extreme: (1) she had suffered much under many physicians; (2) she had spent all that she had; (3) she did not improve; (4) in fact, she became worse after treatment. Hippocrates confirms the problem in his treatise on *Diseases of Women* 1.62:

> Sometimes diseases become incurable for women who do not learn why they are sick before the doctor has been correctly taught by the sick woman why she is sick. . . . At the same time the doctors also make mistakes by not

learning the apparent cause through accurate questioning, but they pro-
ceed to heal as though they were dealing with men's diseases. I have already
seen many women die from just this kind of suffering. (translation by
Lefkowitz and Fant 1992, 237)

Indeed, when one reads the descriptions of treatments for uterine hemorrhage that were practiced in Mediterranean antiquity, it is easy to see why
the author of Mark would characterize the woman as having "suffered much
under many physicians" and as having become worse rather than better as a
result. The second-century CE physician Soranus describes treatments
developed by his predecessors of the previous two centuries and expresses a
preference for "relatively drastic vaginal suppositories, for instance oak gall,
pulverized frankincense, chalcites in equal parts, together with sweet wine; or
ashes of . . . a sea sponge soaked in raw pitch and then put inside. . . ."
(*Gynecology* 3.10.41). Soranus knows that some physicians use bloodletting
as a treatment for hemorrhage, but he opposes this on the grounds that it
may "quickly kill the woman" (3.10.42). It is no wonder that Rabbi Judah is
said to have held that "the best among physicians is going to Gehenna"
(Qidd. 4:14, Neusner trans.).

But the woman in Mark's story has not given in to despair. She takes
bold action on the basis of what she has heard about Jesus (5:27; cf. 3:10).
Jesus calls her bold confidence "faith" and sends her into new life with a
blessing that combines the traditional Jewish "shalom" (peace) with the
Hellenistic "keep healthy" (5:34) (Robbins 1987, 510).

By the end of this unit the audience has witnessed four victories in the
eschatological warfare manifested in Jesus' ministry; Jesus has saved people
from the threat of chaos, from spiritual bondage, from illness and isolation,
and from death. If the parables emphasized the assurance of final victory
despite opposition, the miracles promise present help for those who call on
Jesus with confidence in his power.

The final sentence of the section has puzzled interpreters. After raising
Jairus' daughter, Jesus "strictly ordered them that no one should know this"
(5:43). This, of course, is absurd. The funeral was in progress (5:38). There
was no mistake about the girl's death, as the mocking of the mourners at
Jesus' words of assurance makes clear (5:40). It would have been impossible
for the parents to call off the funeral in such a way that "no one would
know" that things had changed. Obviously, this sentence functions not at the
story level, but at the level of discourse. It is not meant to fit into a realistic
plot structure, but to signal the audience that these demonstrations of Jesus'
power to heal and deliver do not give a complete understanding of his

mission and identity. They are not unambiguous proof of God's reign. That will become abundantly clear in the next scene when Jesus returns to his hometown.

Misinterpretation by Associates in Hometown (6:1-6)

Jesus' encounter with his compatriots in his hometown (*patrida*, identified in 1:9 as Nazareth) synagogue presents the evangelist with the opportunity to clarify the audience's understanding of "faith" and "unbelief." It is not enough to believe that Jesus has the power to exorcise and heal; true faith recognizes in these activities the inbreaking of God's reign.

This second instance of misunderstanding of Jesus' miracle-working activity by intimate associates corresponds to 3:20-35 in the author's chiastic outline of 3:13–6:30. It follows immediately after the panel of miracle stories in 4:35–5:43 and provides important insights into how the evangelist wanted the miracles to be interpreted.

The passage may be outlined as follows:

Narrative introduction—Jesus entered and taught, the people were amazed (6:1-2b)
A—Reaction of the people in direct discourse (6:2c-3b)
B—Narrative interpretation (6:3c)
A'—Reaction of Jesus in direct discourse (6:4)
B'—Narrative interpretation (6:5)
Narrative conclusion—Jesus was amazed; he left and taught (6:6)

The amazed response of the people of Nazareth appears at first to be much like responses to Jesus everywhere until the audience hears exactly what they say. Like the scribes of 3:22, they raise questions about the source of Jesus' power and wisdom (*pothen* = from where?). They recognize that Jesus is doing miraculous things (*dunameis*) and that he has been given (*dotheisa*) extraordinary wisdom, but they do not see in these phenomena the inbreaking of the reign of God, and they do not recognize that God is the source of Jesus' power and wisdom. They point to Jesus' ordinary occupation (*tektōn*, carpenter, by contrast with a scribe or a teacher) and to his nontraditional family ("son of Mary," rather than the traditional "Bar Joseph"). "Who does this fellow think he is anyway? We knew him when he was in swaddling clothes. He's getting something from somewhere, but who knows where?"

The narrator interprets for the audience: *eskandalizonto in autō*. The verb *skandalizomai* is important in Mark, appearing in 4:17, 9:42-47, and 14:27, where it means to be caused to commit apostasy—to abandon allegiance to Jesus after beginning as a disciple. Here, however, it is used of outsiders and means to be prevented from becoming a disciple. The people of Nazareth are like the seed that fell beside the path; they never take root. Their opinions about who Jesus is stand in their way. Jesus' combination of human ordinariness and divine power makes no sense to them. In 8:33 Jesus will call this kind of posture "human thinking" by contrast with "God's thinking." Here, Jesus is amazed by their non-faith (*apistian*). This is a development beyond the concept of faith assumed by the miracle stories just narrated. Merely recognizing that Jesus has power is not faith. Faith is confidence in the saving power of *God* as manifested in the ministry of Jesus.

The statement in 6:5-6a is a curious one: "And he was not able to do any miracle there, except that he put his hands on a few sick people and healed them. And he was amazed because of their unbelief." The clause containing the exception completely nullifies the independent clause. Logic demands that either Jesus was *not* able to do *any* miracle, or he *was* able to do *a few* miraculous healings. Defying this logic, the author insists that *both* things were the case. That is because the evangelist's view of the relationship between faith and miracle is more complex than is usually recognized.

Interpreters of the Markan miracle stories have often made two assertions: (1) The stories make faith a condition of miracles; that is, faith must precede a miracle. (2) Miracles do not lead to faith in Mark, by contrast with pagan miracle stories and even by contrast with the other Gospels. The first assertion is only partially true, and the second assertion is completely false.

It is certainly the case that the evangelist advocates faith on the part of those who seek healing or exorcism. This is clear in the story of the hemorrhaging woman (5:24b-34), the story of blind Bartimaeus (10:46-52), and the story of the paralytic (2:1-12). When the Markan Jesus urges Jairus to believe (5:36), the implication is that if he believes, as the woman did, then his daughter will be healed, even as the woman was healed. The father of the demon-possessed boy interprets Jesus' "If you can! All things are possible to the one who believes" to mean that if he had faith, his faith would lead to the healing of his son. That is why he responds as he does in 9:23, "I believe; help my unbelief!" Faith as a condition for miracles in Mark is made explicit in the prayer teaching in 11:22-24. The Markan Jesus tells the disciples that things that are possible only for God "will be done for" the person who has "faith in God" and "does not doubt." Clearly, faith leads to miracles in Mark.

The assertion that miracles do not lead to faith is based on the fact that the author of Mark never states that the recipient of a miracle "believed" as a result of the miracle. There is no Markan equivalent to the Johannine, "This . . . Jesus did . . . and . . . they believed in him" (2:11; cf. 7:31; 9:38; 11:45).

There is a real sense, however, in which miracles do lead to faith in the sense of confidence in the possibility of miracles, or confidence in God's power at work through Jesus.

In the Markan narrative it is often made clear that the people who come to Jesus seeking miraculous help do so because of his reputation as a miracle worker. In 2:1-12 the four men who bring the paralytic are part of the crowd that is gathered in Capernaum (2:1-3) as a result of Jesus' reputation as a healer and exorcist, both in Capernaum and in "all Galilee" (1:21-45).

About the hemorrhaging woman the narrator tells the audience that "she had heard [things] about Jesus" (5:27) and that she said to herself that just touching his clothes would result in her healing (5:28). The narrator portrays the woman as having heard miracle stories about people who were healed by touching Jesus (3:10). Similarly, Bartimaeus began to cry out "because he heard, 'It's Jesus of Nazareth!' " (10:47). There is a direct connection between the reputation of the healer and the faith of those seeking healing. They believe that Jesus can heal them because they have heard about his healing others. It is in this sense that miracles, or rather reports about miracles, do lead to faith in the Gospel of Mark.

This suggests that the author of Mark understands miracle stories to function in much the same way that inscriptions and votive offerings functioned in the Asclepius cult at Epidauros and Corinth. At Corinth plaster models of body parts, each representing a healing of the limb or organ represented, were hung on the temple walls. These functioned partly as offerings of thanksgiving, but also as an encouragement to sick people coming to the temple for a cure. At Epidauros the votives took the form of tablets inscribed with accounts of the cures. One of these is particularly relevant to the issue of the relationship between faith and miracle.

> A man who was paralyzed in all his fingers except one came as a suppliant to the god. When he was looking at the plaques in the sanctuary, he didn't believe in (*apistei*) the cures and was somewhat disparaging of the inscriptions. Sleeping here, he saw a vision. It seemed he was playing the knuckle-bones below the temple, and as he was about to throw them, the god appeared, sprang on his hand and stretched out the fingers. When the god moved off, the man seemed to bend his hand and stretch out his fingers one by one. When he had straightened them all, the god asked him if he would still not believe (*apistesoi*) the inscriptions on the plaques around the sanctuary and he answered no. "Therefore, since you doubted (*apisteis*) them before, though they were not unbelievable (*ouk apistois*), from now on," he said, "your name shall be 'Unbeliever'" (*Apistos*). When day came he left well. (A3, LiDonnici trans.)

In this story the inscribed miracle stories around the sanctuary do not have the desired effect at first; the patient does not have faith after reading them. In his healing dream he abandons his unbelief after Asclepius heals his hand. The miracle leads to faith. Of course, the point of this inscription is to inspire faith in those who read it, but it bears witness to the notion that though faith in Asclepius' healing power is expected of suppliants, unbelief does not necessarily prevent the desired healing.

The relationship between faith and healing that is promoted by the Gospel of Mark is very similar to that reflected in this inscription. The evangelist demands faith and forbids doubt (11:22-24) without going on explicitly to exclude doubters from God's miraculous help. In 6:5b Jesus' inability to any miracles in Nazareth is quickly qualified with the words, "except that he put his hands on a few sick people and healed them." When we examine the Markan miracle stories carefully, we discover that faith cannot be said to be a condition for miracles in any absolute sense.

In the story of the stilling of the storm (4:35-41), the text states explicitly that the beneficiaries of the miracle did not have faith either prior to or as a result of the miracle. In the second sea miracle, 6:45-52, the disciples are again in trouble in a boat, they are again afraid, and Jesus rescues them again (6:51). Faith is not mentioned in this story, and it certainly is not demonstrated by the behavior of the disciples. In some of the miracle stories where faith is not mentioned, people nevertheless behave in ways that indicate they have confidence in Jesus' power to heal or exorcise. In that sense, people like the Syrophoenician woman are legitimately cited by scholars as examples of faith. In other miracle stories, however, no one evidences confidence in Jesus' power or expectation of his help prior to a miracle. This is the case in both the feeding accounts (6:35-44; 8:1-10). Thus, it is not the case that faith is an absolute prerequisite for miracles in Mark. This is most obviously the case in the story of the demon-possessed boy, which will be discussed later in the commentary.

To sum up: Although it is the case that faith leads to miracles in Mark, it is not the case that miracles do not lead to faith. In the Markan narrative some people have faith in Jesus' power because they have heard miracle stories. The reporting of miracles is expected to lead to faith in the possibility of miracles (not necessarily to discipleship, however). In addition, it is not the case that faith is always a condition for miracles in Mark. The narrative preserves the freedom of God to intervene when faith is not present, and even when unbelief is present. The miracle stories and the prayer teaching illustrate faith and call for faith without limiting the freedom of God.

Commissioning of Disciples (6:7-13, 30)

The mission of the twelve disciples concludes the chiastic section 3:13–6:30 by having Jesus send his followers out to do the ministry to which he had called them at the beginning of the section. The organization is simple:

(6:7)	Disciples are sent out on mission
(6:8-11)	Jesus' mission instructions
(6:12-13)	Disciples go out on mission
	[Intercalated narrative of Herod and John the Baptist in 6:14-29]
(6:30)	Disciples give an account of their mission

The combination of 6:7 and 6:12-13 reproduces the content of the mission described in 3:14-15. Having now been with Jesus (3:14b) and observed his ministry of word and deed, the disciples are ready to be sent out in pairs to proclaim repentance (3:14c; 6:12; cf. 1:15) and to participate in Jesus' warfare with the demonic spirits (3:15a; 6:7c; 6:13a; cf. 1:21-27; 1:34b; 3:11; 5:1-20). They also bring God's healing to the sick (3:15b; cf. 1:29-34; 1:40-45; 2:1-12; 3:1-6; 5:25-34).

The point is this: Jesus' followers are empowered and sent out to continue the activities that characterized his ministry. They are to call humanity to a reversal of thinking and action (*metanoia*), and they are to bring God's power to bear on the demons and diseases that prevent human wholeness and oppose God's reign. They do not do this alone, but with others. Finally, they are accountable. Mark 6:30 is not merely a narrative conclusion; it suggests that disciples will give an account of their faithfulness to the one who sent them out.

There is no sense here of the kind of dispensationalist understanding of mighty works that came to characterize the church in later generations. The author of Mark does not view preaching, exorcism, and healing as activites that only Jesus did; they are the mission of Jesus' followers in every generation. Gerd Theissen writes:

> Where a protest against human suffering takes place through a revelation of the sacred, the elimination of that suffering is not just desirable; it is no less than an obligation. This remains true even when that obligation contradicts all previous human experience. This is the final implication of the miracle stories: they will rather deny the validity of *all previous experience* than the right of human suffering to be eliminated. (Theissen 1983, 302 [emphasis mine])

The center of this pericope focuses on the instructions to the disciples. These very likely reflect the views of the evangelist, whatever relationship they may have had to any actual instructions given by Jesus (cf. the different and at points contradictory instructions in Matt 10:5-42 and Luke 10:2-16). Myers points out that these are instructions "for 'the way' (*eis hodon*)—that is, paradigmatic of discipleship lifestyle (6:8)" (Myers 1988, 213). The effect of the instructions is to make the missionaries dependent upon God to provide for them through the hospitality of the communities to which they witness. They are allowed to have a walking stick and a pair of sandals; they have what they need to get from one place to another. They are not allowed to carry bread, money, a begging bag, or an extra tunic; for the necessities of life they will have to depend on God and God's people. Like the wandering Israelites who lived from one day's supply of manna to the next, they are radically dependent on God's providential care.

The instructions on how to respond to rejection assume that the message and the messengers will sometimes be rejected. This is not a surprising development that becomes an occasion for self-pity and a change of vocation. Neither does it justify vindictive reprisal. The rejected preachers are to shake the dust off their feet and go on.

These prescriptions for the ministry lifestyle are perfectly coherent with the character of the ministry. The only people who are truly qualified to minister healing and deliverance and to preach repentance are people who know from experience that their own lives depend absolutely on daily miracles from God.

Removing Barriers between Jews and Gentiles
(6:14–8:30)

This third and final section of the narrative of Jesus' ministry picks up on and expands the inclusion of the gentiles that was introduced in 5:1-20. The section is framed by identical speculations about Jesus' identity: Is he John the baptizer *redivivus*? Is he Elijah, the forerunner of the Messiah? Is he some other prophet? (6:14-16; 8:27-30). In Mark 6 the question of Jesus' identity is left hanging, but the question of whether his opponents will succeed in destroying him (3:6, 19) is clarified in a chilling flashback. The execution of John the baptizer suggests that the prospects are grim for those who run afoul of Herod and his partisans.

Beginning at 6:31, Jesus feeds and heals first Jews (6:31-56) and then gentiles (7:24–8:10). Between the ministry to Jews and the ministry to gentiles the evangelist has placed a preparatory discussion with Pharisees over the proper understanding of religious defilement (7:1-23).

The section closes with summaries illustrating the failure to perceive the significance of Jesus' ministry by his opponents (8:11-13) and by his disciples (8:14-21). The arrival at Bethsaida in 8:22 marks the end of the sea crossings that began in 4:35, and the healing of the blind man symbolizes the bringing of sight to the gentiles. Thus, the final section of the ministry narrative has the following structure:

Frame— Discussion of Jesus' identity (6:14-16)
      [John the baptizer, Elijah, prophet]
      [Death of John the baptizer (6:17-29)]
A—Ministry to Jews (6:31-56)
      (a) Feeding miracle followed by epiphany (6:31-52)
      (b) Healings (6:53-56)
B—Redefinition of clean/unclean (7:1-23)
A'—Ministry to Gentiles (7:24–8:9)
      (b') Healings (7:24-37)
      (a') Feeding miracle (8:1-9)
Summaries illustrating blindness/deafness
      Outsiders are blind and deaf (8:10-13)
      Insiders are blind and deaf (8:14-21)
      Sight to the blind (8:22-26)
Frame— Discussion of Jesus' identity (8:27-30)
      [John the baptizer, Elijah, prophet]

Discussion of Jesus' Identity (6:14-16)

The audience of Mark's Gospel has been confronted with the demons' knowledge ("I know who you are, the Holy One of God!" "You are the Son of God!" "You son of the most high God!") and the disciples' ignorance ("Who then is this?"). Now the omniscient narrator informs the audience about what is being whispered in the court of Herod Antipas. Some say Jesus is Elijah, the miracle-working prophet who was expected to be sent by God to prepare the people for the coming of the Lord in judgment (Mal 4:5-6). Others say Jesus is a prophet "like one of the prophets." Herod's opinion is stated at the beginning and at the end of the list for emphasis: Jesus is John the Baptist raised from the dead. The Hellenistic magical papyri suggest that magicians used the spirits of murdered people to perform supernatural acts, so Herod may be portrayed here as believing that Jesus is a magician (Smith 1978, 97-98).

The only thing that is really important about these speculations is that all of them are wrong. Nobody suggests that Jesus is the Messiah, the royal

Son of David, the Son of God, or the Danielic Son of Man. The "powers at work" in Jesus are explained by Herod and his courtiers in various ways, but it occurs to no one that God is at work in the ministry of Jesus. Like the scribes, the family, and the people of Nazareth, Herod and his minions have eyes, but do not see.

Death of John the Baptizer (6:17-29)

The execution of John by Herod Antipas is confirmed by Josephus (Ant 18.5.2), who understood it as an attempt to prevent John's organizing a political revolution. Josephus also understood the interfamilial relationships within the Herodian dynasty differently from the author of Mark; Josephus has Philip the Tetrarch married to the daughter of Herodias, not to Herodias herself, who had instead been married to a different half-brother of Herod Antipas. Mark seems to think that the banquet and subsequent execution of John took place in Galilee, whereas Josephus places these events at Macherus in Perea. The evangelist, however, is less interested in such details than in the way his macabre interpretation of the episode can be used to foreshadow the passion of Jesus and perhaps also to suggest future suffering for Jesus' followers, who have just been sent out on their first assignment.

It is important to notice the artistry of this story, which is one of the more obvious of the Markan "sandwiched" narratives. The story is told between the sending of the disciples in 6:7-13 and their return in 6:30. After the disciples have been sent out, the narrator informs the audience that "King Herod heard, for [Jesus'] name had become known." Herod's participation in the speculation about Jesus' identity prepares for the narrative flashback of 6:17-29.

The Markan account of the circumstances leading to John's death is the longest and most melodramatic that has come down to us. It is also replete with Old Testament allusions. By calling Herod the tetrarch a "king" and by making John's criticism of Herod's immoral marriage (Lev 18:16; 20:21) the reason for his imprisonment, the evangelist identifies John with the long line of prophets who rebuked kings (1 Sam 15:17-29; 2 Sam 12:1-15; 2 Kgs 20:16-18; Jer 38:14-23) and of martyrs who upheld the law in the face of royal opposition (2 Macc 6:18–7:42; 4 Macc 5-18) (Guelich 1989, 331).

Gentile members of Mark's audience would have recalled similar traditions in which philosophers accepted martyrdom rather than compromise their convictions and message, Socrates being the paradigmatic example of such courage. Plutarch says of the orator Demosthenes that once he had taken a position he never changed it, "but actually gave up his life that he might not change it" (*Demosthenes* 13.1-2).

All of the Markan narrator's sympathies lie with the martyred prophet. The ruling elite are portrayed as either wicked and ruthless (Herodias) or profligate and spineless (Herod Antipas) (Myers 1988, 215-17; Waetjen 1989, 16, 126-27). Although Herod Antipas was never a king, the evangelist calls him one (*basileus*, 6:14). This places Herod in contrast with God, whose kingship (*basileia*) Jesus announces in 1:14-15. Those who, like John and Jesus, insist on relativizing the claims of human rulers will necessarily find themselves at risk from kings who must protect their own right to reign.

The author of Mark consistently uses the prophet Elijah as a model for his portrait of John the baptizer (1:6-7; 9:11-13). In this story Herodias plays Jezebel to John's Elijah. But whereas Jezebel was unsuccessful in eliminating Elijah, Herodias succeeds in destroying John.

The positive counterparts of Herodias in the biblical tradition include Jael (Jdgs 4:17-22; 5:24-27), Esther, and Judith, all of whom use cunning and/or deceit to secure the death of a powerful enemy. Jael and Judith each inflicts a mortal head wound to the enemy of God's people. Herodias uses cunning to arrange for the beheading of John, God's prophet.

The involvement of the young daughter is a particularly chilling detail. Textual variants make it uncertain whether the evangelist regards her as the daughter of Herodias only, or also of Herod. Commentators usually assume that the dance was erotic, although the evangelist never suggests this. However, it is plain that she is put by the Gospel writer into the same age group as Jairus' twelve-year-old daughter. The same word, (*korasion*) is used for both. One little daughter is restored to life; one participates in a grisly murder. It is the child who adds the detail of the platter. John's head is the final course in this macabre banquet (Much of the above discussion is based on Anderson 1992, 120-32).

John's headless body is claimed by his disciples and laid in a tomb. When Jesus' time for burial comes, however, his disciples will be nowhere to be found.

Ministry to Jews (6:31-56)

This section includes a feeding miracle followed a by sea-walking epiphany (6:31-52) and a series of healings (6:53-56). The feeding and healing stories take place on the western side of the Sea of Galilee, that is, in Jewish territory. The section opens and closes with references to the crowds that surround Jesus and the disciples (6:31 [cf. 3:19]; 6:54-56).

In the first of the two feeding miracles in the Gospel, Jesus is pictured as the faithful shepherd promised to Israel in the prophetic and apocalyptic literature (Ezek 34:23; Jer 23:4; Pss Sol 17:40). Both Moses (Exod 3:1) and David (1 Sam 16:11) had been shepherds, and the shepherd had become a metaphor for the religious and political leaders of Israel. The ultimately faithful shepherd of Israel remained Yahweh, who stood in judgment on all human leaders. (The following discussion is based in part on Vancil 1992).

The prophets criticized Israel's leaders for being irresponsible shepherds (Isa 56:11-12; Jer 23:1-2; Ezek 34:1-10), or for leaving the people unprotected, without a shepherd (Ezek 34:5 [cf. Num 27:17; Isa 53:6]). Through the prophets Yahweh promised to replace the unworthy shepherds, either by shepherding the people himself or by raising up a faithful shepherd, usually a Davidic leader (Ezek 34:11-16; Jer 23:3-6; Isa 40:11; 49:9b-10). Of course, Psalm 23 contains an extended metaphor of Yahweh the shepherd; this is probably the source of Mark's "green grass" (6:39; cf. Ps 23:2 [Guelich 1989, 341]). Because being "without a shepherd" could mean being vulnerable to military defeat (1 Kgs 22:17, Jud 11:19b), the motif of the divinely empowered warrior is not far in the background of the Israelite concept of the shepherd as leader. The war leader as shepherd is much more explicit in Greek tradition, where the royal military leader is known as "shepherd of the host" (*Iliad* 2.75-109 and *passim* ; *Odyssey* 3.156) Later the shepherd metaphor was applied to the ideal king in peacetime (Dio Chrysostom *On Kingship* 1.13-28; 2.6; 3.41; 4.43).

By invoking these images in 6:34, the author of Mark proclaims the good news that the eschatological shepherd has arrived to provide for the needs of God's people. As their shepherd, Jesus teaches the crowds (6:34b), provides them with food (6:42; cf. Ezek 34:2, 8; Isa 40:11; Ps 23:2), and heals their sick and injured (6:53-56; cf. Ezek 34:4). There is also an implicit criticism of the religious leaders who oppose Jesus; they are the irresponsible shepherds condemned by the prophets.

The wilderness setting of the feeding miracle (6:34-35) reminds the audience of the Isaian theme of the new exodus and of God's miraculous provision of manna during the original exodus (Exod 16). Interestingly enough, the disciples, who have just returned from a mission on which they were forbidden to take bread (6:8), manage, when pressed, to produce five loaves and two fish (6:38), behaving like the Israelites who, unable to trust God for daily provision, hoarded yesterday's manna (Exod 16:20). Jewish members of the Markan audience might also have recalled the miraculous multiplication of food supplies by Elijah (1 Kgs 17:8-16) and Elisha (2 Kgs 4:1-7, 42-44).

Both this story and its gentile counterpart (8:1-10) foreshadow the last meal Jesus will share with his disciples (against Fowler 1981). There, as in the feeding stories, Jesus takes bread, pronounces a thanksgiving or a blessing, breaks the bread, and gives it to his disciples (14:22). Not only is the hunger of the crowd satisfied, but also the leftovers fill twelve large baskets (*kophinos*) typically used by Jews for carrying loads (Guelich 1989, 343). The number twelve further reinforces the Jewish cultural setting.

After the feeding the Markan Jesus sends the disciples across the sea toward Bethsaida on the "other side," that is, in gentile territory. Jesus dismisses the crowd and, like Moses and Elijah before him, retires to the mountain to meet with God.

This is the second time that the Markan Jesus withdraws for private prayer (cf.1:35). The portrayal of Jesus as a person of prayer establishes his dependence upon God and contributes to the defense of Jesus and the Christian miracle workers against the charge of practicing magic. When Apollonius of Tyana was accused of practicing magic because he had success-fully stopped a plague at Ephesus, he defended himself by explaining that he had merely prayed to Hercules to stop the plague (Philostratus, *Life of Apollonius* 8.7.9). A magician conjures the gods with spells, but a religious person entreats them with prayers. This distinction may look like hair-splitting to Mark's modern readers, but an ancient audience would have rec-ognized it as a legitimate defense. Its power to persuade would have depended upon whether one were an opponent or a disciple of the miracle worker in question (for more detail, see Dowd 1988, 138-45).

It soon becomes apparent, however, that without Jesus' leadership the disciples are not going to make it to gentile territory; again they are meeting with opposition, as in 4:35-41. Seeing this, the Markan Jesus again demon-strates his superiority over the hostile sea power by striding across the sea, an activity attributed to God in Job 9:8 and Isa 43:16. His intent was to walk ahead of them—to lead them, like a good shepherd, to their destination (cf. Exod 33:2; 12-17; Ps 23:2b; Isa 40:11d). However, the disciples do not recognize him and cry out in fear.

Continuing the imagery of the new exodus, the narrator has Jesus iden-tify himself with the self-designation of Yahweh, "I am" (Exod 3:14, Is 41:4, 43:10-11). Thus the author of Mark provides the audience with a definitive answer to the question raised by the disciples in the previous sea-rescue story: "Who then is this?" (4:41). The promise of deliverance is reinforced by an echo of Deutero-Isaiah's "Don't be afraid" (Is 43:10, 43; 45:18; 51:2). Sadly, none of this provides clarification for the disciples, who remain "utterly astounded."

Their astonishment reveals that they have missed the exodus allusions completely. They "did not understand about the loaves" (the renewal of provision in the wilderness) or about Jesus' being the eschatological shepherd who takes care of his own, or about the way being made for God's people through the sea and the desert, or about Jesus' revelation of the character of God and God's reign in his person and ministry.

Worse yet, the narrator informs the audience that, like Jesus' opponents (3:5) and "those outside" (4:10-12, alluding to Isa 6:9-10), their hearts have been hardened. Despite their having been chosen and sent out on a successful mission, despite their having just participated in Jesus' own miraculous ministry, the disciples seem to be in danger of becoming outsiders. The narrator leaves the audience no room for complacency.

The trip to gentile territory aborted, Jesus and the disciples disembark at Gennesaret on the Jewish shore and are immediately surrounded by people seeking healing (6:53-55). As their shepherd, it is Jesus' responsibility to heal them (Ezek 34:4), and he does so. Echoing 3:10 and 5:24b-34, the narrator reports that people were healed merely by touching Jesus' clothes (6:56).

This series of three episodes repeats the pattern seen throughout the Gospel in which Jesus' ministry has three components: teaching, healing, and domination of the demonic powers. The pervasive image throughout this series is the Jewish expectation of the eschatological shepherd who will feed, heal, and lead his flock to safety through watery chaos and threatening wilderness. The next section of the Gospel redefines religious purity in a way that will mean radical changes in the ethnic make-up of this flock.

Redefinition of Clean/Unclean (7:1-23)

The controversy with Pharisees over the nature of purity links the Jewish mission of 6:31-56 to the gentile mission of 7:24–8:9 by challenging the understanding of defilement represented as that of the religious establishment and by asserting Jesus' authority to replace ritual purity standards with ethical ones. The pivotal position of 7:1-23 in the chiastic pattern emphasizes the critical content of the passage: The Markan Jesus does not eliminate the notion of impurity, but redefines it. The redefinition, however, renders religious purity impossible to achieve. The net result is that although all *foods* are declared to be "clean" (7:19d), no *people* are. The passage thus prepares for the mission to gentiles by assigning equal status to Jews and gentiles: both are equally in need of Jesus' cleansing power.

This complex passage has three overlapping patterns of arrangement. The *literary structure* follows the pattern set in 3:20–4:34: a controversy with authorities "from Jerusalem" is followed by a parable and its private interpretation to the inquiring disciples. The parable and its interpretation (7:14-23) deny the polluting character of non-kosher foods and insist that impurity is caused by behaviors that destroy human community. That this material was understood as similar to the material in chapter 4 is indicated by the addition of verse 16: "Let anyone with ears to hear listen," which is a scribal attempt to achieve conformity with 4:9, 23.

In terms of its *topical content*, the passage falls into four subsections, of which three belong to the controversy and one to the parable and its interpretation:

A—Purity and eating (7:1-5), including an explanation directed to the audience (vv. 3-4)
B—Human tradition versus God's will (7:6-8) with an appeal to the prophetic tradition
B'—Human tradition versus God's will (7:9-13) with an appeal to Torah
A'—Purity and eating (7:14-23), including an explanation to the audience (v. 19d)

In terms of its *rhetorical structure*, the passage may be seen as a chreia elaboration in response to a challenge (the controversy—7:1-13) followed by an argument from a contrary (the parable and interpretation—7:14-23) (Robbins 1994). The point of the argument is not to answer the Pharisees' question, which the Markan Jesus never does. Rather, the rhetoric aims to discredit the opponents and to redefine the category of "impurity" on the authority of Jesus, an authority that he has received from God. The evangelist thus reiterates the claims made in the opening chapters (1:21–3:6): Jesus' authority is greater than that of the religious establishment. As this new controversy scene opens in 7:1-2, the audience has every reason to expect that Jesus will win the argument. They will not be disappointed.

The introduction of the Pharisees and scribes "from Jerusalem" (cf.3:22) prepares the audience for conflict. Earlier confrontations had focused on eating with the wrong people (2:15-17), eating at the wrong times (2:18-20), and eating food obtained in the wrong way (2:23-28). Now the issue is eating without performing ritual ablutions (7:2).

The narrator explains Pharisaic practice—which he attributes to "all the Jews" (7:3a)—indicating that at least some members of the audience would have needed such an explanation. This would have been the case, not because gentiles would have been unfamiliar with the concept of ritual purity, for such concerns were important in virtually all religions of antiquity, but because Mark's audience would have needed specific information about *Jewish* purification practice.

The narrator identifies the source of the purity regulations as "the tradition of the elders," repeating the noun *paradosis* for emphasis (7:3c, 4b). The

opponents are then made to emphasize the importance of tradition in their
challenge to Jesus; their primary accusation is nonobservance of the tradition, of which the omission of ritual ablutions is a glaring example (7:5b).
All this focus on tradition justifies the response of the Markan Jesus, who
attacks the validity of the tradition before returning to the question of eating
and impurity.

The Markan Jesus' response begins with the citation of a chreia (a short
pithy saying from a well-known and admired person, in this case the prophet
Isaiah), preceded, in good Greco-Roman rhetorical style, by praise of the
speaker (7:6a). The quotation from LXX Isa 29:13 has two functions in the
overall plan of the passage: It introduces the external/internal contrast that
will become crucial in 7:14-23; and with its paraphrase in 7:8 it sets up the
contrast between God's will and commandment and merely human
tradition.

At the beginning of 7:9-13 the charge of substituting human traditions
for God's commands is repeated and followed by another scripture quotation, this time from Torah. This kind of appeal to authority is typical of the
rhetoric of chreia elaboration.

The "corban" issue of 7:11-12 serves as an illustration of one of the
"many" (7:13b) ways in which the religious leaders "abandon" or "nullify"
the divine commandment in favor of human tradition. The example concerns the practice, not otherwise attested as early as this Gospel, of using a
dedicatory vow to put one's property out of reach of the specific persons
named in the vow. H. W. Basser gives the example: "my car is as off-limits as
a sacrifice would be in respect to my son" (Basser 1994).

It cannot be known whether such vows were actually being used to cir-
cumvent the fifth commandment in the time of Jesus or of Mark. The theo-
retical possibility is discussed much later in the Talmud at B. Ned. 64a-b.
But from the evangelist's point of view the choice of loyalty to parents as an
illustration is rhetorically appropriate because the obligation to parents was a
high value in both Jewish and Greco-Roman societies. Plato, for example,
held that violence done to a parent was equivalent to manslaughter and
would cause the offender to be thrown into Tartarus (*Phaedo* 113e-114a).

The point of the subunit 7:9-13 is driven home by the fourth statement
setting human tradition over against the word of God (7:13a). Again, as in
the controversies over plucking grain or healing on the sabbath, the Markan
Jesus insists that God is not honored when religiosity is put ahead of human
need. Since the evangelist has to explain the meaning of "corban" and the
handwashing issue to the audience, it is clear that he cannot be attacking
Jewish practices familiar to and controversial among Christians or defending

Christians against Jewish opponents. Rather, the author may have been critiquing the tendency within the Christian community itself to prefer the practice of religion over obedience to God. Human traditions and lip service substitute for wholehearted self-surrender, as Isaiah said so well.

The final subsection, 7:14-23, returns to the theme of eating and impurity, but not to the Pharisees' original question. All the previous rhetoric had decried the replacement of God's commandments by human traditions, and the handwashing requirement for laypersons did fall into the category of human tradition. But when the Markan Jesus declares that "there is nothing outside a person that by going in can defile," he is not rejecting oral tradition, but the food laws laid down in the Torah itself (Lev 11). Why, then, is he not guilty of the charge that he had brought against the Pharisees? Has he not "made void the word of God" in order to establish his own position in its place?

The Gospel narrative as a whole provides the negative answer. The Markan Jesus speaks not for himself but for God. He is God's Son and bears the divine stamp of approval (1:11); the heavenly voice commands the disciples to "listen to him" (9:7). Jesus heals a leper (1:40-45) and forgives sins (2:7)—acts that only God can do. He performs exorcisms through the power of the Holy Spirit (3:20-35). The one who welcomes Jesus (in the person of a child) is really entertaining God (9:37). The audience had already learned in 1:22 that Jesus taught as one "who had [his own] authority," and that in that respect his teaching differed from that of the scribes. So here in 7:14-23 it becomes apparent that the one who is lord of the sabbath (2:28) is also lord of the scriptures.

But the christological claim is not the only claim being made by the text. The rhetorical structure of the passage makes the quotation from LXX Isa 29:13 (7:6b-7) the hermeneutical key to the whole argument; the Isaiah text is the original chreia of which the rest of the passage is the elaboration. Thus, the hermeneutical point is as important as the christological one, especially since, according to Mark, the good news of Jesus happened "just as it stands written in the prophet Isaiah" (1:1-2).

Isaiah had written that God's people honor God with their lips, while their hearts are far from God; they teach human precepts as though they were divine teaching. In the citations of "Moses" and the corban example the Markan Jesus had developed the second half of the Isaiah quote (human tradition replaces divine command). Now in the argument from the contrary he uses the lips/heart contrast of the chreia to redefine the source of impurity as that which comes from the heart rather than that which passes through the lips.

It is vanity to pretend to honor God with the lips (by ritual washing before eating or by abstaining from unclean foods) when the heart is far from God (and so produces the manifold vices catalogued in 7:21-22). That which goes into a person from the outside does not affect the heart, but passes through the digestive system and into the latrine. (Conveniently for the evangelist, excretion had never been thought to make a person ritually unclean, though experiencing certain other bodily discharges had.)

This redefinition of impurity as ethical rather than ritual is often read in the context of Acts and the Pauline corpus and thus reduced to the issue of the conditions of the gentile mission. However, more may be at stake here.

In fact, the connection between ritual purity and abstinence from certain foods was by no means unknown in the pagan cults of Greco-Roman antiquity. The followers of Pythagoras, for example, did not eat meat (Coxon 1970), and according to Pythagoras' biographer Porphyry, beans were also forbidden food (*Life of Pythagoras* 43). According to Lucian of Samosata, some worshippers of the Syrian goddess Hera-Derketo-Artargatis would neither sacrifice nor eat swine, while others abstained from fish and doves, although they ate other birds (Meyer 1987, 134, 140). According to Plutarch, the Egyptian worshippers of Isis abstained from the lepidotus, the seabream, and the pike because these fish had fed upon the penis of the dismembered Osiris (Meyer 1987, 165). And in his account of the initiation of Lucius into the priesthood of Isis, Apuleius has Lucius say, "Meanwhile, I should abstain from all profane or forbidden foods like the other devotees, that I might hasten the more uprightly into the secret bosom of the faith" (Meyer 1987, 187). Although the classical Greeks had no concept of foods that were inherently impure, abstinence from certain foods was associated with various cult practices, and Robert Parker asserts that "contact between Greeks and Egyptian and oriental cults meant that the Hellenistic period saw not a decline but an increase in ritual abstinences, which were not confined to marginal superstition but were treated by a cultured Greek such as Plutarch with interest and respect" (Parker 1983, 324, 357).

Although the Greek tradition sometimes assimilated moral and ritual purity, it never eliminated the latter altogether (Parker 1983, 324). Of course, the Old Testament also links purity with right behavior, particularly in the prophetic traditions, without undermining the prohibitions against unclean food. Thus, when the Markan Jesus says, "there is *nothing* outside a person that by going in can defile, but the things that come out are what defile," his statement is a radical one in any ancient cultural context. It is not merely a practice that sets the gentile Christians over against observant

Jewish believers; it is what makes the members of the Markan community different from *all* their religious neighbors.

Furthermore, the Markan Jesus does not replace the ritual rules of the Pharisees with ethical rules that, if scrupulously followed, would render a person "pure" before God. In fact, there is nothing in this passage to suggest what steps a person might take to guarantee or protect her purity. Jesus states as a matter of simple *fact* that people are defiled by the evils that arise out of the human heart. There is no hint that humans might, by some discipline or ethical rigor, prevent or minimize their defilement. Nor does the Markan Jesus redefine "clean" and "unclean" in order to establish the principle that no one is impure in the sight of God. On the contrary, he redefines the categories in such a way that *all* human beings are impure, regardless of their ritual practice or lack of it.

From the evangelist's point of view, neither gentiles nor Jews can purify themselves. Neither ritual observance nor ethical behavior purifies. Unclean persons become clean only when Jesus removes the impurity by the power of God. That is what happens in 7:24-30.

Ministry to Gentiles (7:24–8:9)

This section completes the A-B-A' structure of 6:31–8:9. It corresponds to the section 6:31-56, which describes Jesus' ministry to his own people: a miraculous feeding and multiple healings. In this parallel section the ministry to gentiles is similarly characterized, but in reversed order: the Markan Jesus first heals two gentiles and then feeds a gentile crowd.

Both sections begin with frustrated attempts by the Markan Jesus to escape from the crowds (6:31-33; 7:24-25). But need never takes a vacation; it presses in on Jesus wherever he goes.

The story of the Syrophoenician woman begins and ends with geographical markers (7:24, 31) that recall 3:7-12, particularly 3:8 ("the region around Tyre and Sidon"). The audience had learned that among those who were attracted to Jesus at the beginning of his ministry were Syrophoenicians from Tyre and Sidon. These people were among those healed and exorcised in Galilee (3:10-12). The narrator has prepared the audience for the information that when the Syrophoenician woman heard that Jesus was in the area, she expected him to be able to exorcise her daughter (3:25-26).

The Markan narrator is careful to credit the woman with an appropriate approach to Jesus. Like Jairus, whose previous request was successful, the woman bows at Jesus' feet and asks for help for her little daughter (7:25-26; cf. 5:22-23).

But Jesus' response presents a striking contrast with every other healing situation in the Gospel. Only here does the initial request meet with refusal; only here is persuasion required; only here does Jesus' dialogue partner get the best of the argument.

This dialogue is not a controversy with opponents like those in 2:1-3:6; 7:1-23; or 11:27–12:34. Although most of the comment on this pericope has focused on the problem of Jesus' apparent insult to the gentile woman, this concern misses the point of the story. Jesus is not testing the woman's faith; unlike the author of Matthew, the writer of Mark never mentions faith in this pericope. In any case, the woman has already demonstrated adequate faith according to the Markan understanding of faith; she has come with a request, confident of Jesus' power to cast the demon out of her daughter.

Nor is the Markan Jesus expressing his (limited) view of his mission—a view that the woman will change by her clever response. Jewish priority is not the perspective of the Markan Jesus, who has already healed and exorcized gentiles (3:7-12; 5:1-20). And, to the extent that the riddle is to be allegorized, the "bread" in question is not the preaching of the gospel to "the Jew first, and also the Greek" (cf. Rom 1:16; 2:9-10; Acts 3:26; 13:46), but in this context must be the meeting of human needs.

The closest parallel in antiquity to the conversation between Jesus and the Syrophoenician woman is the riddle contest in which the solution of the riddle gains for the protagonist access to the desired reward or status (e.g. Jdgs 14:12-18; Oedipus and the riddle of the Sphinx). So the woman does not so much win an argument as solve a puzzle. The problem requiring a solution appears to be the result of a misreading of Isaiah, the prophet so important to Mark's community. Isaiah had been a major source for the interpretation of Gen 12:1-3 as a prediction of the conversion of the Gentiles to Yahwism after the restoration of Israel from exile (Isa 2:2-4; 11:10; 19:21-25; 25:6; 42:6). This, then, became the "Jews first, then gentiles" mission strategy reflected in the writings of Paul and the author of Luke-Acts. But in Acts 6:1 we find a suggestion of a problem that could easily have arisen in many early Christian communities. If in Jerusalem the Hellenized Jewish Christians could be neglected in favor of the "Hebrew" Christians, how much more likely that in racially mixed communities the Jewish Christians might claim pride of place over gentile Christians? After all, hadn't Isaiah portrayed the former idolaters as Johnny-come-latelies in the covenant community? (Isa 56:8; 61:5-11; 66:18-21).

The author of Mark resists this transformation of salvation history into privileged status for some Christians over others. But he resists it, not with a rhetorical sledgehammer, but indirectly with a contest of riddles. He has

Jesus pose the problem: It isn't right to deprive God's chosen people in favor of gentile outsiders. Let the descendants of Abraham be taken care of first. Didn't God choose them first? Then the narrator allows the Syrophoenician woman, representing the voice of the gentile Christians, to solve the riddle.

Clearly the Markan Jesus' statement in 7:27 refers to the privileged status of Israel as God's elect. They are the "descendants" (*tekna*), whose bread must not be tossed out (*balein*) to the dogs. The choice of vocabulary is important.

The noun *teknon* can be used figuratively as a term of affection or compassion (2:5; 10:24), but its literal meaning is descendant or offspring (10:29-30; 12:19; 13:12). It is used of Abraham's son Isaac in LXX Gen 17:16 and 22:7-8 and later (along with *sperma*) of the subsequent descendants of Abraham (John 8:39) and Sarah (Gal 4:28, 31) in general.

The verb *balein*, meaning throw or toss, implies a typically Jewish understanding of the relationship between dogs and human beings. Jews did not keep dogs as house pets. In rural settings dogs might be used to guard sheep (Job 30:1), but overall could be characterized as lazy and gluttonous (Isa 56:9-11a). In urban settings dogs were scavengers (Ps 59:14-15; 1 Kgs 21:24; 22:38; 2 Kgs 9:35-37). In *Joseph and Aseneth* 10:14 a distinction is made between the house dogs of the Egyptian princess Aseneth and the wild dogs outside to which she "throws" all her food as she begins a fast. Even in the Diaspora, where Jews learned from their neighbors that dogs might be kept for companionship, the dogs are seen only outside (Tobit 5:16, 11:4).

The woman solves the riddle by changing the terms. In her answer the "descendants" (*tekna*) become "little children" (*paidioi*), and the street curs become puppies "under the table" (7:28).

Unlike the Jews, the Greeks and Romans kept house dogs, as we know from literary sources (e.g. Plutarch, *Aemilius Paulus* 10, 4; Pliny *Letters* 4, 2.3), relief sculptures (Payne 1931, 302, pl 27, n. 780), and vase painting (Becatti 1967, 33). In reliefs and vase paintings of meal scenes it is common to find a dog depicted as sitting or lying under the diner's couch or table, sometimes munching on a tidbit apparently claimed from its master.

Thus, by changing the cultural context, the Syrophoenician woman solves the problem of priority by replacing the image of sequence and implied scarcity (the dogs eat last *if* there is anything left) with an image of simultaneity and abundance. The puppies will do fine on what the children feed them from their own plates. In addition, the woman's image transforms the Jewish believers from *tekna*, jealously standing on their privileges to *paidia*, those with no status or claim who alone will receive the reign of God (10:15).

The gentile woman has solved the riddle, and the reward is hers. Because of her *logos* (the same word is used for Jesus' preaching in 2:2; 4:33) her daughter is made clean, and a place is reserved at the table for all the gentile underdogs who will follow her (so Betty Grimes).

The transition sentence 7:31 reflects the author's ignorance of or lack of interest in precise geography. The Markan Jesus travels north to Sidon in order to arrive in the region of the Decapolis, southeast of Phoenicia on the eastern (gentile) side of the Sea of Galilee.

Here Jesus heals a man who, although he has ears, cannot hear (cf. 4:9, 12; 23: 8:18). The glance toward heaven (7:34) acknowledges that the healing is accomplished by the power of God, and not by the magical efficacy of foreign words or spittle. Having made it possible for the man to hear and also to speak, Jesus promptly commands him and the witnesses to the miracle to keep silent, but to no avail. Like the Jewish leper, these gentiles ignore Jesus' instructions and proclaim (*kerussein*, 1:45; 7:36) his mighty works. Their response has two functions in the Markan narrative: it further clarifies the source of Jesus' power and interprets the miracle by reference to Isaiah's eschatological vision.

That the healing is the work of God is reinforced by the first part of the accalamation of the bystanders: "He has done all things well!" (7:37b). This allusion to LXX Gen 1:31 (and, secondarily, perhaps to Ecc 3:11 and Wis 8:1) attributes the deeds of Jesus to the Creator and rules out other sources of power (cf 3:20-35).

The second part of the response of those who witness the miracle makes a clear connection between the work of Jesus and the eschatological exodus of Isaiah. In an allusion to LXX Isa 35:5-6 their unison acclamation, like the speech of the chorus in a Greek drama, interprets the significance of the action for the audience. Isaiah 35 comforts the exiles with the promise of redemption and deliverance (35:4, 9-10). The blind will see, the deaf hear, the lame leap, and the speechless sing (35:5-6a). A holy highway (*hodos hagia*, 35:8) will provide safe passage for the exiles to return to Jerusalem. The connection between the miraculous speech of the deaf and the exodus motif in Isaiah is also picked up in Wis 10:21, where it is retrojected into the time of the original Exodus.

Thus, the miracle is interpreted as a sign of the inbreaking of the eschatological reign of God when those who have ears will be enabled to hear. But the context of Isa 35 also foreshadows the healing of the blind man in 8:22-26, as well as the journey on the way (*hodos*) to Jerusalem (8:27–10:52), where Jesus will accomplish the redemption (10:45) promised by Isaiah.

The second feeding story closes this three-part section as well as the larger chiastic structure of 6:31–8:9. The scene does not change between the healing of the deaf mute and the feeding of the four thousand; the setting of the second feeding miracle is still "the region of the Decapolis" (7:31).

The disciples, having been absent in the last two stories, now rejoin Jesus. Since they apparently never got out of the boat back in chapter 5, this is their first time to set foot in gentile territory (5:1—*they* came . . . to the country of the Gerasenes; 5:2—*he* got out of the boat). Faced with the same situation with which they had been confronted in 6:35-36, the disciples demonstrate that they have learned nothing. They have no idea how such a large crowd is to be fed. Their desperate query, "How will anyone be able to satisfy these people with bread out here in the wilderness?" echoes the unbelief of their ancestors: "God is not able to spread a table in the wilderness is he? . . . He is not able to give bread . . . for his people is he?" (LXX Ps 77:19-20). Although the audience might have forgiven them for not expecting a miracle the first time, this time their dismay is maddening and inexcusable.

The audience's frustration is mirrored by the Markan Jesus, who asks (through clenched teeth?), "How many loaves do you have?" He again lays claim to the meager supplies the disciples are hoarding and feeds the whole crowd with seven loaves and a few little fish.

So the Syrophoenician woman turns out to be right after all. The gentile "dogs" eat from the provisions of Abraham's descendents, and the disciples are not deprived in the least. They collect enough leftovers to fill seven baskets, each large enough to hold a man (*spuris*, 8:8b; Acts 9:25). At the eschatological banquet that this meal prefigures, everyone has a place at the table, everyone eats at the same time, and everyone has enough (*echortasthesan*, 8:8a).

Summaries Illustrating Blindness/Deafness (8:10-26)

The ministry of Jesus in Galilee and in gentile territory closes with three scenes that summarize the major themes of 1:14–8:9: words and deeds, controversy and opposition, blindness and deafness, scarcity and bread. The failure to hear, see, and understand that the audience has come to expect from the "outsiders" who oppose Jesus has by this time clearly become a problem for the "insiders" as well.

The last Galilean encounter with opponents (8:10-13) is bracketed by trips across the sea. In 8:10 Jesus and his disciples leave gentile territory and cross over to Dalmanutha. The place is unknown, but the encounter with Pharisees suggests a Jewish setting. Besides, the concluding boat trip, which begins in 8:13, is a crossing "to the other side," and the boat lands at Bethsaida on the eastern (gentile) side of the sea. Thus the setting of 8:11-12 is a Jewish one.

There are few surprises here. The audience already knows that the Pharisees and the Herodians are plotting to kill Jesus (3:6). The Pharisees are often associated with the scribes (7:1) who have been Jesus' opponents from the beginning (2:6, 16, 24).

The Pharisees' request for a sign is not equivalent to the requests for healing and exorcism that have been made to Jesus so far in the narrative. The evangelist makes this clear in two ways. First, they ask for a "sign," rather than making a specific request for a situation of need. Mark's word for miracles that are portrayed in a positive light is *dunamis*, "powerful act" (6:2, 5, 14; 9:39); *semēia*, "signs," on the other hand, are understood negatively as acts done to establish one's identity or status (13:22). That is what the Pharisees request here: a sign "from heaven" as proof that Jesus is someone they should take seriously.

Second, their motive is revealed to the audience by the omniscient narrator who knows everyone's motives in the story: they ask in order to put Jesus to the test. They are contrasted with another Jewish religious leader, Jairus, who had come to Jesus to make a humble request for healing. His motive was a desperate concern for his dying daughter; these Pharisees demand a sign to test Jesus. Since the activity of "testing" Jesus has already been identified as the program of Satan (1:13), it is clear that the Pharisees remain opposed to Jesus' mission.

If Jesus were to accede to their demand, he would be implicitly acknowledging their right as the religious establishment to define and categorize him according to their standards of legitimation (Waetjen 1989, 140). This, of course, he will not do. Their demand that he provide proof of his insider status is the final straw that confirms them as outsiders. Their status as outsiders is due not to their religion, to their race, or even to their elite status, but to their hardened hearts (3:5), manifested in their blindness to God's activity in the ministry of Jesus.

When in the next scene the Markan Jesus warns his disciples against the "leaven" of the Pharisees and the "leaven" of Herod, he refers to the corrupting tendency to make Jesus fit into one's preexisting categories. The Pharisees want a legitimating sign. Jesus' family diagnoses him as a mental case (3:21). The scribes from Jerusalem have him pigeonholed as a demon-possessed magician (3:22). Herod knows that he has to be John the Baptist come back to haunt his executioner (6:16). Those who are certain that they "know" who Jesus is are inevitably misguided. That the disciples need this warning will become evident in 8:32-33. In the boat scene (8:14-21), however, the focus is not on what they know, but on what they do not know.

The last of the three boat scenes in the Gospel (8:14-21) brings to a climax the disciples' incomprehension. In 4:35-41 they had asked, "Who then is this?" and Jesus had asked, "Don't you have faith yet?" In 6:45-52 the disciples had failed to recognize Jesus, and he had answered their previous question with the divine self-definition, "I am." The narrator had remarked that "they did not understand about the loaves, but their hearts were hardened" (6:52).

In this final scene it becomes clear that the disciples still do not understand about the loaves. Even after two miraculous feedings they are worried about their scarcity of bread. This is more than the Markan Jesus can tolerate, and he fires questions at them faster than they can answer: "Why are you talking about having no bread? Do you still not perceive or understand? Are your hearts hardened? Do you have eyes and fail to see? Do you have ears and fail to hear, and do you not remember?" Even his review quiz on the number of baskets of leftovers after each feeding leaves them baffled.

The audience comes to the chilling realization that indeed the disciples are deaf and blind, indeed their hearts are hardened. Worse yet, these are the characteristics of "those outside" (4:10-12; Isa 6:9-10). This scene poses a serious threat to an audience that has been led to identify with the disciples as followers of Jesus and recipients of the "mystery of the reign of God" (4:10).

The long tradition of the mystery religions and their revival during the Hellenistic period had produced a high level of confidence in the efficacy of initiation. To be one of those to whom the mystery had been given was to be transformed from a mere mortal into a true spiritual insider. This revelation that the disciples are blind, deaf, and hard of heart despite their insider status shatters the complacency of the audience of this Gospel. If the disciples, recipients of the mystery and chosen companions of Jesus, are to be counted among the outsiders, who is left on the inside? And how can one be sure of remaining inside, when the boundaries seem so fluid?

Finally in 8:22 Jesus and the disciples arrive in gentile Bethsaida, their destination ever since 6:45. There, Jesus heals a man of a particularly stubborn case of blindness. The story is narrated in such a way as to provide a parallel to 7:31-37 (the healing of a deaf man):

- Jesus arrives (7:31; 8:22a).
- People bring to him an afflicted person and beg Jesus to touch him (7:32; 8:22b).
- Jesus takes the person aside and performs a healing action (7:33; 8:23).
- The healing is confirmed (7:35; 8:25b).
- Jesus attempts to conceal the healing from public notice (7:36; 8:26).

After the devastation of 8:14-21 these two stories hold out hope that Jesus may yet be able to heal the disciples' spiritual blindness and deafness as well. If the eyes of the gentiles are being opened, can sight not be given to Jesus' closest associates?

Discussion of Jesus' Identity (8:27-30)

The issue of Jesus' identity closes the frame on the large section 6:14–8:30. The same questions heard in Herod's court are repeated and in the same order: Is Jesus John the baptizer come back to life? Is he Elijah? Is he some other prophet? Just when it appears that the disciples have found the right answer ("You are the Messiah"), the audience learns that there is more to messiahship than anyone bargained for. With that unsettling revelation, the evangelist begins the third major section of the Gospel.

On the Way to the Cross

(Mark 8:22–10:52)

The healing of the blind man at Bethsaida (8:22-26) and the story of Peter's confession at Caesarea Philippi (8:27-30) have dual functions in the structural plan of the Gospel. Having previously discussed their functions in the narrative of the Galilean ministry, we now turn to a study of the third major section of the Gospel in which the Markan Jesus teaches his disciples about the community implied by God's reign and about the role of suffering in Jesus' life and in the lives of his followers. Of course, the teachings of Jesus in this section have become the vehicle by which the evangelist teaches *his* audience on these topics.

We have already seen how Mark takes over Isaiah's imagery of sight and hearing, blindness and deafness. The material in 8:27–10:45 is framed by two stories about the healing of blindness—the only two such stories in this Gospel. Within this frame there is a narrative introduction (8:27-30) that sets the stage for the section. The subsequent material is arranged in three units of similar structure but differing length: 8:31–9:29, 9:30–10:31, and 10:32-45.

Each of these units begins with a prediction of Jesus' suffering, death, and resurrection (passion prediction). The prediction is followed by the disciples' response, indicating that they do not understand the significance of what Jesus is telling them. This response provides the Markan Jesus with an opportunity to engage in further teaching about the nature of discipleship. Thus the section may be outlined as follows:

Frame—Healing of a blind man in two stages (8:22-26)
Narrative introduction—The problem of human thinking that opposes God's thinking (8:27-30)
First passion prediction unit (8:31–9:29)
Second passion prediction unit (9:30–10:31)
Third passion prediction unit (10:32–45)
Frame—Healing of a blind man immediately (10:46–52)

The author of Mark has already indicated that although the disciples have eyes, they cannot see (8:18). Even though they have been given the secret of the reign of God, they have not perceived or understood it because their hearts are hardened (4:11; 6:52; 8:17). The teaching on the way to Jerusalem represents the Markan Jesus' attempt to penetrate their blindness with the light of understanding. To indicate that purpose, the evangelist begins the teaching section with the story of the healing of a blind man.

Healing of a Blind Man in Two Stages
(8:22-26)

This is the only healing story in any Gospel in which Jesus seems to experience difficulty in achieving the desired result. In the parallel account of the healing of a deaf mute (7:31-37) the result was apparently instantaneous; furthermore, the man was able not only to hear and to speak, but also to speak correctly (*orthōs*, 7:35). Prior to that healing, Jesus had cast an unclean spirit out of a child at a distance, without even encountering the patient (7:24-30). This story is such a contrast to the other Markan healings that it immediately grips the attention of the audience.

Jesus leads the blind man out of the village (cf.7:33), spits into his eyes, and puts his hands on the man. Then he checks with the patient to see how the healing is going: "Do you see anything?" (8:23). The result is partly successful. The man can look at and identify objects ("I see people"), but he does not see them as they really are; he perceives them "as trees walking around." The choice of verbs is noteworthy. In the citation of Isaiah 6:9 in Mark 4:12, people are said to "look but not see" (*blepō/horaō*). In 8:24 a man looks at (*blepō*) people and sees (*horaō*) them as trees. He needs a second touch.

After Jesus lays his hands on the man's eyes again the healing is complete, and he sees "everything clearly" (8:25). This two-stage healing prepares for the conversation with the disciples that follows it.

That conversation takes place *on the way* to the villages of Caesarea Philippi. Of the sixteen references to "the way" (*hodos*) in Mark, half are concentrated between 8:27 and 11:8. In this section "the way" is the way to the cross, which becomes clear for the first time in the passion predictions. It is also "the way of the Lord" about which Isaiah wrote in the citation that began the Gospel (1:2-3). This way out of bondage to freedom, this second exodus, is a way the disciples are going to find especially distasteful. But then Isaiah also wrote, "My plans are not like your plans, nor are your ways like my ways (*hodoi*) says the Lord" (LXX Isa 55:8).

Narrative Introduction
(8:27-30)

This is the moment the audience of Mark has been waiting for. In 4:41 the disciples had asked, "Who then is this, that even the wind and the sea obey him?" In 6:50 Jesus had answered their question: "I am" (cf. Exod 3:14; Isa 43:10, 25; 45:18; 51:12). But their concern over bread in the last boat scene (8:14-21) showed that they were still blind to what they had seen.

Now the Markan Jesus asks them directly about his identity, beginning with what others are saying (8:27). The speculations are those heard in Herod's court in 6:13-15. Then comes the question that has challenged would-be disciples in the centuries since Mark first wrote it: "But who do *you* say that I am?" (8:29).

Peter, speaking for the other disciples as he often does in Mark, replies, "You are the Messiah" (8:29). This is the first time that the title Messiah (Christ, "anointed one") has been used since 1:1, where Jesus' identity was announced to the audience by the heavenly voice. The disciples' progress from "Who is this?" to "You are the Messiah" is considerable. Peter has given the correct answer. The audience breathes a sigh of relief. At last the disciples have seen the light.

But Jesus interrupts the applause with a command to silence: "He rebuked them in order that they should tell no one about him." This surprising response recalls the exorcism stories, in which Jesus rebukes and silences demons (1:25) because they know his identity (1:34; cf. 3:11-12). The audience is dumbfounded. They know that Jesus is the Messiah because the omniscient narrator said so in 1:1. How can the disciples be rebuked and silenced for being correct? Obviously there is more to learn about who Jesus is before the news can be spread.

First Passion Prediction Unit
(8:31–9:29)

In this five-part unit, the hints pointing toward the passion (2:20; 3:6) are replaced by explicit predictions. The first sub-unit, 8:31-33, insists on the passion and resurrection as necessary components of Jesus' role as Messiah. In 8:34–9:1 the Markan Jesus explains the implications of his own passion for the definition of faithful discipleship: his followers must be prepared to take up their own crosses and lose their lives for the sake of Jesus and the gospel. These startling revelations receive the strongest possible confirmation in the transfiguration scene, 9:2-8. Here, expanding the exodus theology of

Isaiah, the evangelist portrays Jesus as the prophet-like-Moses who suffers and dies because of the sins of others, but is glorified by God after his death. This is followed by a clarification of John's role as forerunner, 9:9-13. The unit closes with an exorcism of a demon-possessed boy (9:14-29), underlining the tension between Jesus' power to relieve suffering and the approach of his own agony and death for which his most earnest pleading will provide no relief.

The evangelist places the first passion prediction unit immediately after Peter's confession of Jesus as "the Messiah" and Jesus' command to silence in order to show that before Jesus can be proclaimed as the Messiah, the component of suffering must be integrated into the messianic role.

This was no easy matter for the early Christian interpreters of Jesus' life, death, and resurrection. In order to sustain the claim that Jesus was Israel's promised Messiah, Christians had to find a way around the fact that no interpretive tradition prior to the resurrection had understood Scripture to predict a Messiah who had to suffer and die to fulfill his role as deliverer of Israel.

The Gospel of Mark makes that very claim: "It is necessary" (*dei*) for Jesus, who has just been correctly identified as the Messiah, to suffer many things; specifically, he must be rejected by the religious authorities, be killed, and rise after three days. In this Gospel the impersonal verb *dei* suggests the necessary sequence of events leading to the consummation of God's eschatological reign, which is already breaking in through Jesus' ministry of healing and exorcism. In 9:11 the Markan Jesus confirms the judgment of the scribes that "it is necessary" for Elijah to come first, but that has already taken place. Now "it is necessary" for Jesus to suffer, die, and be raised. But before the final consummation, "it is necessary" that there be wars and rumors of wars (13:7), and "it is necessary" that the good news be proclaimed to all the gentiles (13:10). The Gospel thus interprets Jesus' death and resurrection as an essential part of the coming of the reign of God announced in 1:14-15. By contrast with Jesus' usual mode of speech in parables, this passion prediction is all too clear (8:32).

Peter, again representing the disciples as a group, rejects Jesus' reinterpretation of Messiahship. He "rebukes" Jesus as arrogantly as he and his fellows "rebuke" the parents of the children in 10:13. Jesus responds with a rebuke of his own, but in this Gospel when Jesus is the subject of the verb *epitimaō* the object is the demonic (1:25; 3:12; 4:39; 9:25). The refusal to accept the necessity of the Messiah's death is the program of Satan, Jesus' cosmic opponent (1:13; 3:22-27). The audience's hopes for the rehabilitation of the disciples are crushed again. The insiders (4:10-12) become outsiders

(8:14-21) have not regained their status by giving the right answer (8:29). Instead, their partial sight is no better than that of the demons who correctly proclaimed Jesus as "Son of God" (3:11; 5:7; cf.1:24).

Jesus goes on to accuse the disciples of the same error of which the religious authorities are guilty: they are substituting human attitudes and values for the values and attitudes characteristic of God (8:33; 7:6-13). From the evangelist's point of view, thinking like a human being is not a result of natural limitations, but a result of bondage to the demonic. But what hope can the disciples or the audience have of ever "thinking the things of God"?

The answer is, "None whatever," if the change of perspective depends upon their own efforts. But they are keeping company with the master exorcist, and he remains their only hope for freedom from demonic influences. Though they have already begun to participate in the ministry of exorcism themselves (6:13), their own deliverance is still partial. Like the blind man at Bethsaida, they need for Jesus to continue to work on them before they will be able to see clearly and to "think the things of God" (Juel 1994, 73-75).

The deliberate inclusion of the crowd with the disciples in 8:34 is designed to emphasize that the definition of discipleship that follows applies to all would-be followers of Jesus. After the brief narrative introduction (8:34a), the rest of the subunit consists of Jesus' speech:

Definition (8:34b)
    a—Goal: If anyone wishes to *follow me*
     b—Action: Deny self
     b'—Action: Pick up cross
    a'—Goal: *Follow me*

Explanation (*hos gar*, 8:35)
    a—Whoever wishes to *save* life
     b—will *lose* it
     b'—whoever *loses* life on account of me and the gospel
    a'—will *save* it.

Positive Argument—Two Rhetorical Questions (*ti gar*, 8:36).
    Question 1: What does a person profit *to gain* world   (a)
                                   to lose life   (b)
    [Implied answer: "Nothing."]
    Question 2: What will a person give (*lose*)   (b')
               in exchange for [*gaining*] life?   (a')
    [Implied answer: "Everything."]

Negative Argument—Two Warnings (8:38–9:1)
    Warning 1: Judgment on apostasy is severe
    a—Whoever should be ashamed of me and my words
    b—in the present evil age
    a'—The Son of Man will be ashamed of that person
    b'—in the future judgment
    Warning 2: Judgment on apostasy is near; some standing here will see it.

The first thing to note here is that the noun "life" (*psyche*) is used in two different senses. This play on the sense of "life" is also found in similar sayings from Mark's cultural setting. Sayings of the Wise Menander, 65 is an example: "Whoever despairs not in war, and offers himself to death directly wins life, fame therewith, and is celebrated." Similarly, Epictetus says of Socrates that "dying he is saved" in a way that he could not have been by escaping (*Diss* 4.1.165. References from Beardslee 1979, 57-72).

In Mark the life that is not saved, but lost on account of Jesus and the good news, is a follower's physical life. To pick up one's cross is to assent to one's own execution rather than to be ashamed of Jesus and his message. The life that is saved by martyrdom or lost by foolish self-preservation is eschatological life in the reign of God that will soon come "in power." Resurrection life is life in the presence of "the God of the living" (12:27).

The language of shame in 8:38 contributes to the paradox; the shameful death by public crucifixion in this adulterous and sinful generation prevents the ultimate shame in the judgment. Similarly, Xenophon writes that soldiers who try to save their lives will die in shame, but those who try to "die well" often outlive cowards (*Anabasis* 3.1.43). And Epictetus claims that Menoeceus, in dying to save Thebes, gained honor (the opposite of shame), which he would have lost if he had preserved his life (*Diss* 3.20.5-6; citations from Beardslee).

This, then, is the second calling of disciples. In 1:16-20 and 2:13-14 Jesus had called, and the disciples had followed. Now the Markan Jesus calls (*proskalesamenos*, 8:34a) again. The stakes are higher now because the disciples and the audience must decide whether to continue to follow, not only a preacher and healer, but also a life-giver whose way leads to a shameful death. The difference between the Greco-Roman exhortations and the words of the Markan Jesus is that in the Greco-Roman examples the protagonist dies a heroic death to avoid shame, whereas Mark's audience is called to embrace a shameful death in the present as preferable to the ultimate shame of apostasy.

A final word is needed on the concept of self-denial. In her award-winning book, *Journeys by Heart* (New York: Crossroad, 1988), Rita

Nakashima Brock rejects the Markan Jesus' call in 8:34-9:1. She argues that the oppression of women and minorities is perpetuated by Mark's call to self-denial and that wholeness comes only through self-affirmation and the shar-ing of "erotic power" (Brock 1988, 90-91 and *passim*). Although Brock's concerns are legitimate, her solution assumes that human beings in commu-nity have within themselves the capacity for self-definition and wholeness. The author of Mark, on the other hand, assumes that true self-understand-ing comes to human beings only from their Creator.

The concept of self-denial in Mark must be interpreted in the context of the Gospel narrative as a whole. It does not mean adopting the posture of a doormat by abandoning all sense of self. It does not mean giving up certain pleasures or desires. It means, rather, abandoning all claims to self-definition and accepting and asserting God's program for and God's claim upon one's life (so Kristen Bentley).

This is what the Markan Jesus does in 14:36. He has a will of his own, but he chooses God's will instead. In 14:62 Jesus denies himself publicly by the parodoxical act of boldly *claiming* his God-given identity and role. As a result, he takes up his cross and saves his life by losing it. Peter, by contrast, becomes the example of one who tries to save his life by denying *his* God-given identity and role as a follower of Jesus (14:66-72). Peter forfeits eschatological life by his attempt to save his physical life.

For a Christian to deny herself, then, is to have the courage to claim her true identity—to be the person God says she is no matter what the cost. A Christian who tries to protect himself from persecution as a follower of Jesus denies Jesus, loses the ground and center of his life in the present, and forfeits life in the reign of God.

The next scene in this passion prediction unit is traditionally labeled "the transfiguration." The scene has two functions in the Gospel narrative: to allow God to confirm Jesus' interpretation of messiahship in terms of suffering and to interpret Jesus' role by using Exodus/Moses motifs.

Jesus selects only Peter, James, and John to accompany him, not because they are his favorites, but because in this Gospel they are singled out as hav-ing special difficulty understanding the point he has just made in 8:31–9:1 about the necessity of suffering. Just as the voice from heaven at Jesus' bap-tism identified him as God's Son who would exercise the power of the Holy Spirit to heal and deliver from bondage to the demonic, so in this scene the voice from heaven identifies Jesus as God's Son whose predictions of the pas-sion and resurrection will be vindicated and whose insistence on the implica-tions of the passion for the life of faithful discipleship are correct (Myers 1988, 251).

The evangelist continues to follow Isaiah's lead by giving an eschatological interpretation to motives associated with the exodus, and particularly with the figure of Moses. He does this by combining the expectation of a prophet like Moses (Deut 18:15) with the expectation of Elijah as forerunner to the Messiah (Mal 4:5-6, LXX 3:22-23). Following the order of LXX Mal 3:22-24, he mentions Elijah first, then Moses (9:4, with Gundry 1993, 458). But the application of the two eschatological expectations is developed in chiastically reversed order: Jesus as Moses (9:2-10), then John as Elijah (9:11-13).

Joel Marcus has demonstrated that in Mark the entire transfiguration scene depends upon motifs derived from a conflation of two accounts of Moses' ascent of Mt. Sinai in Exodus 24 and 34 (Marcus 1992b, 80-93). Marcus charts the parallels (82):

Mark		Exodus
9:2a	six days	24:16
9:2a	three disciples	24:1, 9
9:2b	ascent of mountain	24:9, 12-13, 15, 18
9:2b-3	transfiguration	34:29
9:7b	cloud	24:15-16, 18
9:7b	voice out of cloud	24:16
9:15	people astonished	34:29-35

As promised, God has "raised up" a prophet like Moses from among the people of Israel (*anastesei*, LXX Deut 18:15; cf. *anaste*, Mark 9:9). That promise in Deuteronomy was accompanied by a command to "listen to him" (Deut 18:15, 19). The voice from heaven in this scene repeats that command: "Listen to him." Peter and the others would do well to listen to Jesus' teaching on his crucifixion and their martyrdom, rather than trying to correct him (9:7; cf. 8:32b).

Marcus points to three developments in the interpretation of the Moses story in Hellenistic Judaism that seem to contribute to the Markan portrayal of Jesus in the transfiguration scene: Moses' enthronement, Moses' translation, and Moses' divinization.

Ezekiel the Tragedian (2nd century BCE) and Philo of Alexandria (1st century CE) both interpret Moses' ascent of Sinai as an enthronement in ways that imply that Moses participates in the kingship of God. Since Jesus' transfiguration is narrated immediately after the prediction of the imminent "kingdom of God come in power" (9:1), it would appear that the transfiguration is to be interpreted as an indication that Jesus the royal Son of

God participates in God's kingship, which is beginning to break through in his ministry (cf. 1:14-15).

Philo (*Questions on Genesis* 1.86) takes the absence of a known burial place for Moses to mean that he had been translated into heaven, an event that "was believed to have been foreshadowed by the ascent of Sinai" (Marcus 1992, 88). Josephus (*Antiquities* 4.326) denies that Moses "returned to the divinity," but his account seems designed to refute a current interpretation resembling Philo's. This pattern, which Talbert has called "the myth of the immortals," would have been quite familiar to a Greco-Roman audience: a wise, powerful, and/or virtuous person is exalted to heaven as a reward for a life of obedience to the gods and as a result is able to offer assistance to devotees still living on earth (Talbert 1977, 25-43). Since the Markan arrangement makes explicit mention of the resurrection of Jesus in connection with the transfiguration (9:9-10), a connection between the two is implied.

Closely related to the notion of translation and kingship is the notion of divinization. Philo writes in his *Life of Moses* 1:158 that Moses "was named god and king of the whole nation." It may have been this connection that caused Josephus to deny the translation of Moses as vigorously as he did. "The title 'Son of God,' therefore, is a perfect one for the Markan Jesus, since it bespeaks both his unique familial likeness to God and his subordination to the one whom he calls 'Father' (see 8:38; 13:32; 14:36)" (Marcus 1992b, 92).

Thus, the Moses typology enables the evangelist to portray Jesus as the prophet-like Moses who proleptically enters into his kingship at the transfiguration and who, in the present experience of the Markan audience, shares the rule of the universe with his Father by virtue of his translation and divinization.

The transfiguration narrative provides only a partial fulfillment of the promise of 9:1 that some would see the coming of God's reign in power. Complete fulfillment awaits the coming of the Son of Man in the clouds (13:26; cf. 8:38), but this experience should give the disciples confidence that Jesus' interpretation of his identity and mission is the one that God endorses.

It should, but it does not. Peter, for lack of a better response, suggests a building program (9:5), but that is not what God has in mind. To think as God thinks is to listen to Jesus and take his words to heart, but the disciples are not up to that. When the cloud lifts, they find themselves alone with Jesus again, and they stumble down the mountain to be confronted with the report that their failure to understand the transfiguration has been matched by the failure of the other disciples to exorcise a demon.

On the way down, the Markan Jesus warns the three not to report what they had seen until after "the son of Man should rise from among the dead" (9:9). This combination of a reference to the resurrection with the vision of Elijah they have just experienced causes the disciples to realize the eschatological significance of the transfiguration. Their question about the sequence of events in the last days foreshadows their similar questions in 13:4. Here, as there, the function of the question is to provide an opportunity for the Markan Jesus to clarify things for the audience.

The question the disciples put to Jesus is, "Why do the scribes say that Elijah must come first?" (9:11). This has to mean that the Markan disciples attribute to Jewish tradition a belief that Elijah would appear as a forerunner to the Messiah. Whether or not there was such a belief is not relevant for the analysis of the Markan narrative (see Marcus 1992b, 110). The narrative logic is plain: Jesus has been recognized as the Messiah (8:29); he has predicted his suffering, death, and resurrection (8:31); and he has been seen in his eschatological glory by Peter, James, and John and identified by the heavenly voice as God's Son, the prophet-like Moses whose words are to be taken seriously. In short, the Messiah has appeared in glory. The disciples now want to know why the Messiah was not preceded by the coming of the forerunner promised in Malachi 4:5-6 (LXX 3:22-23).

That Mark is dependent on LXX Malachi at this point is made clear by the word "restore," found in both texts. The disciples have identified a legitimate problem. If Elijah must come before the Messiah, and if, when he comes, Elijah will "restore all things" (i.e. repair fractured human relationships according to the context in Malachi and its later interpretation), then obviously Elijah has not yet come, since the predicted suffering of the Son of Man (8:31) presupposes a continuing breach in human relationships.

Marcus argues that the sentence attributed to Jesus in Mark 9:12b is interrogative, not declarative: "Does Elijah, when he comes first, restore all things?" (Marcus 1992b, 98-99). The evangelist has Jesus respond to that suggestion with another question: "[If the scribes are right that Scripture predicts that Elijah will restore all things], then how [will we solve the contradiction between two Scriptural predictions, since] it is written about the Son of Man that he must suffer and be treated with contempt?" Jesus has stated the problem implied by the disciples' question.

Of course, there is no place in the Old Testament where "it is written" that the Son of Man must suffer and be rejected. However, Marcus has shown that "it is written" can indicate a Christian exegetical conclusion rather than a specific Scriptural citation, as in Mark 1:2-3, Gal 4:22, and John 7:38 (Marcus 1992b, 95-96). The evangelist means that Scriptures having to do with the Son of Man of Daniel 7, the suffering servant of Isaiah 53, and the Psalms of the Righteous Sufferer, all taken together, show that "it is written of the Son of Man that he should suffer many things and be rejected."

The further claim that "it has been written" about Elijah that he, too, must suffer at the hands of his enemies whatever they wished to do to him seems to have been arrived at by logic something like this:

Major premise—The forerunner of the Messiah must foreshadow the Messiah's own mission.
Minor premise—The mission of the Messiah includes suffering and death (8:29-33; 9:12).
Conclusion—The forerunner must also have undergone suffering and death. John the baptizer fits this description (9:13).

Because he finds this kind of argument in the *Mekilta* and other rabbinic midrashim, Marcus assumes that the Markan audience must be familiar with rabbinic modes of argument (Marcus 1992b, 106). However, this very same kind of argumentation appears in Hellenistic rhetoric in the form of the enthymeme, a syllogism in which one of the components is implied rather than explicit. Anyone who had listened to rhetors arguing on the street corners could have been exposed to this device. Sophisticated Jewish exegetes may have been part of Mark's audience, but they need not have been.

Thus, the response of the Markan Jesus to the disciples' question can be paraphrased as follows:

The scribes were correct to predict that Elijah would come first, but does he come to "restore all things" and reconcile people to one another? No, as the forerunner of the suffering Messiah, he must suffer an unjust death at the hands of the powerful. I tell you, Elijah has come in the person of John the baptizer and they did to him whatever they wished.

John the baptizer is established as the suffering forerunner of the suffering Messiah, Jesus. The eschatological timetable implied by *dei* (9:11) is on schedule.

In the story that completes this large unit the discontinuity between Jesus' impending suffering and death and his remarkable power to heal and deliver becomes present to the audience in jarring clarity. This is the story of the healing of the demon-possessed boy (9:14-29). Here the author of Mark has two points to make: (1) God's miraculous power and human confidence in that power are inextricably linked, and (2) God's power is not an impersonal force to be manipulated, but a gift to be prayed for. In order to make these two points, the evangelist uses this story of a botched exorcism to criticize the father and the crowd for their lack of faith and to criticize the disciples for their prayerlessness.

The Markan audience is surprised to learn that the disciples are not able to exorcise the boy, since Jesus gave them authority to cast out demons in 3:15 and 6:7, and the narrator has reported that they were successful in "many" cases (6:13). Their failure here catches the attention of the audience and prepares for Jesus' success and for his diagnosis of their failure.

This story may be outlined as follows (Lang 1976, 322):

A—Focus on the failure of the disciples (9:14-18)
   B—Focus on the boy and the crowd (9:19-20)
      C—Conversation between Jesus and the father (9:21-24)
   B'—Focus on the boy and the crowd (9:25-27)
A'—Focus on the failure of the disciples (9:28-29)

The pericope opens with Jesus, Peter, James, and John approaching the other disciples (9:14). Standing with Jesus and the three, the narrator says, "They saw a great crowd around *them* and scribes arguing with *them*." In both instances in this opening scene *them* refers to the disciples left behind at the foot of the mountain. In 9:15 the crowd leaves the disciples and runs up to greet Jesus. From this point on, the disciples are out of the picture altogether until the private scene in 9:28 "in the house." Thus, the disciples' failure is not blamed on *their* lack of faith, but on the faithlessness of the father and the crowd. They are the ones Jesus addresses as "O faithless generation" in 9:19.

In response to Jesus' question about the duration of the boy's demon possession, the father again gives a dramatic description of his son's symptoms. Having been disappointed once, the father is understandably skeptical about Jesus' ability to exorcise: "*If* you are able to do anything, have pity on us and help us" (9:22). But in Mark, Jesus' *ability* to help is never at issue; the leper was right when he said, "If you choose, *you can!*" (1:40). So Jesus answers, " '*If* you are able!'—All things are possible for the one who believes" (9:23). This response makes it clear that to regard as conditional the *possibility* of the requested miracle is to be unbelieving. Jesus repeats the father's words, "If you can," in order to challenge them.

The sense of the second part of Jesus' response is deliberately ambiguous. The Markan Jesus claims that he has faith, and therefore God's power to do the impossible is available in response to his prayers. At the same time he urges the father to have faith also.

Still desperate and still honest, the father cries out, "I believe; help my unbelief!" To this request Jesus immediately responds by exorcising the boy. This demonstrates three things: (1) Jesus does have the faith for which nothing is impossible; (2) inadequate faith on the part of either victim or advocate does not prevent miracles; and (3) the answer to the father's prayer that Jesus help his unbelief is the miracle itself, which would certainly destroy any doubts the father had about Jesus' power.

This story completes the Markan picture of the relationship between faith and miracles. The father's response to Jesus' insistence that "everything is possible for the one who believes" is that he *does* believe, but his faith is inadequate. The father's faith is similar to that of the Syrophoenician woman. He must have had confidence that God's power through Jesus could help his son; otherwise, he would have stayed at home instead of seeking out Jesus and his followers. His faith is demonstrated by his actions. The failure of the disciples to exorcise the demon, however, has discouraged him. He needs to have his confidence strengthened. The only thing that happens in the narrative after the father's request, "Help my unbelief," is the healing of his son. From the evangelist's point of view, the miracle constitutes the "help" for the father's unbelief. Faith is needed for miracles in Mark, but sometimes miracles are needed to awaken the confidence in Jesus' power that the evangelist labels "faith" (Dowd 1988, 107-114).

But the father's lack of faith is not the whole story. When the disciples get Jesus alone "in the house," where all private teaching takes place, they ask the reason for their failure (9:28). Jesus' answer is that "this kind" of demon comes out only for those who are persons of prayer like Jesus himself (1:35; 6:46). Since the Markan Jesus has not prayed in this particular story, this must be a reference to the necessity of a regular practice of prayer. The disciples' power for ministry depends upon the quality of their time spent in the presence of God.

In 1:36 "Simon and those with him" pursue Jesus out to his place of private prayer, demonstrating that they have little or no patience with someone who merely *prays* when there is so much to *do*. This may reflect a problem in the Markan community that the evangelist addresses using the disciples as bad examples. If the Christian community lacks spiritual power, the problem may be an over-emphasis on action to the neglect of prayer.

Second Passion Prediction Unit
(9:30–10:31)

This second passion prediction unit begins like the previous one: the Markan Jesus predicts his betrayal, death, and resurrection (9:31; cf. 8:31), and the disciples make an inadequate response indicating their failure to understand or accept Jesus' prediction (9:32-34; cf. 8:32b). Their failure to understand the implications of Jesus' coming suffering for their lives as followers of Jesus leads naturally to their argument over which of them is the greatest. What follows is a collection of teaching material on the nature of discipleship that is held together by an inclusion that provides a paradoxical solution to their argument: "Whoever wants to be first will be last" (9:35) and "Many who are first will be last, and the last will be first" (10:31). This, of course, parallels the paradox of saving life by losing it (8:34–9:1).

Within this frame the teaching material is divided into two main parts by the use of two geographical settings. All the teaching in 9:35-50 takes place "in the house" in Capernaum (9:33). Jesus sits down in 9:35 (*kathisas*) and gets up again in 10:1 (*anastas*) in order to continue his journey south. The setting for 10:1-31 is no longer Galilee, but rather the region of "Judea [and] Transjordan (10:1).

The teaching "in the house" begins with Jesus' awareness of an argument among the disciples (9:33) and ends with his admonition that they be at peace with each other (9:50). The Markan Jesus first addresses the topic of the argument: "Who is the greatest" (9:34). By this time the audience is not surprised to learn that the answer is exactly the reverse of what would be expected. Jesus predicts that those who are now concerned about being first will in the future be the last and the servants of all (9:35). Gundry correctly notes that the Markan Jesus does not say, "Whoever wants to be first *must* be last," but rather, "Whoever wants to be first *will* be last" (Gundry 1993, 509). By casting this formula for greatness as a prediction rather than as an imperative, the evangelist remains consistent with the emphasis on the priority of grace that pervades this Gospel and prepares for the announcement in 10:27 that the salvation human beings cannot achieve is "possible for God."

The child in this scene (9:36) is a concrete example of one who would be regarded as "last of all" in the ancient social order. The high infant mortality rate in antiquity contributed to the marginalization of children. Perhaps fewer than half lived to their fifth year. They had only recently come from the divine realm and were likely to leave this life at any time; thus, they were not fully human beings (Wiedemann 1989). Indeed in the Gospel narrative all the children who have been portrayed up to this point have been either terminally ill (5:23), demon-possessed (7:25; 9:17), or under the control of evil and manipulative adults (6:22-25).

On the other hand, this marginal status conferred on children a certain mystery. They were thought to be closer to the gods than adults, and sometimes even their casual utterances were regarded as omens. (The best-known instance of this belief occurs in Augustine's account of his conversion, *Conf.* 8.12.)

This cultural context enables the evangelist to portray Jesus as identifying with those diminuitive non-persons who nevertheless are in a mysterious way the bearers of the divine presence when they are welcomed in his name. To welcome a powerless child is to welcome not only Jesus himself, but also the One who sent him (9:37). The logical corollary is that the community in which the non-persons of society find no welcome is a community without the presence of God.

The phrase "in your/my name" links this pronouncement story with the one that follows. The disciples, although unable to perform the most recent exorcism requested of them (9:14-29), nevertheless want to make sure that no one outside their group is allowed to cast out demons in Jesus' name. In addition, the narrator portrays the disciples as trying to usurp Jesus' role as leader; the problem with this outsider is that "he was not following *us*." But the Markan Jesus insists that all who minister wholeness in his name are to be recognized as "for us" (40). The use of "the name" makes it clear that the issue is not the ultimate status of "anonymous Christians" (non-Christians who perform acts of compassion); rather, the issue is the necessity of openness toward the ministry of Christian groups other than one's own. But in 9:41 the audience learns that anyone (even a non-Christian) who shows mercy toward members of the Christian community will be rewarded (cf. Matt 25:31-46).

Calling attention back to the child in his arms, the Markan Jesus pronounces an ominous warning against influencing a believing child (or any new Christian?) to commit apostasy (9:42). On the topic of apostasy in general, the sayings in 9:43-48 make it clear that "it is better to enter life having renounced certain cherished acts than to go into hell having done it all without restraint" (Via 1985, 18). Self-fulfillment is not to be equated with "entering into life," and self-indulgence may lead to self-destruction. This is essentially the same warning that was issued in 8:34–9:1 with the emphasis shifted from abandoning one's confessional identity ("being ashamed of me and my message") to actions leading to apostasy.

Once again the boundaries between insiders and outsiders have been blurred. One who appears to be outside may be an insider, and even outsiders can earn a reward by kindness to insiders. Furthermore, those who are confident of their status as insiders may put themselves outside by their treatment of weak believers or by self-indulgent behavior.

In light of all this the disciples would do well to "be at peace among [themselves]."

The second subsection of this passion prediction unit is made up of teaching by the Markan Jesus on three topics: marriage and divorce (10:2-12), receiving the reign of God (10:13-16), and the problem of wealth (10:17-31). The geography is confused, as the textual variants indicate, but the mention of Judea (10:1) reminds the audience that the Markan Jesus is coming ever closer to the scene of his suffering and death. The first pericope begins with an attempt to "test" Jesus. The final pericope in this subsection closes with the ironic promise of "persecutions" as the final item in the list of the blessings of belonging to the community of Jesus' followers. Like him they can expect to be tested and to suffer (cf. 13:9).

The crowds, who have many times been the recipients of Jesus' help and teaching, come together again, and again Jesus teaches them (cf. 2:13; 4:1; 6:34; 8:34). But this time there is an ominous difference. The crowds question Jesus with the motive of testing him (10:2), thus imitating the behavior of Jesus' opponents (8:11 and 12:15, omitting the reference to the Pharisees here with the Western text in agreement with Metzger and Wikgren: Metzger 1994, 88). In this way the evangelist foreshadows the complicity of the crowd in the crucifixion (15:8, 11).

The precise words of the "historical Jesus" on divorce are not recoverable from the diverse New Testament texts; since all reports are negative, it is probably safe to say that Jesus was against it. The earliest written report of an opinion of Jesus is Paul's, "the wife should not separate from her husband . . . and . . . the husband should not divorce his wife" (1 Cor 7:10-11). Thus Paul agrees with Mark in assuming that women can initiate the breakup of a marriage. Among the Gospels, John does not mention the issue at all; Mark and Matthew describe a question about divorce to which Jesus gives an answer; and all three synoptic evangelists record a formula of case law using the "if . . . then" formula typical of such pronouncements and connecting divorce with adultery. In fact, Matthew has two such pronouncements that are slightly different in content and nuance (cf. Garland 1993, 67-70, 198-99). The author of Mark places the public question-and-answer session first (10:1-9) and the pronouncement afterward as private teaching to the disciples in the ubiquitous house.

The Markan question is not, like the Matthean one, a question about the grounds for divorce (cf. Matt 19:3). The debate between the school of

Shammai and the school of Hillel is not in view here. The crowd is portrayed as asking "Whether it is proper (or permitted, *exestin*) for a husband to divorce a wife" (10:2). It is an odd question because the possibility of divorce was taken for granted by both Jews and gentiles at the time the Gospel was written; thus, the question of divorce must have been a matter of debate in the Markan community for some reason not apparent in the text itself. Because the evangelist makes the question part of a program of "testing [Jesus]," the issue may have been a source of conflict between the Christians and their neighbors of other persuasions.

It is difficult to determine what lies behind the question as to whether divorce is proper at all, but it may have arisen from arguments within the Markan community over the problem of reconciling the prohibition handed down to them from Jesus with conflicting teachings within the Scriptures. The rabbinic debates of the Second Temple period focused on the tension between two Torah texts: the intent of God in creation for permanent union between a man and a woman (Gen 1:27; 2:22-24) and the regulation of divorce procedure (Deut 24:1-4). But the mixed gentile/Jewish congregation of Mark's audience read the Septuagint, which included the prophetic denunciation of divorce (Mal 2:13-16) along with the account in the writings of the divinely mandated divorce of foreign wives (Ezra 10). This mixed message did nothing to clarify matters, which were as complex in Greco-Roman society as they are today.

Most of our information about divorce in Greco-Roman antiquity comes from the upper classes, but at least in those circles divorce was not difficult to obtain. Texts from classical Athens to Hellenistic Egypt to late republican and early imperial Rome confirm that marriages could be ended by mutual consent or by the initiative of either party (sometimes the woman's initiative was exercised by male relatives on her behalf). People readily resorted to divorce for a variety of reasons, despite the belief that marriage was a "great and worthy estate" overseen by "great gods": "first Hera (and for this reason we address her as the patroness of wedlock), then Eros, then Aphrodite, for we assume that all of these perform the function of bringing together man and woman for the procreation of children" (Musonius Rufus, "Is Marriage a Handicap for the Pursuit of Philosophy?"). Similarly, Isis claims, "I have brought woman and man together" (*SIG* 3.1267). Despite such divine sanction for marriage, a Roman widower could write this inscription for his late wife: "Marriages as long as ours are rare, marriages that are ended by death and not broken by divorce. For we were fortunate enough to see our marriage last without disharmony for fully 40 years." (Lefkowitz and Fant 1992, 136; translations of Musonius Rufus and the Isis aretalogy are from Boring, Berger, Colpe 1995, 117; see also Pomeroy 1975, 64-65, 129-30, 154-58, 193-97, 204).

The reasons for divorce varied. Sometimes the original marriage was undertaken for financial advancement. In a first century CE papyrus from Roman Egypt, a woman complained that her husband married her for her dowry, spent it all, and then deserted her. She demanded the return of her dowry with interest. Indeed, it was generally agreed that the dowry must be returned in case of divorce; if the wife were at fault, the husband might keep a portion of the dowry.

If the marriage did not produce children, the fault was assumed to be the woman's and she could be divorced for this cause (Pomeroy 1975, 158). However, insanity was not considered a valid cause for divorce (Lefkowitz and Fant 1992, 114).

Marriage and divorce were sometimes political. Tiberius, the son of Augustus' second wife, was forced to divorce his beloved first wife in order to marry Augustus' daughter Julia, whom he loathed (Suetonius, *Tiberius* 7.2). This prepared the way for his adoption by Augustus and subsequent accession to the throne.

Augustus allowed, but did not compel, women to divorce their husbands for adultery (Pomeroy 1975, 158). Women who committed adultery had to be divorced by their husbands during the imperial period, but this was an improvement, since earlier the husband, or sometimes the father, had been allowed to kill a woman caught in adultery along with her partner. The sources vary as to the specifics of these laws, and it is difficult to determine how often such executions occurred.

In general, then, it appears that the causes for many marriages and divorces were political expediency, financial greed, the desire for progeny, and the serial waxing and waning of sexual attraction.

The frequency of divorce was deplored by some Romans. Plutarch writes nostalgically of the laws of Romulus forbidding divorce initiated by the woman and severely restricting a man's right to divorce to three circumstances: the wife's "poisoning her children, or counterfeiting his keys, or for adultery" (*Romulus* 22, LCL). Plutarch advises the woman who suspects her husband of being unfaithful to refrain from "entering a writ of divorce" because this is just what her rival desires. Moreover, when an man indulges in sexual relations with a *hetaira* or a slave, "his wedded wife ought not to be indignant or angry, but she should reason that it is respect for her which leads him to share his debauchery, licentiousness, and wantonness with another woman" (*Moralia,* "Advice to Bride and Groom," 144a, 140b, LCL).

Augustus, concerned lest the Roman nobility fail to reproduce itself in adequate numbers, "assessed heavier taxes on unmarried men and women without husbands, and by contrast offered awards for marriage and child-bearing. And since there were more males than females among the nobility, he permitted anyone who wished (except for senators) to marry freedwomen, and decreed that children of such marriages be legitimate" (Dio Cassius, *Hist.* 54.16.1-2). And according to Suetonius, "when he found out that the law was being sidestepped through engagements to young girls and frequent divorces, he put a time limit on engagement and clamped down on divorce" (*Augustus* 34; translations from Lefkowitz and Fant 1992, 103). These texts demonstrate both the (to Augustus) alarming frequency of divorce in the early imperial period and the demographic consequences of the Roman prac-tice of exposing rather than rearing female children. Of course, Augustus made an exception for his successor Tiberius, "allowing" a divorce that Tiberius did not even desire.

Meanwhile, debates among Jewish legal experts in this period reflected no doubt about the *possibility* of divorce for the male partner, but consider-able disagreement over the legal *grounds* for such action. Theoretically, divorce was not initiated by Jewish women (On the Jewish background relevant to the Matthean texts, see Keener 1991, 38-49).

This cultural confusion, combined with conflicting texts in their Greek Bible regarding marriage and divorce and a clear prohibition from the Jesus tradition, may well have led members of the Markan community to raise the question as to whether divorce were permissible or not. That the community rejected the serial monogamy of the ruling classes is suggested by the Gospel's negative attitude toward Herod's marital escapades.

The Markan Jesus responds to the question with a question of his own: "What did Moses command you?" The response is taken from Deut 24:1, and the questioners are portrayed as construing divorce entirely from the male point of view. They speak only of writing the certificate; they omit the formal step of putting it into the woman's hand, thus guaranteeing that she can show the specific reason for her ex-husband's rejection of her, leaving nothing to rumor and speculation.

Further, the Markan Jesus' dialogue partners admit that the passage in Deuteronomy is not a command to divorce, as Jesus' language had sug-gested, but is a mere permission. That is, Deuteronomy takes it for granted that husbands will divorce their wives. The only imperative in the passage is the one forbidding the first husband to remarry a woman he has divorced.

Mark 10:5-9 then proceeds to interpret the reason for the Mosaic divorce permission and God's true intention for relationships between men and women. Jesus treats the Mosaic legislation as a concession to human "hardness of heart," a condition he had recognized in the onlookers in the Galilean synagogue as early as 3:5. But this concession does not reflect God's intention. In creating humankind male and female, God had intended a permanent union between husband and wife, a point that the Markan Jesus makes by combining Gen 1:27 with Gen 2:24.

This presents an interesting contrast with Jubilees 3:4-7 (2d century BCE), in which the creation of the *female* is for the purpose of marriage. For the author of Mark, God created both female *and* male in sexual differentiation from each other so that they might be joined in marriage and become one. According to the evangelist, then, marriage is *not* about political or economic alliances, or increasing the upper-class population or improving the gene pool, or providing help for the male who cannot make it on his own, or sexual gratification, or getting one's needs met. From the point of view of the Markan Jesus, marriage is only and emphatically about fulfilling the perfect design of the Creator. This being the case, Jesus says, it is not a human prerogative to subvert the purposes of God by divorce (10:9). It is not God's will that human hardness of heart have the last word.

In the private conversation "in the house" with the disciples (10:10-12), however, the present reality of hardheartedness is taken into account. Not divorce, but divorce *with* remarriage, constitutes adultery on the part of the person initiating the divorce. Only the author of Mark entertains the idea that a man can be considered to have committed adultery against his rejected wife (*ep'autēn*, 10:11). And among the Gospel writers only the author of Mark sees women not as victims but as responsible moral agents. No longer merely passive in marriage and divorce, they too must take responsibility for their decisions and actions: "if she divorces her husband and marries another, she commits adultery."

A few observations are necessary at this point. First, the person said to be adulterous in this text is the person who initiates the divorce and then marries someone else. Nothing is said about the appropriateness of remarriage by the rejected partner. It would appear that what is being condemned is the dissolution of marriage as it was being practiced in the Greco-Roman cultural context; the Markan Jesus warns that when a person leaves a spouse because the dowry has run out or because she can't have children, or because he bores her and they have "nothing in common," that person has run afoul of the will of God as surely as the person who is sexually unfaithful.

Second, this passage is not about the details of pastoral care and family therapy; it is about human rebellion against God. Here, as in 8:31-33, the Markan Jesus draws a sharp contrast between the way God thinks and the way humans think and act. As in 7:6-13, he criticizes the way in which human religiosity uses Scripture to avoid God's will and justify the neglect and abuse of the helpless. It is no less than blasphemous to use the Markan prohibition of divorce to encourage terrified people to remain in abusive relationships that should not even be dignified with the term "marriage."

Third, in the Gospel of Mark, adultery, though serious, is not the "eternal" sin for which one cannot obtain forgiveness. That offense is blasphemy against the Holy Spirit, or the attribution of the work of the Spirit to Satan (3:28-30).

The neighbors of the Markan congregation would have found the prohibition of divorce and the equation of remarriage with adultery amazing. Even Augustus had not succeeded in his attempts to reform the sexual immorality and serial monogamy of his subjects (or even his own daughter, whom he had to exile for adultery). It is possible to imagine a Markan Christian's being "tested" in debate as Jesus is "tested" in the story. Who do these Christians think they are, anyway?

The answer is, of course, that the members of the Markan community think that they are the recipients of the baptism in the Holy Spirit promised in 1:8 but not narrated in the Gospel itself—a baptism that effected the transformation of life that the demand for repentance had not accomplished for John's disciples.

In 9:35 Jesus had announced that because of the transforming power of the Spirit those who now want to be first will instead be last and the servants of all. Because of this power, which signals the eruption into the present of the eschatological future, God's will for male-female relationships revealed in creation becomes a possibility within the eschatological community: "Indissoluble marriage is a possibility enabled by the miracle of the eschatological new creation" (Via 1985, 115).

This is the "already" of Markan inaugurated eschatology. The case law in 10:10-12 represents the "not yet;" hardness of heart has not been completely eliminated even in the church. Of course, when God's reign comes in fullness, not even marriage will be necessary (12:24-25). For now, transformed women and men are empowered to live counterculturally in lifelong faithful marriages, but sadly, they do not always do so.

Some persons from among the same crowd with whom Jesus had engaged in the divorce discussion now bring children "in order that he might touch them" (10:10). The vocabulary (*paidia*, children; *dechomai*, receive; *enagkalisamenos*, taking up in the arms), the setting of children over against the attitude of the disciples, and the use of the "whoever" (*hosan*) construction for the final pronouncement all recall the scene of 9:36-37. Just as in the second feeding story, the disciples have learned nothing from their previous experience. Despite Jesus' teaching in 9:37 that whoever receives a child in his name receives not only him but also the One who sent him, the disciples try to prevent children from having access to Jesus (Tannehill 1977, 401). Instead of welcoming them as Jesus himself, they rebuke (*epetimēsan*) the people who bring the children, as an exorcist rebukes a demon.

Indignant, Jesus demands that the children be permitted, not forbidden, to approach him because the childlike are the primary citizens of God's realm (10:14). Revising the structure of 9:37 ("Whoever welcomes one of such children . . .), he announces that "whoever does not welcome God's realm as a child [welcomes it] will certainly not enter into it."

This is "not an invitation to childlike innocence and naiveté but a challenge to relinquish all claims of power and domination over others" (Schuessler Fiorenza 1983, 148). The disciples are obsessed with being in control: Who is the greatest? Who is authorized to exorcise? Who can have access to Jesus? They are not prepared to welcome the imminent reign of God that Jesus announces (1:14-15), because they cannot control it; it is, after all, *God's* reign.

Children in antiquity, who had no control, no claim, and no status, could welcome whatever came their way with open arms, not because they were innocent and trusting, but because they had nothing to lose and everything to gain. According to the Markan Jesus, people enter God's realm, not in a proud triumphal procession, but in complete vulnerability, with no claim to any rights or status. It was not what the disciples had in mind, and the next incident proves even more devastating to their preconceptions.

Mark 10:17-31 concludes the second passion prediction unit. This pericope, like the one that begins this subsection of the unit, consists of a narrative about Jesus' response to a question (cf. 10:2-9 with 10:17-22) followed by a dialogue between Jesus and the disciples (cf. 10:10-12 with 10:23-31). In this case the question is raised, not by the crowd, but by an individual. A man (neither young, nor a ruler) interrupts Jesus' preparations to set out again with a question about eternal life.

The man's approach identifies him as a positive character; like Jairus (5:22) and the Syrophoenician woman (7:25), he adopts a posture of humble supplication (10:17) and addresses Jesus as "Good Teacher." The narrator indicates no negative ulterior motive for this questioner (contrast with 10:2), who asks Jesus, "What must I do in order that I may inherit eternal life?" The question refers to the state of the righteous after the final judgment. According to *Pss. Sol.* 14:9-10, sinners' "inheritance is Hades, and darkness and destruction; . . . but the devout of the Lord will inherit life in happiness" (cf. *Pss. Sol.* 3:11-12; 13:11; 15:10; 2 Macc 7:90). To "inherit eternal life" here is equivalent to "enter life" (9:43, 45, 47), to "receive/enter the Realm of God" (10:15, 23, 24, 25), to "be saved" (10:26), and to "receive eternal life" (10:30). The question about what one must do to achieve this is attested in *b.Ber.* 28b:

> Our Rabbis taught: When R. Eliezer fell ill, his disciples went in to visit him. They said to him: Master, teach us the paths of life so that we may through them win the life of the future world. He said to them: Be solicitous for the honour of your colleagues, and keep your children from meditation, and set them between the knees of scholars and when you pray know before whom you are standing and in this way you will win the future world.

Before the Markan Jesus deals with the man's question he corrects his anthropology: "No one is good except one, [that is,] God." The man is portrayed as addressing one whom he assumes to be a person deserving of eternal life; his question implies that inheriting life is somehow related to goodness. Jesus' rhetorical question in response to the man's address says in effect that since being good is not a human possibility, the man may as well give up his ambitions in that regard before the conversation even begins.

Jesus then refers to the section of the Decalogue having to do with human relationships, substituting "do not defraud" for "do not covet," perhaps specifying the tactics by which a rich person might acquire what is coveted. Immediately the man claims to have avoided (*phylassō* in the middle voice) all the vices since his youth. The effect of the combination of the man's claim to unblemished virtue with the desperation signaled by his running up, kneeling like a suppliant, and blurting out his question is to suggest to the audience that he is not convinced that all this commandment-keeping will lead ultimately to life. Had he been confident of his spiritual condition, he would not have raised the question in the first place.

The Markan narrator now tells the audience that Jesus looked intently at the man and loved him. It is this love that motivates the call to sell whatever he has, give to the poor, and "Come here! Follow me." This repetition of the language of 1:16-20 and 2:14 indicate a summons to discipleship; the man is being invited to join the company of disciples, to exchange everything he has for the presence of Jesus, which is the "one thing [he] lack[s]." To inherit eternal life, to enter the realm of God, is to give up everything to follow Jesus. Further, there can be no turning back after a trial period of discipleship; the man is not told to put his funds in escrow, but to give them away to the poor where they would be beyond retrieval.

This invitation produces shock and grief in the man, who turns away without a word, becoming the only person in the Gospel to refuse the invitation to discipleship. A typical Markan *gar* clause gives the reason: "for he had many acquisitions (*ktēmata*)." The noun is unusual for its generality; one would expect "possessions/means" (*chrēmata*) or "riches" (*ploutos*), both of which are used in the discussion that follows in 10:23-31. The use of the more general term suggests that what stands in the man's way is more than his material wealth. Following Jesus would also involve the renunciation of the reputation for righteousness he had acquired by not breaking even one commandment (10:20b). After all, one did not acquire much of a record for commandment-keeping by following Jesus (cf. 2:1–3:6; 7:1-5). Unable to trade his material and spiritual acquisitions for companionship with Jesus, which is eschatological life, the man turns away.

Droge points out that such "unsuccessful call stories" were also known in the Cynic tradition. Diogenes Laertius relates the following story about Diogenes the Cynic:

> Someone wanted to study philosophy under him. Diogenes gave him a fish to carry and commanded him to follow him (*ekeleusen akoluthein*). But the man threw it away out of shame and departed. Some time later Diogenes met him and laughed and said, "Our friendship was broken by a fish." (*Lives* 6.36; Droge 1983, 255)

Note the parallel structure: A person makes a request; the teacher gives a difficult assignment related to defying convention and follows it up with the command to "follow." The person called departs with a negative emotional response (cf. Matt 8:19-22 = Luke 9:57-62, which, however, lack any mention of the person's final response).

The dialogue with the disciples that follows in 10:23-27 interprets this scene. The Markan Jesus' initial comment on the difficulty that riches present for entry into the realm of God astonishes the disciples, but they are even more amazed when Jesus says that entry into God's realm is difficult for anyone but *impossible* for the rich.

The impossibility is expressed by the literary device of the *adynaton*—the juxtaposition of two events or conditions, one of which is regarded by common consent as utterly impossible. The effect is to render the other member of the pair impossible or unthinkable as well. So Herodotus (5:92) has Socles tell the citizens of Sparta that "the heaven shall be beneath the earth and the earth aloft above the heaven, and men shall dwell in the sea and fishes where men did dwell before, now that you . . . are destroying the rule of equals and making ready to bring back despotism into the cities . . ." An epigram attributed to Lucian says, "You will sooner find white crows and winged tortoises than a Cappadocian who is an accomplished orator" (*The Greek Anthology*, LCL, 11.436). Similarly, Jer 13:23 asks, "Can the Ethiopian change his skin or the leopard his spots? Then also you can do good who are accustomed to do evil" (RSV).

Mark 10:25 employs the "sooner than/easier than" form of the device similar to that employed in the epigram attributed to Lucian; the blatantly impossible is said to be more likely than the thing being compared to it. It is impossible for a camel to pass through the eye of a needle; therefore, it is impossible for a rich person to enter God's Realm.

The disciples' astonishment shows that this time they have understood Jesus all too well. In fact the statement is outrageous in its cultural context. In the Greco-Roman world riches were a religious asset, not a liability. The wealthy could be initiated into more mysteries and offer more and better sacrifices in support of their prayers to various deities. In the Jewish tradition the Deuteronomic equation of prosperity with the blessing of God upon the righteous had been reinforced and individualized by the wisdom school. The Old Testament recognized that some rich people exploited the poor or broke the commandments, but in the foregoing narrative the rich man who rejected Jesus' invitation had been identified as a commandment-keeper, and yet he had become the type for those who can no more enter God's realm than a camel can squeeze through the eye of a needle.

Various manuscript copiers and interpreters throughout the centuries have attempted to soften the statement of the Markan Jesus. Several manuscripts read, "How hard it is for those who trust in riches to enter God's realm" in 10:24, suggesting that it is not the rich *per se*, but merely those who trust in their riches who have difficulty. Perhaps the best known dodge is the fiction, introduced in the eleventh century by the commentator Theophylact, that Jesus was referring to a low gate in the wall of Jerusalem called "the eye of a needle" through which a camel might pass only by bending its knees. This would make the entry of the rich into God's realm possible on the condition that they "bent their knees" in humility before God, rather than being haughty and self-righteous. The problem is that there was no such gate; the saying stands as a stark *adynaton* like the later Rabbinic saying in *b.Ber.* 55b, in which an elephant replaces the camel.

The disciples' question, "Who *is able* to be saved (enter God's Realm)?" means, "If the most likely (the rich) are not able to be saved, then how is anyone else able to be?" The answer is that—like the healing of the paralytic (2:1-12), the cleansing of the leper (1:40-45), the calming of the storm (4:35-41), the exorcism of a legion of demons (5:1-20), the raising of Jairus' daughter, and the healing of the hemorrhaging woman (5:21-43)—the salvation of the rich, though impossible for humans, is possible for God (10:27). This is not mere acceptance without transformation. The Markan Jesus does not accept the sick and demon-possessed while leaving them in their bondage; he heals and sets them free. Jesus had "loved" the rich man (10:21) and offered him freedom from the bondage of his wealth, but he had turned away. He was not able to be saved. God's power at work in Jesus was able to save him, but he preferred the security of bondage to the insecurity of freedom with Jesus. Apparently the author of this Gospel does not know of Christian communities made up of both rich and poor converts; he seems to think that the formerly rich have been enabled by God's power to redistribute their wealth.

What follows in 10:28-31 answers the unspoken question raised by what has preceded: How will an individual survive financially after conversion to Christianity, and why would anyone want to convert to such a life of downward mobility? Peter's comment on the disciples' having left everything to follow Jesus merely sets up the situation so that the Markan Jesus can answer the question for the audience. His response is that the eschatological community that lives out the "not yet" reality of God's reign in the present evil age more than makes up for the losses entailed in conversion.

The Markan narrator has already made it clear that Jesus' family members who think him mad have been replaced by the circle of his followers (3:20-35). This experience of Jesus is now expanded to all disciples: those who leave house, brothers, sisters, mother, father, children, and fields on account of Jesus and the good news will receive, even in the present, a hundredfold replacement: houses, brothers, sisters, mothers, children and fields, and the Markan Jesus adds an ironic "with persecutions." That is to say, giving up everything is not loss, but gain, because to follow Jesus is to have provisions and relationships within the new family of the Christian community. In "the age to come" Christians enter "eternal life," which had been the focus of the rich man's question in the first place. The promise is community and provision in abundance in the present and life in the eschatological reign of God. The persecutions are also seen as a benefit in this upside-down value system (cf. Phil 1:29; Acts 5:41).

It is worth noting the inclusions and omissions in the relationships given up and compensated for. Wives and husbands are not included in the list; they are neither left nor "received a hundredfold." The Markan community is no free love commune. Further, though parents may be left and new mothers received, the Markan Jesus has made it clear that he does not sanction neglect of parents for "religious" reasons (7:10-13; Via 1985, 150-52). The leaving/receiving saying is not permission to escape reponsibility, but the promise of compensation for relationships lost through rejection by the family of origin.

These themes are also found in the conversion literature of Judaism. In the Hellenistic Jewish novel *Joseph and Aseneth* (1st century BCE–2nd century CE), Aseneth, the ideal prosylete, begins her conversion by giving her rich clothes and the gold from her idols to the poor (10:10-13). She then prays, "Behold, I left behind all the good (things) of the earth and took refuge in you, Lord, . . . (13:2; trans. *OTP*). Later, the second-century Christian Acts of Paul and Thecla portrays Thecla as rejected by her family (20), but given a new mother in Tryphaena (27-30, 39).

The most striking feature of the lists of relationships left and received in Mark 10 is the treatment of fathers; they are left, but not received. The Roman *patria potestas* is not in force in the Christian community. No human being exercises autocratic power in this new family. Just as the Markan emphasis on the *basilea* of God means that God reigns alone and does not delegate power to the Roman emporer or other human rulers, so the omission of father here and the use of "Father" as designation for and address to God in the Gospel mean that within the family of God no individual has the power to make decisions for or to discipline others as did the Roman *pater*.

The fatherhood of God as a substitute for the lost relationship with one's natural father is also found in Joseph and Aseneth:

> because my father and my mother disowned me and said, "Aseneth is not our daughter," because I have destroyed and ground (to pieces) their gods, . . . I have no other hope save in you, Lord, . . . because you are the father of the orphans . . . Have mercy upon me, Lord, . . . because you, Lord, are a sweet and good and gentle father. (12:12-14)

The context is parallel in that Aseneth's loss of parental relationships is caused by her conversion to the one true God.

The Markan Jesus closes out this unit with the saying, "Many who are first will be last, and the last first" (10:31; cf. 9:35). For Peter, the disciple who was called first, this could be construed as a warning.

Third Passion Prediction Unit
(10:32-45)

The third passion prediction is the longest and most detailed of the three, but the literary unit that it begins is the shortest of the three. After the setting of the scene on the road up to Jerusalem, the familiar pattern is repeated: the Markan Jesus predicts his betrayal, death, and resurrection (10:33-34); representative disciples make an inadequate response indicating their failure to understand (10:35-37); Jesus corrects them (10:28-40) and teaches about discipleship (10:41-45). The unit then closes abruptly with the story of the healing of blind Bartimaeus (10:46-52), completing the frame around the "way" section of the Gospel.

This short unit combines features of the other two. Lest the audience misunderstand the presence of Peter, James, and John at the transfiguration as an indication of their exalted insider status, the author of Mark uses all three as representatives of the opacity of Jesus' disciples; Peter serves this function at the beginning of the first (8:32b) and the end of the second units (10:28), and James and John do so in the third (10:35-37). Peter's misunderstanding is marked by his refusal to accept Jesus' suffering and its implications for his own life. The misunderstanding of all the disciples in the second unit (9:32-34) and of James and John in the third (10:35-37) is manifested by their jockeying for positions ahead of others in the pecking order that the Markan Jesus has worked so hard to abolish in all his teaching "on the way" to his own ironic fulfillment of his role as divine warrior-king.

The passion prediction itself (10:33-34) is virtually an outline for Mark 14:43–16:8. Jesus will be "handed over" to the religious elite, who will "condemn him to death" and "hand him over to the gentiles." The gentiles will "mock him, spit upon him, flog him, and kill him; and after three days he will rise again."

Immediately after the Markan Jesus completes this litany of humiliation and torture, James and John step up, not to console him or to offer their support, but to ask a favor. It is as though they have heard and seen nothing since their vision of Jesus' glory on the mountain. The result is a grim comedy of boorish *non sequitur* that cannot have been lost on the Markan audience.

The brothers' approach is cagily manipulative; they want a yes before they make their specific request. But Jesus demands to know what they want before he commits himself (10:35-56). Having seen a glimpse of Jesus' glory (9:2b-4), they seek reserved seats on either side of him. Jesus' response, "you don't know what you're asking" (10:38a) and his later comment that the places on his right and left have already been assigned (10:40) is proven true in 15:27. Those places will be occupied by condemned criminals. Truly the sons of thunder do not know what they are asking.

Picking up on the royal imagery suggested not only by the brothers' request, but also by the heavenly voice at the transfiguration, the Markan Jesus reminds James and John that those closest to the king have to drink from his cup; if the wine is poisoned, they share the death intended for the ruler (10:38b; cf. Gen 40:1-13; 41:9-13; Neh 1:11b–2:1; Xenophon, *Cyropaedia* 1.3.9; Suetonius, *Claudius* 44.2). Jesus' cup is in fact the cup of suffering that he will ask God to take away in 14:36.

There may be a pun on the word "baptize" in 10:38c, since one of the meanings of the verb was "to destroy (e.g., a person by drowning, or a ship by sinking)" (Beasley-Murray 1990, 85). Although it would be inappropriate to read a fully developed theology of baptism into this simple question of the Markan Jesus, two implications are worth noting. First, within the Gospel itself, Jesus' baptism by John already foreshadowed his death by the allusion to Gen 22:2. God's beloved son, unlike Abraham's, will get no last-minute reprieve by substitution. Second, within the larger early Christian context, the question of the Markan Jesus suggests the earlier Pauline understanding of the baptism of Jesus' followers as baptism "into his death" (Rom 6:3). The prediction of a future "baptism" of James and John certainly influenced the later development in Christian rhetoric in which martyrdom was equated with baptism (Tertullian, *On Baptism* 16; Anon, *On Re-Baptism*, 15; Origen, *Commentary on Matthew* 16.6; Cyprian, *Epistle* 53.4).

James and John respond to Jesus' question as to whether or not they are able to drink his cup and be baptized with his baptism with a prompt and naive, "We are able!" This naivete is perpetuated by the American Protestant practice of repeating their response in the song based on this passage (Marlatt 1995). Nevertheless, the Markan Jesus predicts that the brothers' current self-aggrandizing behavior will finally be replaced by faithfulness (cf. 13:9-13).

The anger of the other disciples upon learning that James and John were seeking special privileges gives the Markan Jesus an opportunity to teach about the upside-down values of Christian leadership (10:41-45). The Christian community will not be modeled on secular Roman ("gentile") structures. The teachings of 9:35 and 10:31 are recapitulated for emphasis: The one who wants to be great will be a servant; the one who wants to be first will be the slave of all.

Here, as in 9:35, the future tense is predictive, not imperative. Following logically after the use of the future in 10:39 to predict the faithful martyrdoms of James and John despite their present self-serving attitudes, the use of the future here indicates that although some among the disciples (and within the Markan community) may wish to be "great" or "first," such people will *not* act on their wishes. Instead, transformed by the promised immersion in the Holy Spirit (1:8), they will resist the temptation to lord it over others and will serve rather than seek prominence or greatness. This reading, effectively argued for by Robert Gundry (1993, 580), is the only one that prevents servanthood from becoming merely an alternative path to greatness and prominence. Thus, all translations that employ the word "must" or other signals of command should be rejected in favor of the simple future. James and John *will* drink Jesus' cup of suffering and *will* be baptized into Jesus' death, and those among Jesus' followers who may harbor a desire for greatness *will* instead become the servants of the Christian community.

As usual in the Gospel of Mark, the actions of Jesus function as the model and ground of the actions of Jesus' followers. This is made clear in the notoriously difficult *gar* clause in 10:45: "For even the Son of Man did not come to be served, but to serve, and to give his life a ransom for many (*lutron anti pollōn*)." The saying looks both backward and forward in the Markan narrative. All that Jesus has done so far falls into the category of serving. His teaching, preaching, exorcizing, and healing were done not to call attention to himself, but as examples of his service to others. In the upcoming passion narrative Jesus' service will take an additional form: giving his life *lutron anti pollōn*.

The previous servanthood sayings in Mark did not include the phrase "not to be served" as a contrast to serving. The introduction of that phrase here suggests that the servanthood of Jesus is remarkable because he is one who should, by rights, receive service rather than give it. Indeed, the Markan Jesus has been portrayed throughout as the warrior-king who, like the Davidic monarch, is "Son of God," and like Deutero-Isaiah's Cyrus, is "the anointed one" of Yahweh. Such a royal figure should be served rather than serving. It is not just "the gentiles" (10:42) who make a distinction between the ruler and the servant; there is no precedent either in the Old Testament or in the Jewish context for the ruler who serves rather than being served. However, David Seeley has shown that such a concept did exist in the Greco-Roman philosophical tradition, particularly among the Stoics and Cynics (Seeley 1993, 234-50).

In the same century that Mark was being written, Dio Chrysostom wrote a series of treatises on kingship in which he argued that the good king puts the welfare of his subjects above his own: "In the title 'master,' . . . he can take no delight, nay, not even in relation to his slaves (*douloi*), much less to his free subjects; for he looks upon himself as being king, not for the sake of his individual self, but for the sake of all [people]" (1.22-23, LCL). According to Dio Chrysostom, the sun is an exemplary monarch because he "does not grow weary in ministering to us and doing everything to promote our welfare (*sotēria*)" (3.73), while experiencing "a servitude (*douleian*) most exacting" (3.75). Seeley argues that the position expressed by Dio Chrysostom goes back to Musonius Rufus, slightly earlier in the first century CE, and is paralleled by fragments of the Pythagoreans Archytas and Diotogenes with similar ideas expressed as early as Plato and Xenophon (Seeley 1993, 237-38).

The Greek tradition even knew of a king who went so far as to die for the sake of his subjects. Lycurgus, an orator of the 4th century BCE, holds up the example of Codrus, legendary king of Athens during the Dorian invasions. According to legend, the invading Dorians learned from an oracle that their success depended upon their preserving the life of the king of Athens. When Codrus heard this, he entered the Dorian camp in disguise, started an argument with some soldiers, and died at their hands. Because the king had been killed, Athens was saved. Lycurgus comments that Codrus "thought it better to die for the salvation (*sotērias*) of his subjects" than to live (*Against Leocrates* 86). In a construction similar to that used by the author of Mark, Lycurgus uses the preposition *anti* followed by the genitive: Codrus is said to have sacrificed "his own life for the common salvation" (*idian psychēn anti tes koines sotērias*; 88). Although the king is not said to have given his life as a ransom, the concept of a substitionary death is very close to that of the tradition employed by the author of Mark at 10:45.

The importance of this tradition is quite different from that of the traditions about kings who offer their lives in atonement for suffering brought on their people by the sins of the king himself. Oedipus goes into exile when he realizes that he is the one whose sin of parricide has caused the plague in Thebes (Sophocles, *Oedipus Rex*). David offers (somewhat belatedly) to take upon himself and his descendents the punishment he brought on the people by ordering the census (2 Sam 24:17 = 1 Chron 21:17). But the offer of substitutionary death is not accepted. The stories of Codrus and Jesus have in common a threat to or enslavement of the people by hostile powers; the evil averted by the death of the king is not sent by God or the gods as a punishment for the sin of the king or of the people.

We have already seen that the theology of Mark is at least in part a reading of the new exodus theology of Deutero-Isaiah. It is within that context that the notion of ransom/redemption must be understood. Mark, like Isaiah, understands God's saving action in terms of deliverance from slavery.

Although the noun *lutron* appears in LXX Isaiah only once (45:13), the verb is important in Deutero-Isaiah's understanding of redemption (41:14; 43:1, 14; 44:22-24; 51:11; 52:3; 62:12; 63:4, 9). God is understood to be the one who redeems or sets free captive Israel. But interestingly enough, no ransom is paid to their alien master: "I have aroused Cyrus in righteousness and I will make all his paths straight; he shall build my city and set my exiles free, not for ransom or reward" (*ou meta lutron oude meta doron*; 45:13).

Herein lies the difference. The triumphal march of the divine warrior at the head of his rescued people, the victory procession along "the way of the Lord" "undergoes an almost alchemical transformation when it collides with the theology of the cross" (Marcus 1992b, 41). Instead of destroying the forces that oppose God's reign, Jesus will die at their hands. But "for those with eyes to see . . . Jesus' suffering and death . . . *are* the prophesied apocalyptic victory of the divine warrior" (Marcus 1992, 36). Unlike the new exodus of Deutero-Isaiah, the new exodus led by Jesus *will* require a ransom, and that ransom will be the life of the warrior-king himself.

Although the author of Mark does not specify who or what it is that holds Jesus' rightful subjects captive, there is one likely candidate: the adversary (*tou satana*, 1:13, 3:20), the prince of the demons (3:22), who has set up a kingdom and a royal house in opposition to God's (3:24-25). It is this adversary whom Jesus has bound and whose house he is plundering by his exorcisms (3:27); Satan's minions recognize that Jesus has come to destroy them (1:24) and to set free those they are holding hostage.

The logic of the Markan narrative suggests that not only do the demons know Jesus' true identity as Son of God, but Satan also knows that Jesus' death will be his defeat. This is suggested by the fact that Jesus calls Peter "Satan" when Peter opposes the statement that Jesus' death carries with it an apocalyptic necessity (8:31-33).

It may be that for the writer of this Gospel, those who are obviously plagued by demons merely manifest the human condition in general; what is true for all people, Jews and gentiles alike, is that they are in bondage to Satan and need to be set free. Through the power of the Holy Spirit (3:29) Jesus can set free one captive at a time. To effect the ransom of "many" (10:45), the king must die. The Greek notion of the ideal king who serves his people even to the point of giving his life for their freedom provides the missing element not present in apocalyptic warfare mythology.

As Gundry (1993, 590-93) points out, the many attempts that have been made to make Mark 10:45 dependent upon Isaiah 53 or 43:3-4, 25 have all failed to persuade. The concept of redemption in Isaiah is independent of the concept of forgiveness for sin. Israel is forgiven because she is guilty; she is redeemed because she is in bondage to an alien power. The author of Mark also regards forgiveness for sin as important, but does not seem to relate forgiveness to the cross. Jesus' authority to forgive sin is connected with his power to heal physical ailments and his authority to interpret Scripture (2:1–3:6). Certainly forgiveness, like healing, continues to be available to Jesus' followers after his death and resurrection, but it is not *contingent* upon his death in the Gospel of Mark. In terms of typologies of atonement theory, then, Mark 10:45 should be categorized as part of the "*Christus Victor*" motif (cf. Col 2:15) rather than the motif of sacrifice for sin.

Immediate Healing of a Blind Man
(10:46-52)

The "way" section of the Gospel closes with the healing of blind Bartimaeus (10:46-52), recalling the healing of the blind man at Bethsaida (8:22-26) and forming a frame around the entire section. The contrast between the two stories is dramatic; in the first, Jesus has to lay hands on the sufferer twice; in the second, he heals with a word. The first blind man is nameless, but this one not only has a name, but also has his name interpreted for the Greek-speaking audience of the Gospel. The prefix "bar" means "son of," thus, "Son of Timaeus." This detail, while irrelevant to the healing story, will become significant in the passion narrative to follow.

Bartimaeus is the only person healed in the Gospel of Mark who is said to become a follower of Jesus as a result (although the former demoniac desired to do so in 5:18). The logic of a narrative about a healer would suggest that many of the healer's followers would come from among the beneficiaries of his power, and this is recognized by the author of one of the spurious endings of the Gospel, who identifies the follower Mary Magdalene as a former demoniac whom Jesus had exorcised (16:9). But the Gospel's original author reserves the explicit connection of healing and following for the case of Bartimaeus in order to connect Bartimaeus' following "on the way" (10:52) to his gaining his sight. In this way the narrative exploits the Isaianic equation of sight and blindness with faithful and unfaithful responses to covenant relationship with the God of Israel. Recovering from blindness enables one to follow Jesus "on the way" to suffering and martydom, and such recovery is possible only through a miracle given by Jesus.

The exploitation of the blindness/sight metaphor is reinforced by Jesus' repetition of the question he had asked James and John in the pericope immediately preceding this one. When they asked for a favor, Jesus had asked, "What do you want me to do for you?" (10:36). Now, when Bartimaeus calls for mercy from the ideal monarch (Son of David), Jesus again asks, "What do you want me to do for you?" (10:51). This sets up the audience to expect an appropriate answer from Bartimaeus to replace the inappropriate answer of James and John; the appropriate request is not for positions of honor, but for the recovery of sight. In one form or another blindness afflicts all categories of people in this story: opponents, disciples, and members of the crowd. So far, Jesus has had much greater success at restoring physical sight than at removing the spiritual blindness that identifies a person as one of "those outside" (4:11), but the healing of Bartimaeus and his consequent following "on the way" gives the audience hope, if not certainty, that the disciples may finally "see" as well.

Ministry and Passion in Jerusalem

(Mark 11:1–15:47)

The fourth division of the Gospel of Mark is set entirely in Jerusalem and has two major parts: chapters 11–13 concern Jesus and his actions related to the temple (11:1-25) and his teaching in the temple (11:27–12:44) and opposite the temple (13:1-37); chapters 14–15 concern the suffering and death of Jesus.

Jesus and the Temple

(11:1–13:37)

Chapters 11–13 again reflect the author's coordination of Jesus' deeds with Jesus' words, as in the portrayal of the Galilean ministry. This unit of deeds and words is bracketed by references to the Mount of Olives. In 11:1-11 Jesus leaves the Mount of Olives and enters Jerusalem and the temple; in 13:1-37 Jesus leaves the temple, predicting its destruction, and goes to the Mount of Olives, where he delivers an apocalyptic discourse on the coming of the Son of Man.

The subsection focusing on the actions of Jesus (11:1-25) is structured in a double intercalation or "sandwich": entry into Jerusalem and the temple (11:1-11); fig tree incident (11:12-14); expulsion of merchants and money-changers from the temple (11:14-19); interpretation of fig tree incident (11:20-25). The material that begins the subsection of teaching and contro-versy (11:27-33) is part of this intercalation as well, since it is clearly a reaction to the expulsion of merchants and moneychangers.

The effect of this arrangement is to give a double significance to the strange story of the withered fig tree: On the one hand, the fig tree represents the temple establishment, which, despite the approach of God's eschatologi-cal reign, is failing to bear fruit and is therefore destined for destruction; on the other hand, the power that withered the fig tree is an example of God's power to do the impossible in response to the prayers of the believing community. The relationship between these two themes is the shift from sacred space to sacred community that is a part of the Markan cultural and religious milieu.

Deeds (11:1-25)

The first of the dramatic actions in this subsection is the entry into Jerusalem and the temple (1:1-11). The finding of the colt for the ride into Jerusalem (11:1-6) and the similar story of the finding of the room for the final meal (14:12-16) demonstrate Jesus' powers of prediction and his royal authority to requisition what he needs. Now that he has three times redefined his role as anointed warrior-king by combining access to divine power with vulnerability to rejection and death, the Markan Jesus has no further need to obscure his identity as the one who inaugurates the reign of God.

The acclamation of the disciples in chiastic form (11:9b-10: hosanna, blessed, blessed, hosanna) is based partly on Ps 118:26. This psalm portrays a procession of thanksgiving to the temple and emphasizes national sovereignty and defeat of Israel's enemies. In Mark, however, nationalism has been transmuted into world-transforming apocalyptic; the patriotic shout becomes a cry of welcome for the eschatological savior promised by Isaiah (33:22), whose coming inaugurates the inclusion of all the nations into the people of God (56:7).

Both Jewish and gentile members of Mark's audience would have recognized this as the processional entry of a warrior-king enacting a ritual associated with divine epiphany in pre-imperial religions. Unlike the group of disciples pictured in the narrative, the audience would have appreciated the irony of the scene. Breaking the pattern of expectation associated with such processions, the author of Mark has Jesus enter Jerusalem and the temple, look around, and quietly return to Bethany (11:11). The anti-climax is stunning. Even on the following day, instead of offering sacrifice in the temple, which would have symbolized the "appropriation" of the temple by the conquering ruler, the Markan Jesus cancels temple worship altogether (Duff 1992). As before in this story, expectations are overturned and traditional concepts redefined. The "triumphal entry" that begins in Mark 11 will end in Mark 15 with the execution, not of the prisoners of war as in Roman custom, but of the divine warrior-king himself.

Although this division of the Gospel is set in the spring near the time of Passover (14;1), and therefore "not the season for figs" (12:13b), it is legitimate for the Markan Jesus to expect fruit on the fig tree (11:12-14) because his ministry has inagurated the reign of God, which was supposed to be characterized by unlimited fruitfulness and abundance (Telford 1980). The barrenness of the fig tree reflects the faithlessness of the temple leadership. Although Isaiah (56:7) had written that the temple was to be called "a house of prayer for all the [gentile] nations," the temple hierarchy had made it into a "robbers' hideout," where they huddled together, claiming the protection of the holy place despite their failure to recognize the inauguration of the eschaton when "all the gentiles" will make the pilgrimage to Jerusalem (Isa 2:2) and "every knee shall bow" to the God of Israel (Isa 45:22-24) because Israel has become "a light to the gentiles" (49:6; cf. 60:3). Both tree and temple are condemned for their failure to manifest the signs of God's reign. The withering of the fig tree prefigures the destruction of the temple by the Romans—an event in the Markan Jesus' future but in the Markan church's present.

The saying in 11:17, which is a combination of Isa 56:7 and Jer 7:11, should not be understood as an objection to inflated pigeon prices or dishonest exchange rates. In the first place, the word *lēstēs* means not cheats, but muggers or pirates, who use their "dens" not for robbing people, but for evading detection and punishment. This was Jeremiah's original complaint; the priests were relying on the supposed inviolability of the temple to protect them from the consequences of their faithlessness.

In the second place, the actions of the Markan Jesus are not designed to improve or reform the exchange and selling practices in the temple, but to cancel temple worship altogether. What the merchants and moneychangers were doing was not dishonest, but essential. Few could manage to transport a flawless animal all the way from Galilee or Transjordan to Jerusalem for sacrifice. It made more sense to purchase one upon arrival. The Markan Jesus makes it impossible, not only for proper sacrifical animals to be procured and money changed into temple currency, but also for the priests to carry through the temple the vessels necessary to perform the rituals (*skeuos* — 11:16). Of course, the author understands the incident as a proleptic gesture; as described it would not have prevented temple functions for longer than a few minutes. Anything seriously disruptive would have resulted in the preemptory arrest of the perpetrator. But the symbolic gesture is the nonverbal equivalent of Jesus' prediction of the temple's destruction in 13:2. Since the temple leadership has not transformed it into a "house of prayer for all the gentiles," the Markan Jesus acts to shut it down completely.

The teaching that follows the observation that the fig tree has withered to the root interprets the tree's demise as an example of the dramatic power available to the believing community through prayer. It follows here precisely because the predicted destruction of the temple requires a reconsideration of the conditions for effective prayer. Like all ancient religions, Judaism had a tradition of understanding the temple of the deity as the place where petitions were sure to be granted. Egyptian temples, for example, had rooms in which holes in the walls represented the ears of the deity into which petitioners could speak their requests (See Dowd, 1988, 45-55 for secondary references supporting what follows.).

In the Old Testament the prayer of Hannah at Shiloh (1 Sam 1:1-29) and the intercession of Hezekiah in the Jerusalem temple (2 Kgs 19:14-37) illustrate the principle that prayers prayed in the holy place are efficacious. Even when Jonah prays from the belly of the fish his prayer is said to come "into thy holy temple" (Jonah 3:2). The Psalms also stress the importance of the sanctuary as a place where prayers are heard.

The Deuteronomist links the efficacy of prayer with the temple in the dedication speech attributed to Solomon (1 Kgs 8:14-61). Solomon's prayer lists seven situations in which prayer is offered: in individual disputes involving a curse (8:31-32); defeat of the nation by an enemy (vv. 33-34); drought (vv. 35-36); famine, pestilence, and siege (vv. 37-40); prayer by a non-Israelite (vv. 41-43); defeat in battle (vv. 44-45); and exile (vv. 46-51). In each case, prayer is to be offered "in" or "toward" the temple.

In the literature from the period of the second temple the same emphases appear. In Judith 4:9-15 the people prostrate themselves in front of the temple when they pray for protection from Holofernes. In 3 Maccabees the priest and people rush to the temple to pray in the face of the threat to the Holy of Holies by Ptolemy Philopator (3 Macc 1:20-24). The high priest prays, "thou didst promise that if . . . we should come to this place and make our supplication, thou wouldst hear our prayer." The enemy is struck down (3 Macc 2:1-22). In 2 Maccabees 3:15 the priests pray before the altar as Heliodorus prepares to sack the temple treasury. In response to the prayer, Heliodorus is flattened by a divine apparition and subsequently converted (2 Macc 3:24-40). After Judas and his men pray before the altar (2 Macc 10:25-26), the Lord gives them victory over Timotheus by sending angels into battle with them.

The assumption that effective prayer must be offered toward the temple is so basic in Josephus' thought that he commits a gross anachronism by introducing the temple into his (somewhat garbled) account of Abraham's prayer for the recovery of his wife: " . . . uplifting pure hands towards this spot which you have now polluted, [Abraham] enlisted the invincible Ally on his side" (*War* 5.380).

Given this background, it is not hard to see why the destruction of the second temple would cause some rabbis to question whether prayer were any longer possible:

> R. Eleazar said: From the day on which the Temple was destroyed, the gates of prayer have been closed, as it says, "Yea, when I cry and call for help, He shutteth out my prayer," {Lam 3:8} . . . R. Eleazar also said: Since the day that the Temple was destroyed, a wall of iron divides between Israel and their Father in Heaven; as it says, "And take thou unto thee an iron griddle and set it for a wall of iron between thee and the city." (Ezek 4:3) *b.Ber* 32b

However, this level of despair was overcome by the necessity of coping with the loss of the temple. One rabbi argued that:

> The gates of prayer are never closed, for it is written, "As the Lord our God is whenever we call upon Him;" and calling is nothing else but praying, as Scripture in another context has it, "And it shall come to pass that before they call I will answer." (Isa 65:24) *Deut Rab.* 2:12

The Mishnah and both Talmudim advocate prayer in the direction of the temple (*m.Ber.* 4.5; *y.Ber.* 4.5; *b.Ber* 30a).

Of course, the presence of the Shekhina in the temple had never meant that it was not also everywhere in the world. Thus the sages were able to assert that even though the temple had been destroyed, the Shekhina was present in the synagogues and houses of study (*y.Ber.* 5.8d). In the final analysis, rather than being made impossible by the loss of the temple, prayer was seen to be all the more necessary because it was all that Israel had left (Heinemann 1977, 20).

The transition from a religion of animal sacrifice to a religion of prayer and study was forced upon Judaism by the destruction of the temple in 70, but it had already been made, to some extent, by the Jews of the diaspora, to whom the temple was inaccessible even before it was destroyed. The replacement of the temple by the praying community had also taken place before 70 at Qumran and in some Christian groups. In these cases the shift took place not because the temple had been destroyed, but because it had been rejected. While the sectarian authors of some of the Dead Sea Scrolls regarded the Jerusalem temple hierarchy as corrupt, early Christians who would have identified with the Lukan Stephen regarded temples "made with hands" as inherently inadequate (Acts 7:44-50). The substitution in Mark 14:58 of the community of the resurrection for the destroyed temple "made with hands," reflects a critique of sacred objects and sacred places going back to a much older Greek tradition.

The Greek anti-temple polemic was not directed against any particular temple, but against temples in general. This critique became especially prominent in the last century BCE and the first two centuries of the Common Era. Seneca writes that natural places of worship "not made with hands" are more inspiring than temples (*Ep.* 41.3, LCL). Similarly, for Plutarch and the author of the fourth Epistle of Heraclitus, the whole world was the temple of deity. Even Philo regards the Jerusalem temple as a mere concession to the human need to offer material sacrifices, and he thinks that "the highest, and in the truest sense the holy, temple of God is the whole universe" (*Spec.* 1.66-67, LCL).

The devaluation of temples had implications for attitudes toward the practice of prayer. When Lucian's ideal philosopher Demonax was asked by a friend to accompany him to the temple of Asclepius to pray for healing for the friend's son, Demonax is supposed to have replied, "You must think Asclepius very deaf, that he can't hear our prayers from where we are!" (*Demonax* 27, LCL). Seneca again expresses the Stoic attitude:

> We do not need to uplift our hands towards heaven, or to beg the keeper of a temple to let us approach his idol's ear, as if in this way our prayers were more likely to be heard. God is near you, he is with you, he is within you. (*Ep.* 41.1, LCL)

As sacred places became relatively less important in antiquity, religious communities gathered around the person or the memory of a holy man began to take their place. This is the pattern reflected in the Gospel of Mark. From the viewpoint of the author of Mark, the temple had been rejected as a failure long before the Romans destroyed it, but because of its traditional role as the guarantor of the efficacy of prayer, the rejection of the temple required a reassertion of the importance of community prayer and the power available to it. Thus in chapter 11 the author arranges his material so that the proleptic destruction of the temple is followed immediately by the necessary assurances about the efficacy of prayer.

For the Markan community prayer takes place, not in a temple "made with hands," but in the groups that meet together in homes—"in the house" where the Markan Jesus teaches his often confused and frightened disciples. The efficacy of prayer is guaranteed by the power of God to do that which is impossible for humans and is available to a community in which faith and forgiveness are of primary importance.

As we have seen, "faith" in the Gospel of Mark is unswerving confidence that the power of God at work in Jesus is able to heal and transform those who seek Jesus' help. It is the certainty that "everything is possible for God" (10:27; 14:36) and, by extension, for the person who places trust in God's power (9:23; 11:22-24). This belief that the divine could and would intervene in events in the world was held by some philosophical and religious groups in antiquity, but was denied by others. By portraying Jesus as demanding "faith" and forbidding "doubt" in the prayer teaching, the author of Mark locates the Christian community among those who held to the notion of the freedom of the deity to intervene in nature and history, despite the scoffing of those others in the society who insisted that the world was a closed system of cause and effect (For what follows, see Dowd 1988, 78-94).

Among the groups that denied "everything is possible for God/gods" were the Epicureans. Founded by the philosopher Epicurus (341–271 BCE), this philosophical community was still influential during the time Mark was written. Epicurus believed that human unhappiness was caused by mistaken beliefs, those about the gods being among the most harmful. Epicureanism combated the superstition and fear engendered by these mistaken beliefs by denying that the gods had any influence over natural events or human affairs. There is nothing to be feared from the gods, nor is there anything to be hoped for from them. The Epicurean Lucretius ridicules religious persons who revert to "the old superstitions, taking to themselves cruel taskmasters, whom the poor wretches believe to be almighty . . ." (*De Rerum Natura* 5.86-90, LCL).

The Epicureans also held to an early version of atomic theory. They believed that everything was made up of tiny bits of indivisible matter, atoms, and that everything that happened in the world was caused by the collision of these atoms. Therefore, divine intervention was neither required nor desired as an explanation for anything.

The followers of Plato held to the metaphysics laid out in their founder's treatise *Timaeus*. Here Plato had argued that the creator was not omnipotent, but achieved only those results that were possible, given the limitations of the material with which he worked. In *Timaeus* 73E-74B, Plato explained that had the creator been omnipotent, he would have made human bones both hard and flexible, but since that was impossible, he had to choose the property of hardness. Thus, bone is able to protect the marrow and the brain because it is hard, but it is unfortunately also brittle and breaks easily. The properties of bone are not ideal, but they are the best that could be achieved, given the limitations.

In about 170 CE the physician Galen appealed to the position of Plato against the view of "Moses" that "everything is possible for God." On the contrary, Galen wrote, "We say that some things are impossible by nature and that God does not undertake these things, but rather chooses the best out of the possibilities of becoming" (Walzer 1949, 11-13). In other words, God cannot do anything that is contrary to the ordinary course of nature. The followers of Aristotle agreed with the Platonists in denying the possibility of supernatural intervention by the gods.

Stoic philosophers, on the other hand, insisted that "there is nothing which god is unable to do," (Cicero, *On the Nature of Gods* 3.39.92; *On Divination* 2.41.86). They believed in omens, oracles, and portents, extraordinary happenings by which the gods sought to warn humans and enable them to make the appropriate response. The Stoics, however, were also determinists; they believed that everything that happened was caused by the universal divine *logos* that pervaded and controlled all nature and human life. Therefore, the Stoics did not believe in petitionary prayer. People should accept the life circumstances decreed for them by the divine and not seek to change those circumstances in any way.

The Pythagorean philosophers were pantheists like the Stoics, but they believed not only in divination, but also in miracles. Miracle stories were told about Pythagoras himself. "He got rid of plagues rapidly and stopped strong winds; he caused hail to stop at once; he calmed rivers and seas so that his companions might cross over easily . . ." (Iamblichus, *Life of Pythagoras* 135). The miracles of the Neopythagorean teacher Apollonius of Tyana were so amazing that he was accused of practicing magic and stood trial before the emperor Domitian. According to Iamblichus, Pythagoreans "did not conceive that some things are possible to god but others impossible, as those believe who reason sophistically; but they believed that all things are possible" (*Life* 28.139, LCL).

As might be expected, Hellenistic Jewish thinkers also insisted on the omnipotence of God. In Genesis 18:14 God rebukes Sarah's laughter at the promise of a child with the question, "Is anything too hard for the Lord?" In the Septuagint translation into Greek from Hebrew the question becomes, "Is anything impossible for God?" This and other subtle changes from Hebrew to Greek show that the Jews who translated the Scriptures were aware of the philosophical debate about omnipotence and wanted to make it clear that Jews believed God could do the impossible. The same formula, "everything is possible for God," is found repeatedly in the writings of the Jewish historian Josephus and the biblical interpreter and philosopher Philo of Alexandria.

Thus, the discussion of the relationship of the divine to the natural world and to human lives was a topic of widespread debate in the Greco-Roman world at the time of the writing of the Gospel of Mark. The assertion that "everything is possible for God" was usually associated with a belief in miracles and with the practice of petitionary prayer. Those who denied divine omnipotence, on the other hand, tended to regard believing in miracles and praying for divine help as superstition.

In such a pluralistic society any group that maintained a belief in divine omnipotence would have found it necessary to help its members maintain their worldview against the scoffers and sceptics. The best way to do this would be to repeat the miracle stories of God's intervention in the past and to pray expectantly for God's intervention in the present. The telling of the miracle stories would build faith in the community, and that faith would see new answers from God in response to the community's prayers. In other words, faith leads to miracles, and miracles lead to faith.

When the Markan Jesus says in 11:23 that the person who asks that a mountain be taken up and thrown into the sea, and does not doubt inwardly, but believes, will see the request granted, he is asserting the necessity of unswerving confidence in the power of God to do the impossible. When he broadens the example to a command, "Whatever you (plural) pray for and request, believe that you (plural) received it, and it will be done for you (plural)," he is calling the community of disciples to confidence in the promise God made to Isaiah: "Before they call I will answer; while they are yet speaking I will hear" (Isa 65:24, NRSV).

Despite the apparent absolutism of the demand for faith in the prayer teaching, the evangelist draws back from stating the logical corollary. The Markan Jesus does not say that when doubt is present in the community God will not answer prayers. As we have seen in the examination of 6:6 and 9:14-29, the author of Mark believes that God is free to act whether or not people have faith. Nevertheless, he knows that a community that does not nourish the expectation that God will answer prayer will not see the activity of God in its midst.

In addition to faith as a condition for answered prayer, the Markan Jesus calls for forgiveness. As before, all the second-person pronouns are plural because these instructions are for the community of disciples: "When you stand praying, forgive, if you have anything against anyone, so that your father who [is] in heaven may forgive you your offences" (11:25; v. 26 is not part of the original text, but is a later scribal addition). The connection between forgiving others and receiving answers to prayer is unstated, but understood. Unforgiven sin blocks God's answers to prayer and in order to receive God's forgiveness for their sins, Christians must forgive each other as well. Again the theology comes from Isaiah:

> Behold, the Lord's hand is not shortened, that it cannot save, or his ear dull, that it cannot hear; but your iniquities have made a separation between you and your God, and your sins have hid his face from you so that he does not hear. (Isa 59:1-2, RSV)

The remedy for sin is repentance and confession, to which God responds by forgiving the sin, thus removing the barrier between God and the community. Throughout the Old Testament the connection between confession of sin and effective petitionary prayer is maintained (e.g., 1 Kgs 8:22-53; Neh 1:4-11; Dan 9:3-20). The connection was upheld in postbiblical Judaism as well. In the synagogue prayer of the Eighteen Benedictions, petitions for relief from affliction, for healing, for rain, and for national restoration are preceded by a prayer for an attitude of repentance and a request for forgiveness. Both Philo and Josephus insist that unjust and sinful persons are not heard by God unless they repent, confess their sin, and ask God's forgiveness.

The relationship between sin and ineffective petitionary prayer is also found, to a lesser extent, in Greek and Roman religion. Homer's Achilles knows that the gods listen to the prayers of those who obey them (*Iliad* 1.218). Aeschylus and Euripides insist that the gods do not grant the requests of immoral and unjust persons (*Agamemnon* 396; *Medea* 1391).

In general, the favor of the Greek and Roman gods was sought through the offering of sacrifices, or through vows that promised a sacrifice if the petition were answered favorably. When the gods were offended, however, the promise of a handsome sacrifice might not be enough to persuade them to grant one's request. In such cases the Greeks, and later the Romans, learned from the Oriental cults that confession of sin and pleas for forgiveness could be added to petitionary prayer (Pettazzoni 1937; Hadas 1959, 210-11).

But God does not look favorably upon confessions and requests for forgiveness from humans who are unwilling to forgive each other. Sirach 28:1-5 reads:

> He that takes vengeance will suffer vengeance from the Lord, and he will firmly establish his sins. Forgive your neighbor the wrong he has done, and then your sins will be pardoned when you pray. Does a man harbor anger against another, and yet seek for healing from the Lord? Does he have no mercy toward a man like himself, and yet pray for his own sins? (RSV)

Similar ideas appear in rabbinic literature: "As often as you are merciful, the All-merciful will have mercy upon you" (*Tos. Baba Kamma* 9.30). "He who is merciful to others, mercy is shown to him by heaven, while he who is not merciful to others, mercy is not shown to him by heaven" (*Shab.* 151b in Lohmeyer 1965, 167). This is, of course, the point of the Matthean parable (18:21-35) and of the warning following the model prayer (Matt 6:14-15), which is the source of the scribal addition in Mark 11:26.

The point being made by the Markan Jesus, then, is that a community in which Christians nurse grudges against each other and refuse to let go of real or imagined offences cannot expect the power of God to flow through it. Notice that Christians are commanded to forgive if they have anything against anyone, *whether or not* the other is repentant. One does not forgive because forgiveness is deserved. One forgives because forgiveness is necessary and because unforgiveness blocks the prayers of the entire community.

To sum up: It is through prayer that the inclusive community, the "house of prayer for all the nations," experiences the miracle-working power of God. The God to whom the community prays is not limited in power; rather, this God is one who can do the impossible, symbolized by the mountain-moving image in 11:23. Therefore, nothing the community asks in prayer is impossible for God; they are to regard everything they request as already received from the hand of God (11:24). But in the pluralistic setting of the early imperial period, there were many who would challenge the community's confidence in God's power. The evangelist calls for "faith in God," by which he means a stubborn adherence to the worldview by which the community lives and interprets its experience. Forgiveness within the community is also essential because the power invoked in Christian prayer is not an amoral force. As community members forgive each other they are forgiven by God, and this forgiveness removes the sin that could block the flow of divine power. In this context of faith and mutual forgiveness, the church is to pray for "anything: and "it will be done" for them.

Words (11:27–13:37)

Jesus' Jerusalem teaching falls into two parts: words in the temple (11:27–12:44), made up of a series of controversies with and criticisms of the religious leaders, and words opposite the temple (13:1-37), a lengthy apocalyptic discourse on the coming of the Son of Man as liberator and judge.

Words in the Temple (11:27–12:44). A long collection of teaching and controversy material (11:27–13:37) follows the brief accounts of Jesus' actions and their interpretation in 11:1-25. This collection falls into two divisions: Jesus' words in the temple (11:27–12:44) and Jesus' words on the Mount of Olives "opposite the temple" (13:3-37). These are connected by the move out of the temple and the explicit prediction of its destruction (13:1-2).

The Markan Jesus enters the temple at 11:27 after the prayer teaching outside Bethany. He exits the temple at 13:1a. Within these bracketing movements are nine small units of material organized in a chiastic structure (revised from Dewey 1980, 162 and Donahue 1982):

A—(11:27-33)	Transition: Question of Jesus' authority	
	Looks backward as response to expulsion incident and forward as first of series of controversies	
B—(12:1-9)	Judgment on religious leaders; parable of the vineyard	
C—(12:10-12)	Psalm citation (118:22) in service of christology	
D—(12:13-17)	Question about taxes "Teacher" as address	
	Compliment with reference to truth	
	Question	
	Answer: Caesar/God	
	Response of questioners	
E—(12:18-27)	Question about the resurrection	
D'—(12:28-34)	Question about the greatest commandment	
	Question	
	Answer: God/neighbor	
	Response of questioner	
	"Teacher" as address	
	Compliment with reference to truth	
C'—(12:35-37)	Psalm citation (110:1/8:7) in service of christology	
B'—(12:38-40)	Judgment on religious leaders; critique of scribes	
A'—(12:41-44)	Transition: Widow's offering.	
	Looks backward as contrast to religious leaders and forward, forming frame around apocalyptic discourse with story of anointing woman.	

The opponents in the first three subunits are identified as "principal priests, scribes, and elders," who come to Jesus in 11:27 and leave again at the end of the third subunit, "looking for a way to arrest" Jesus (12:12).

The rhetoric in 11:27-33 is masterful. The opponents try to discredit Jesus by demonstrating that he stands within no authoritative teaching tradition; no one has authorized him to act as he acts or to interpret Scripture as he did in 11:15-17. The Gospel writer has already informed the audience in 1:22 that Jesus did not cite the authoritative teachings of others, but taught as one who had his own authority. In fact, Jesus has so much authority that he presumes to set the terms of the conversation and thus creates a dilemma for his opponents. By refusing to answer their question unless they pronounce on the legitimacy of John's baptism, the Markan Jesus reminds the audience of John's testimony about Jesus and of the events surrounding Jesus' baptism. The opponents' question is answered for the audience, who were the only ones besides Jesus who heard the heavenly voice authorize Jesus' ministry.

In the parable of the vineyard (12:1-9) the author again appeals to Isaiah; the Song of the Vineyard in Isa 5:1-7 provides the equation of the vineyard with Israel that lies behind the parable. But there is a significant difference. In Isaiah the vineyard itself is at fault for yielding sour grapes; in Mark the fault lies not with the vineyard, which yields good fruit, but with the tenants, who refuse to give the owner his portion. Also in Isaiah the vineyard itself is judged and destroyed; in Mark the tenants are destroyed and the vineyard preserved and given "to others." In the Gospel of Mark there is no judgment upon Israel as there is in Isaiah; rather, the judgment falls on the temple leadership whom Jesus has already condemned for not including the gentiles in God's house of prayer.

Joel Marcus has demonstrated that the Song of the Vineyard was associated with the temple in Jewish exegesis approximately contemporaneous with the Gospel of Mark (Marcus, 1992, 120). The evangelist makes that connection also in the way he uses the cornerstone/capstone tradition from Ps 118:22 in the third subunit of this section (12:10-12). Here the parable is interpreted (as though the allegory itself had not been transparent enough). The stone (="beloved son"=Jesus) that was rejected (=killed) by the builders (=tenants=religious leaders) has become the essential element in the new temple "not made with hands" (14:58), that is, the Christian community including both Jews and gentiles (Donahue 1988, 55-56). This is the answer to the opponents' question about the source of Jesus' authority. The rejected stone's becoming the "head of the corner" of the new temple comes about "from the Lord" (*para kuriou*).

The rhetoric of Psalm 118 has been turned back upon itself. Whereas the Psalm celebrates the destruction of the gentile enemies who have scorned and rejected Israel, the Markan interpretation predicts the vindication by God of the one rejected by Israel's leaders and the replacement of the temple with the multiethnic community of Isaiah's eschatological vision. (Marcus 1992, 115-18). The Gospel appropriates the motif of the warrior king against its ethnocentric origins.

The center of the chiastic structure (D-E-D') is made up of three controversy stories, after which Jesus' opponents are afraid to ask him any more questions (12:34b). The first and third of these subunits are structured similarly, and the central controversy story focuses on the resurrection, making that topic the focal point of the entire section 11:27–12:44.

The first question is raised by the Pharisees and Herodians, who have been trying to find a way to get rid of Jesus since 3:6. They address Jesus as "teacher" and offer him the insincere compliment "you are true . . . and teach the way of God truly." The Markan audience would surely have snickered as they heard Jesus' enemies praise his impartiality, the very thing for which they had criticized him in 2:16 when they wanted to know why he ate with sinners.

The question of whether to pay taxes is designed to get Jesus into trouble either with the people, who disliked paying Roman taxes, or with the Romans who demanded the payment. A further complication is the biblical prohibition against images. Later rabbis taught that the use of pagan coins violated the prohibition against idolatrous images (*b. Pesah.*1041; *y.`Abod.Zar.* 3.1). The rhetoric is in the form of an enthymeme:

Major premise—Ownership of anything is established by the image and seal imprinted on it.
Minor premise—The denarius bears Caesar's image.
Conclusion—The denarius belongs to Caesar.

But that is not all. The Markan Jesus' answer is that those things that belong to Caesar are to be given to Caesar, but what belongs to God is to be given to God. This argument runs like the first:

Major premise—Ownership of anything is established by the image and seal imprinted on it.
Minor premise—Human beings bear God's image (Gen 1:27).
Conclusion—Human beings belong to God.

The effect is to shift the focus of the argument. God is entitled to the complete surrender of the human being to God's will. Idolatry consists, not in a triviality like handling coins or paying taxes, but in withholding any part of the self from God (cf. 12:28-34a).

Not incidentally, the Markan Jesus phrases his response in such a way that there is an unmistakable distinction between Caesar and God. The practice of deifying the Roman emperor after his death, which began with Julius Caesar, had by the time of the evangelist been taken by Gaius Caligula to the extreme of demanding worship during his life. The author of Mark makes it clear that Caesar's sphere is a very limited one and must not encroach upon that which belongs to God.

The central pericope is the question about the resurrection, raised by the Sadducees, who, the author helpfully informs the gentiles in his audience, deny that possibility. They intend to show that the Mosaic command that a dead man's brother marry the widow precludes the possibility of resurrection. "Whose wife will she be?" they ask derisively.

Jesus' response is twofold and is framed by the charge, "You are misled" (*planasthe*, 12:24, 27). First, he denies that their objection is relevant, since life in the resurrection transcends sexuality and marriage. His second argument is from scripture; if they can cite Moses, so can he. Again, the structure is that of the enthymeme (adapted from Tolbert 1989, 252-53):

Major premise—God speaks accurately in scripture.
Minor premise—In scripture God speaks of the dead in the present tense (Exod 3:6).
Conclusion—The dead live in the presence of God; resurrection is a reality.

The next question is raised by one of the scribes: "Which commandment is first of them all?" This gives the Markan Jesus an opportunity to reinforce and expand upon the point made implicitly in 12:17. He begins with the *Shema*, Israel's confession of faith in the unity of God (Deut 6:4). The implications of such absolute monotheism are several. First, worship of God cannot be shared with Caesar. Second, the whole self is to be given to God (Deut 6:5 = Mark 12:30). Further, there is a second commandment that flows inevitably from the first. If God is one and is loved with the whole self, then other human beings are understood to be of equal value as oneself —no more and no less. Below God there is no hierarchy of value among human beings. All human beings are the same; only God is different. This principle echoes 10:18: "No one is good except God alone."

Behind this rather straightforward answer, which was the standard rabbinic summary of Torah, lies an important piece of early Christian apologetic. The evangelist makes it clear that his community's christological claims do not abrogate the monotheism of Israel, nor do the Christians teach a different morality from that of their religious heritage. The *Shema* and the love command are affirmed by no less an authority than Jesus himself.

The scribe's positive response repeats the address, "Teacher" and the attribution of truth to Jesus (12:32). The scribe then links Jesus' emphasis on monotheism with its restatement in Deutero-Isaiah (45:21, "There is no other god besides me") and goes on to add the prophetic critique of sacrifice without obedience (1 Sam 15:22; Hos 6:6; Mic 6:6-8). Thus the evangelist delivers a final blow to the temple system. Its fruitlessness is conceded by one of its own scholarly elite. This interlocutor, unlike the previous two groups whose questions and compliments were insincere, is pronounced "not far" from the eschatological reign of God foreseen by Isaiah and inaugurated in Jesus' ministry.

The three central stories in this section (12:13-17, 18-27, 28-34) establish the basic truths about God without which Markan christology would make no sense. The God who has anointed Jesus as eschatological warrior-king to lead humanity out of bondage along the way of the Lord is the one, only, living God who claims the whole self and undivided loyalty of every person created in God's image and whose entire ethical system is to love one's neighbor as oneself. After this, no one puts any more questions to the Markan Jesus (12:34b).

In the final three subunits, then, the initiative shifts. Now it is Jesus' turn to ask the questions. In 12:35-37 there are two assumptions in the logic of Jesus' argument: (1) The title "lord" is used by an inferior to address a superior; (2) Psalm 110 is messianic. Thus:

Major premise—One who addresses another as "Lord" is the inferior of the one addressed.
Minor premise—David addresses the Messiah as "Lord" in Ps 110.
Conclusion—David is the inferior (and therefore not the father) of the Messiah.

This conclusion presents a problem for interpreters of Mark because elsewhere the evangelist clearly makes Davidic claims for Jesus, the use of Psalm 2 by the heavenly voice at the baptism being only the most dramatic. The first feeding story presents Jesus as the shepherd of Israel like the good Davidic monarchs; the acclamation "Son of David" on the lips of Bartimaeus (10:47) and the reference to "the kingdom of our father David" by the crowd (11:10) meet with no correction from the Markan Jesus. From the evangelist's point of view, is "Son of David" an appropriate or an inappropriate designation for Jesus?

The answer is, "Both." Like the related titles, "Messiah" and "Son of God," the designation "Son of David" is affirmed by the Markan narrative, but only after it has been redefined by the plot of the story itself. "Paradoxically, . . . the Davidic image turns out to be both too triumphant and not triumphant enough to encompass the sort of Messiah whom [the author of] Mark wishes to portray to his community" (Marcus 1992b, 149-50). The image is too triumphant because Jesus' victory comes, not as a result of slaughtering his enemies, but as a result of being slaughtered by them. It is not triumphant enough because that victory is won, not merely over human enemies, "but also, as his entire earthly ministry reveals, over their supernatural masters" (Marcus 1992b, 150). The scribes are mistaken, not because they apply the wrong title to the Messiah, but because they do not under-stand the full implications of the Son of David's victory, nor the manner in which the victory is to be won.

Having demonstrated that the scribes are wrong about the Messiah, the Markan Jesus now proceeds to attack their behavior. Most of the charges have to do with making a great show of learning and piety. Scribes are said to enjoy the respect to which their positions entitle them. Like James and John, they seek "the best seats" and "places of honor." They make a pretense (*prophasei*) of piety by praying at great length. But their unethical behavior shows that they have no real respect for the Torah they interpret.

One of the most basic indicators of covenant faithfulness was care for the resident alien, the orphan, and the widow, that is, for those who had no family or clan to protect and provide for them. They were to be included in the sacrificial banquets (Deut 16:11) and provided for by generous leavings for gleaning (vv. 19-22). A widow's clothing should not be taken as surety for a debt (v. 17). When Isaiah calls Israel back to covenant faithfulness, one of his primary charges is that the leadership has neglected to provide justice for widows (Isa 1:16-17, 23). Instead of protecting widows, the leaders have despoiled them (10:2). Ezekiel similarly complains against Jerusalem: "Its princes within it are like a roaring lion tearing the prey; they have devoured human lives; they have taken treasure and precious things; they have made many widows within it" (22:25, NRSV).

Using the same participle as LXX Ezekiel, the author of Mark has Jesus charge the scribes with devouring (*katesthiontes*) the houses of widows, while simultaneously cultivating reputations for holiness. Those who were not even supposed to deprive a widow of an article of clothing long enough to secure a debt are accused of taking away the entire homes of widows. For this dou-ble offense of pretending devotion to God while violating one of God's most basic commands, for honoring with their lips a God from whom they with-hold their hearts (cf. 7:6b), the Markan Jesus says that religious leaders "will receive greater condemnation."

It seems likely that this invective is only partly a critique of a second temple leadership group within Israel. The reference to "best seats" and "places of honor" recalls not only the request of James and John, but also the previous quarrels over who was the greatest (9:34-35) and the Markan Jesus' admonitions against such jockeying for position (10:41-45). This must surely be a word of warning to the Markan community against the tempta-tion to create its own religious hierarchies. It is too easy for today's audience to hear this polemic as one more piece of evidence for the corruption of first-century Judaism. This polemic against scribes who love status and exploit financially those who are without power indicts all religious institutions in which the gaps in status and compensation between the executives and the secretaries and janitors parallel those of the non-Christian society.

In the last periocope set within the temple precincts, the Markan Jesus calls attention to the exemplary conduct of one of the poor widows whom he has just identified as victims of the hypocritical religious leaders. Whereas the leaders make every effort to be noticed and honored, the widow "is so unobtrusive that only Jesus notices her" (Malbon 1991, 595). Their devotion to God is all pretense; they are so self-absorbed that they take away the most basic needs of those under God's special protection. This widow's devotion is so complete and her trust in God so absolute that she does not hesitate to give to God her last two coins. The reading of A. G. Wright ignores the widow's point of view and makes her a naive, if not a stupid, victim of the temple establishment. Wright claims that Jesus *laments*, rather than *praises* her extravagant contribution to the corrupt and doomed temple (Wright 1982, 262). But from her own point of view, the widow is giving, not to the scribes, the priests, or the temple, but to God.

The widow is contrasted not only with the scribes, but also with the other contributors to the temple treasury. They give much, but have much left over; she gives little, but it is all she has. She gives, not a tithe, but one hundred percent. The Markan Jesus' comment condemns the church's subsequent practice of naming buildings after those who contribute large *amounts* and ignoring those who contribute large *proportions* of their resources.

The author chooses two phrases to express the extent of the widow's gift. The first is *autēs panta hosa eichen*, "everything she had." Since that phrase is perfectly clear in itself, the second is superfluous if it is taken to be synonymous with the first. The second phrase is *holon ton bion autēs*, which can be translated, "all she had to live on" (NRSV), but is more naturally translated, "her whole life," since *bios* usually means, "earthly life" (BAG). Indeed, when the author of Mark means only "all her financial resources," as in 5:26, he uses a phrase more like the first phrase in this passage: *ta par'autes panta* (but contrast the variant at Luke 8:43). In Luke 21:4 the author of the Third Gospel conflates the two Markan phrases in order to make them equivalent: *autes panta ton bion hon eichen*, but in Mark the separate phrases are complementary rather than synonymous: "everything she had, her whole life." The Markan Jesus, who knows people's thoughts and motives (2:8), points out that the widow has given to God "that which is God's," that is, her whole life. Her outward piety is completely consistent with her inward surrender (c.f. 7:6b). This is the example the Markan Jesus praises in 12:44 and follows in chapters 14–15.

Words Opposite the Temple (13:1-37). Having been in the temple since 11:27, the Markan Jesus now leaves the temple and predicts its destruction: "There will not be left here a stone upon a stone." What was implicit in 11:15-17 here becomes explicit. This closes the section of teaching in the temple and prepares for the following teaching "opposite the temple" (13:3).

This second long speech by the Markan Jesus has a number of common features with the parable discourse in chapter 4. Both assume the cosmic conflict myth that is so fundamental to apocalyptic thought. Both contain repeated admonitions to pay attention (4:3, 9, 23, 24; 13:5, 9, 23, 33, 35, 37), both use parables from nature (4:3-9, 26-32; 13:28-29), and both contain allegorical applications of parabolic material to discipleship (4:13-20; 13:34-37, Donahue 1988, 61).

It is characteristic of both speeches that an extended discourse punctuated by second-person plural imperatives tends to blur the distinction between the addressees at the story level and the audience of the Gospel as a whole. The "you" of the teaching material reaches out to include the listeners in any subsequent time (Tannehill 1980, 142). The chapter may be outlined as follows:

Prediction of temple's destruction (13:1-2)
Setting of the scene of the discourse (13:3)
Disciples' questions (13:4)
    A—When? (13:4a)
    B—What will be the sign? (13:4b)
Jesus' answers (13:5-37)
    B'—Things that are and are not signs (13:5-27)
        (1) Things that are not signs (13:5-23)
            a—Danger of deception (13:5-6)
                b—Future events are not signs (13:7-8)
                    c—Persecution and mission of the church (13:9-13)
                b'—Future events: appropriate responses (13:14-20)
            a'—Danger of deception (13:21-23)
        (2) The only reliable sign (13:24-27)
    A'—Only God knows when (13:28-37)
        a—Parable (13:28-29)
            b—You, the angels, and the Son do not know when (13:30-32)
        a'—Parable (13:34-37)

The scene in chapter 13 is the Mount of Olives. The cast of characters is exactly the same as that of the first scene of the Galilean ministry (11:16-20): Jesus, Peter, James, John, and Andrew. The only function of the disciples in this scene is to ask two questions. They are not mentioned again.

The disciples' questions are: (1) When will will these things happen? and (2) What will be the sign? They are portrayed as regarding the destruction of the temple, which Jesus has just predicted, as a catastrophic event that would surely be preceded by a significant omen. They understand themselves as insiders who are entitled to be let in on the secret (cf. 4:11).

Jesus, however, has more important information to impart. He never mentions the temple again; rather, he begins to talk about false and true signs of the eschatological consummation of God's reign. Although he is answering a question the disciples have not asked, he takes up the two issues they have raised in reverse order, beginning with how to recognize the sign of the end (13:5-27) and moving to the issue of the time of the end (13:28-37).

He first explains that no historical event can be read as a sign of the eschaton (13:5-23). This chiastically arranged section begins and ends with warnings that there will be deceivers who will make messianic claims for themselves and others and perform miracles in order to lead Christians astray (13:5-6, 21-23). Their apocalyptic interpretations of events are to be ignored (13:21, 23). Here again is the distinction between "mighty works" and "signs." When miracles are used as proof of the claims of the miracle worker, the claims are to be ignored. Jesus refused to give such proof when asked (8:11-12), and those who use miracles in this way are false prophets or messiahs.

The second and penultimate items in the chiasm describe historical and natural events that might be misinterpreted as signs of the end (13:7-8) and prescribe the proper way to respond to such difficult times (13:14-20). Natural disasters and human conflicts are merely the beginning (13:8d) of the apocalyptic birth-pains, but "the end is not yet" (13:7b). Christians must always be ready to move quickly in times of crisis. Attachment to possessions will have to be put aside and even the most natural relationships will pose a problem (13:15-17). But though the suffering will be terrible, God is in control and will provide for God's chosen people. The right response is prayer and trust (13:18-20).

The center of the chiasm focuses on the persecution of the church (13:9-13). Like Jesus, Christians will be handed over, betrayed, brought to trial, and put to death. Here again is evidence that families were being divided by conversion to Christ and family members could be expected to "hand over" Christian relatives to the authorities, just as Jesus was "handed over" by Judas. In their situations of trial, persecuted Christians are not to be afraid, because the Holy Spirit will enable them to bear witness. In the midst of their persecutions they must continue to preach the gospel to the gentiles, because this is part of the divinely ordained prelude to the end (13:10). "The one who endures to the end will be saved" (13:13).

Scholars sometimes assume that the events described in 13:5-23 had already taken place at the time of the writing of the Gospel. According to this interpretation, Jesus is portrayed as speaking in the past about events in the future, which is the evangelist's immediate past. It is likely that the audience of the Gospel is facing some of the things described in this section. Some may already be in the past. But there is no way of knowing that all the events in this description are either past or present. The evangelist may anticipate that some of these difficulties lie ahead for the church and may wish to prepare them to respond appropriately.

After an extensive discussion of events that are *not* signs of the end, the Markan Jesus turns to the real sign of the end: the coming of the Son of Man on the clouds, amid cosmic upheaval, to gather the elect from all over the earth (13:24-27). When they see Jesus coming for them, they will know that the end is about to take place; no natural or political disasters that take place before that time are to distract them from their mission. If the event itself is the only sign, then calculation and speculation are automatically ruled out.

As for the question of "When?" the Markan Jesus takes care of that in short order. This brief section (13:28-37) begins and ends with a parable. The parable of the fig tree makes the point that when the disciples see "these things" (i.e. the coming of the Son of Man, vv. 24-27), they will know that he is "at the gates." In other words, when you see it happening, you will know that it is happening, and not before!

This is reinforced by repeated reminders that "you do not know when" (13:33, 35). In fact, no one knows except the Father. The futility of calculation based on "signs of the times" could not be more dramatically portrayed. But if "biblical prophecy" workshops are not appropriate, neither is complacency. The parable of the returning landlord (13:34-36) emphasizes the suddenness of the arrival of the eschaton. Since you do not know, be ready and alert at all times. This parable reminds the audience that Jesus is the only master (*kurios*); the rest of them are slaves, each with assigned work to do. In this version of the parable no slave is given authority over any other slave in the absence of the *kurios*. They are to keep alert, lest they be found asleep on the job. The final exhortation is addressed explicitly to the audience: "What I say to you [disciples] I say to all [who may hear this narrative]: Keep awake" (13:37).

Suffering and Death of the King
(chs. 14–15)

The section of the Gospel of Mark usually known as the passion narrative draws upon a variety of biblical and cultural resources to interpret the humiliation and crucifixion of God's anointed warrior-king. Some of these have been discussed already in connection with the interpretation of Mark 10:45. The discussion that follows will not attempt to separate the work of the author or final editor of the Markan passion narrative from earlier traditions. Whether the evangelist received a complete account of Jesus' suffering and death already infused with scriptural interpretations or created one for the first time is not one of the concerns of this commentary. This interpretation reads the passion narrative as it stands in the context of the whole Markan narrative.

Marcus (1992b, 153-98) has carefully reviewed the state of the question on the scriptural citations and allusions in the passion narrative and found that "four bodies of Old Testament literature . . . appear to play a decisive role in the Markan narrative: Zechariah 9-14; Daniel 7: the Psalms of the Righteous Sufferer; and the Deutero-Isaian Servant Songs, especially Isaiah 53" (153).

By "the Psalms of the Righteous Sufferer" Marcus means Psalms 10, 22, 27, 35, 37, 38, 41, 42, 43, 69, and 140, all of which are alluded to in Mark —Ps 22 more often than any other. These Psalms are mostly individual laments in which a person complains to God that, although righteous before God, he or she is suffering; sometimes the suffering is caused by others, and sometimes the individual is being despised by others because of the suffering. The psalmist prays for deliverance and vindication in this life.

In the Wisdom of Solomon, on the other hand, the righteous man suffers not only *despite* his righteousness, but also *because* of it (Marcus 1992b, 177). The "ungodly" say to themselves:

> Let us lie in wait for the righteous man, because he is inconvenient to us and opposes our actions; . . . He professes to have knowledge of God, and calls himself a child of the Lord . . . and boasts that God is his father. Let us see if his words are true and let us test what will happen at the end of his life; for if the righteous man is God's child, he will help him, and will deliver him from the hand of his adversaries. Let us test him with insult and torture, . . . Let us condemn him to a shameful death, for, according to what he says, he will be protected. (Wis 12:2-20, NRSV)

This view is also found in Greek thought as early as Plato. In the *Republic* (361e-362a, LCL), Socrates is challenged by dialogue partners who suggest that the truly righteous person will "hold his course unchangeable, even unto death," having "to endure the lash, the rack, chains," and "finally, after every extremity of suffering, he will be crucified." In this dialogue the speakers go on to point out that although the gods are believed to reward the righteous and punish the wicked, it is also believed that the unjust rich are able to appease the gods and thus escape punishment for their wickedness (364b-e). Thus, "the thing to do is to commit injustice and offer sacrifice from the fruits of our wrongdoing" (366a). This is similar to the charge brought by the Markan Jesus against the temple establishment: they tried to use the cultic center as a "robbers' den" in which to hoard their booty and hide from justice. The suffering of the teacher of truth at the hands of the wicked and powerful is the theme of the various interpretations of Socrates' death (Plato, *Apology, Phaedo*; Xenophon, *Memorabilia*).

While it is unlikely that Isaiah 53 influenced the "ransom saying" in Mark 10:45, it does appear that themes from Deutero-Isaiah were used to interpret aspects of Jesus' passion (Marcus 1992b, 186-96). This, of course, is what the audience would expect, given the importance of Isaiah in Markan theology. Daniel and Zechariah are not as pervasive in the passion narrative as are the other biblical resources. Daniel 7 is cited in Jesus' climactic self-identification before the Sanhedrin (14:62; cf. 8:38–9:1; 13:26), suggesting an ironic reversal of the roles of judge and accused (cf. Wis 4:16–5:14). Zechariah 9–14 is influential in the interpretation of Jesus' last meal with his disciples and his predictions on the way to the Mount of Olives (Marcus 1992b, 154-171).

The narrative pace, which had been made so breathless in the stories of Jesus' ministry by the constant use of "immediately," slows in the passion narrative to a day-by-day account in chapter 14. Finally, during the crucifixion the narrator tolls the agonizing hours of Jesus' tortured death: "it was the third hour" (15:25); "at the sixth hour" (15:33). From being the principal actor in Mark 1–13, Jesus becomes the one acted upon in Mark 14–15. It is in the passion narrative that it becomes clear that Jesus is not in control of events, nor does he intend to be. Here, as in the teaching, healings, and exorcisms, he does the will of God instead of his own.

Plot of and Preparation for Jesus' Death (14:1-11)

The story of the anointing woman (14:3-9) has two literary functions in the outline of the Gospel. Besides joining with the story of the women who go to anoint Jesus' corpse to form a frame around the passion narrative, it also frames the apocalyptic discourse in Mark 13 when read with the story of the widow's offering (12:41-44). In both these stories women are praised for their actions, which point forward to Jesus' giving of his life (the widow) and to his burial (the anointing woman). The two women are contrasted with the religious leaders, who exploit them (12:40) and oppose Jesus (14:1-2) (Malbon 1991, 598).

The anointing of Jesus is sandwiched within the narrative about the plot to kill him (14:1-2, 10-11; cf. Ps 10:7-8; Wis 2:12). This conspiracy is not a new development; it began in Galilee (3:6) and was renewed after the temple incident (11:18). For the first time, however, the narration of the plot reflects the language of the passion predictions. In 3:6 and 11:18 Jesus' enemies plotted "how they might destroy him"; now they seek to discover "how, having seized him by stealth, they might kill him" (cf. 8:31; 9:31; 10:34).

But the success of their plan appears to be jeopardized by the presence of the Passover crowd, which is expected by the religious leaders (as well as by the audience of the Gospel) to support Jesus (11:32; 12:12, 37b). That this expectation will finally prove false (15:11, 15) is one of the many ironies of the passion narrative, though it was foreshadowed by the hostility of the crowd around the question of divorce (10:2). Whether Jesus' enemies will find a solution to their problem of how to seize him remains in doubt until 14:10-11, but after Jesus has been anointed for burial, the necessity of that act is sealed by the cooperation of Judas, about whose complicity the audience has known since he was introduced in 3:19. The note about the promise to pay Judas (14:31a) presents a sharp contrast with the anointing woman. As Malbon points out, the woman gives up money for Jesus, while Judas agrees to give up Jesus for money (Malbon 1991, 599).

The setting of the anointing story reminds the audience that the Markan Jesus is in the habit of eating with the wrong people (2:15-17). There is no indication that Simon is a former, but now healed, leper. When the evangelist wants to make that distinction, he is perfectly capable of doing so (cf. 5:15, 18). Here, he deliberately portrays Jesus as reclining to eat in the home of a leper. The Markan Jesus thus acts upon his own redefinition of clean/unclean (7:1-23). After the scene is set, the story falls into three parts:

The woman's action	14:3b
The negative interpretation by "some"	14:4-5
The positive interpretation by Jesus	14:5-9

The anointing itself is narrated only briefly, and the nameless woman's interpretation of her own action is not given. She is silent throughout the story.

That those present criticize the woman's use of the perfumed oil (*muros*) and propose an alternative use of it suggests that the narrator thinks of the woman as the owner of the expensive ointment. In that case the author of Mark may be portraying her as a wealthy matron, since a woman wearing a vial (*alabastron*) of perfume around her neck is the stereotype of domesticity in Greek vase art (Keuls 1985, 120). She is not already in attendance at the meal, as a courtesan might have been, but comes in while the meal is in progress (14:3a).

That a man should have been anointed on the head during a meal would not have struck Mark's audience as unusual. Banquet customs during the centuries before and after Mark called for the use of perfume between courses, and especially between the meal itself and the drinking party or symposium (Didorus Siculus, *Bib. Hist.* 37.3.3; Lucretius, *Rer.Nat.* 4.1131-1132; Plutarch, *Quaest.Conv.* 6166a, 708c, 711d, *Reg. et Imp.* 192d; Athenaeus, *Deipn.* 14.642f, 15.665c, 15.685c-d, 11.462d). Jews (Josephus *Ant.* 19.239-240; b.Ber 43b; b.Keth. 17b) and Christians (Acts of Thomas 5) were familiar with this custom. Men might anoint themselves or be anointed by slaves or courtesans provided by the host to perform this service. But for a wealthy matron to come to a meal in a leper's house and anoint the head of a man who was not her husband would have been regarded as highly irregular. She is portrayed as crossing a number of social barriers to carry out her act of service to Jesus.

"Some" of those present object to the woman's action, not because of its impropriety, but because of its wasteful extravagance. Some members of the Markan audience may have heard echoes of Isaiah 3:13-26, where the wealthy women of Jerusalem are accused of indifference to the poor because of their conspicuous consumption of perfumes, jewelry, and expensive clothing. The woman's critics give her the advice that Jesus gave to the rich man in 10:21; she should have "sold . . . and given to the poor."

But the Markan Jesus is not a lawgiver whose sayings can be transformed into eternal principles applicable in all situations. He defends the woman's extravagant act as "a good thing," attributing to her a prophetic knowledge of his destiny that his meal companions lack. Their apparent concern for the poor does not impress Jesus. He says that they may aid the poor whenever they want to, suggesting that they have not previously manifested any tendency toward sacrificial almsgiving. In any case the woman's act is not a banquet ritual but a burial ritual, which is a meritorious service (Tobit 1:17-20; 2:3-8).

Of all the minor characters whom the Markan Jesus praises, this woman receives the most dramatic accolade. Other characters display faith (5:34; 10:52), speak wisely (7:29; 12:34), or exemplify servanthood (1:31; 15:41), but this woman's action ("what she has done," not her identity) will be repeated "wherever the gospel is proclaimed in the whole world." Why does the evangelist single out this particular action?

This is the last section of a threefold pattern in the Gospel that emphasizes the importance of responding appropriately to the eschatological moment. The time to fast is after "the bridegroom is taken away" (2:18-20). The time for abundance is upon the advent of the Messiah, whether or not it is the normal "season for figs" (11:12-14). There is an appropriate time for action in the interest of the poor (and Mark's audience should have understood that they were now living in that time and under that mandate), but in Markan theology a critical factor in discernment is knowing what time it is. The Markan Jesus establishes a memorial to this anonymous woman because she discerned what to do, when to do it, and acted despite the unconventional character of the action she felt called upon to take. She exemplifies the eschatological alertness called for in 13:37 along with the extravagant generosity characteristic of the widow (12:44) and of Jesus himself (10:45).

The final prediction of the story both draws the audience into the story and brings the story into the present of its hearers. As a first-century audience heard the Markan Jesus predict that this woman's eschatologically appropriate action would be narrated as her memorial whenever the gospel was proclaimed, at least some of its members must have realized that the prediction was being fulfilled at that moment.

Jesus' Last Meal with His Disciples (14:12-31)

The temporal marker, "On the first day of Unleavened Bread, when it was customary to sacrifice the Passover lamb," opens the sequence of three scenes related to the final meal that the Markan Jesus shares with his followers: the preparations (14:12-16), the meal (14:17-25), the transitional walk to Gethsemane (14:26-31). Each scene emphasizes Jesus' prophetic powers, not for their own sake, but for the sake of their emphasis on the eschatological necessity of the unfolding chain of events.

The instructions given to the two disciples who are sent ahead to prepare the meal are reminiscent of those given in connection with the procuring of the colt for the ride into Jerusalem (11:1-6); the narrator provides neither the names nor the genders of the two disciples. As before, the predictive instructions create an atmosphere of mystery. A man will be seen carrying a water jar; Jesus is to be identified to the householder only as "the Teacher"; the "large upstairs room" will have been prepared before it was requested. As before, everything happens just as Jesus predicted.

In the first part of the Gospel the Markan Jesus is remarkable for his power to heal, to exorcise demons, to multiply resources to feed the crowds, and even to control nature. Although he teaches "with authority," his verbal teaching is not recounted in much detail, and he seems to teach as much by what he does as by what he says. After the withering of the fig tree, however, there are no further miracles. Beginning with 11:1-11, the Markan Jesus begins to make specific predictions regarding events within or beyond the end of the narrative. Many of his predictions are fulfilled almost immediately with uncanny accuracy, lending strong credibility to those not yet fulfilled. His role shifts from initiator to interpreter of events.

When Jesus gives instructions about procuring the colt for the ride into Jerusalem, the disciples not only find the colt, but also are, inexplicably, given permission to take it away, just as Jesus said they would be. The tempo of prediction and fulfillment picks up quickly, as Jesus' promise of a memorial for the anointing woman is fulfilled as he speaks it. In 14:12-16 the pattern is repeated, and the prediction is fulfilled in all its mystifying detail. It is this pattern that develops in the audience the habit of expecting that whatever the Markan Jesus predicts will, in fact, happen. The rest of the passion and resurrection narrative exploits and relies upon that expectation.

Another temporal marker, "When evening had come," begins the scene in the upstairs dining room. Before another evening falls (15:42), Jesus will be dead. Now he comes to the supper "with the twelve," bringing the total number of disciples present to fourteen, counting the two who were sent ahead to prepare the meal. Here again, as in 3:34 and 4:10, the author of Mark demonstrates that despite the received tradition about the twelve men named in 3:16-19, he wants to insist that Jesus' circle of intimates was not limited to them alone.

After the group has reclined and begun to eat, the Markan Jesus abruptly announces his coming betrayal by one of those present. Recalling Ps 41:9, he points to the worst possible breach of trust in Mediterranean society—the betrayal of table fellowship. That the betrayer is sharing food with Jesus is stressed by repetition (14:18, 21).

The correct translation of the disciples' response to this prediction is critical for understanding the scene. They are *not* asking, "Is it I?" in a tone of self-doubt, as though they were aware that any one of them might be the betrayer. Rather, their common question is phrased in a Greek construction designed to guarantee a negative answer. The NRSV's translation "Surely, not

I?" comes close. "Well, you certainly aren't talking about me, are you?" would be a good dynamic equivalent. They are "sorrowful" or "distressed" (*lupeisthai*), not because they are convicted by self-examination, but because the generality of the accusation does not clearly exclude anyone. The question, put to Jesus by each disciple individually (*heis kata heis*), is intended by each speaker to establish his or her own innocence.

The Markan Jesus does not take their bait; he gives no answer to these individual attempts at self-justification, merely indicating that the betrayer is "one of the twelve." Again the notion of any special privileges associated with being one of the group of twelve by contrast with other disciples of Jesus is undercut. The apocalyptic presuppositions of the entire Gospel become explicit again in this scene as the Markan Jesus adds the statement of dual responsibility in 14:21. That Jesus' death will happen "just as it stands written" in Scripture indicates the role of his death in the plan and will of God. That "woe" is pronounced against the betrayer, who would be better off if he had never been born, indicates that even within the divine plan, the betrayer is culpable for his perfidy. This needs clarification, lest some in the Markan community who may come under pressure to betray their sisters and brothers should be tempted to excuse their actions as inevitable (13:12). Since the narrator does not have Judas leave the meal, the audience would have assumed that he was present throughout the entire scene, including the sharing of bread and cup that follow the prediction of his act of treachery.

Ignoring the symbolic actions usually associated with Passover meals, the narrator introduces new and shocking ones. Echoing the language of the miraculous feeding stories, the Gospel writer has Jesus "take a loaf," "say a blessing," "break" the bread, and "give it" to his disciples. In the case of the cup, thanksgiving replaces the blessing (cf. 6:41; 8:6-7). The Markan Jesus identifies the bread as "my body," and the cup as "my blood of the covenant, poured out for many." The blood of the covenant sacrifice (Exod 24:8) is that which binds the covenant people to their delivering God. According to Zech 9:11 LXX, it is the blood of the covenant that identifies those whose prisoners will be set free by the divine warrior. The blood of the covenant is "poured out for many," just as the Markan Jesus is said to "give his life a ransom for many" (10:45).

In this way the author of Mark combines the Hellenistic notion of the king who gives his life for the salvation of his people (10:45) with the symbol of the Israelite covenant sacrifice (14:24) and uses both images to interpret the death of Jesus. Both Jews and gentiles were miraculously fed by the loaves and the fish. The covenant people, both Jews and gentiles, are nourished by the body of Jesus and marked by the blood of Jesus, not sprinkled on them (Exod 24:8), but ingested. Here is an image that would have been repulsive to Torah-observant Christians, but more familiar to the gentile Christians hearing this story.

Whatever "the historical Jesus" or the earliest tradents of this material may have meant by these words, the gentiles in the Markan audience cannot have failed to hear in them a challenge to and a replacement for the mystery cults, such as those of Mithras and Dionysus, cults that appealed to Hellenistic men and women respectively. In these cults the flesh and blood of the sacrifice were consumed by the worshippers, who thus took the god into themselves. By becoming monotheists, gentile Christians had rejected such rites to join themselves to the God of Israel who had acted in Jesus to ransom them from spiritual bondage and to include them in a new covenant sealed with his own blood.

The ritual meal, participated in by "all" Jesus' disciples, according to Mark 14:23, required that both the Jews and the gentiles in the Markan community cross significant boundaries in order to be joined to Jesus and to each other. The gentile Christians gave up the easy inclusiveness of polytheism to trust only one savior for their access to the divine—a savior who belonged to a despised ethnic minority, had been crucified as a criminal, and was now being interpreted to them through the categories of long-dead Israelite prophets. The Jewish Christians gave up their exclusive claim to the knowledge of God and swallowed the abrogation of the dietary laws that had set them apart for centuries—even engaging in a new ritual in which they symbolically ate Jesus' body and drank his blood. For both groups, crossing such boundaries meant that there could be no turning back. To "be ashamed" of this strange Jewish savior with his stubborn claim to universal dominion would mean losing everything at the final reckoning toward which the age was rushing (8:38–9:1).

And indeed, the Markan Jesus points them not backward, but forward to the victory celebration in the reign of God (14:25). He will next drink wine when, according to Isa 25:6, "the Lord of hosts will make for all peoples (*pasi tois ethnesin*-LXX)" a banquet of fine food and wine "and will wipe every tear from every face." This Passover meal unlike any the disciples have ever experienced ends with the traditional hymn, and Jesus and his disciples go out toward the Mount of Olives (14:26).

During this transition scene (14:26-31) the Markan Jesus makes three more predictions, beginning with the announcement that all of his disciples will abandon him. He quotes Zech 13:7, changing the original imperative "Strike the shepherd!" to a declarative "I [God] will strike the shepherd, and the sheep will be scattered." But God's people will not be left "like sheep without a shepherd" (6:34) for long. The Markan Jesus promises, "After I am raised up, I will go before you to Galilee."

When Jesus had warned about the dangers of riches in 10:23-27 Peter had been quick to point out that he and the others had left everything to follow Jesus (10:28). Now Peter hastens to distance himself from the other disciples in the face of this new threat. True, all these others may desert Jesus, but he, Peter the Rock, will stand firm (14:29). At this point Jesus becomes excruciatingly specific: Peter will deny him three times before the night is over (14:30). Peter will have none of it. He blusters that he will never deny Jesus, even if it costs him his life (14:31). The rest of the disciples join in this claim, which is reminiscent of James and John's bold proclamation: "We are able!" (10:39). But by this time Jesus' record of accurate predictions has convinced the audience that he is the one to be believed, not Peter and the others.

Whatever shred of inclination the audience may have had to identify with the disciples is by now frayed to the breaking point. The disciples were attractive travel companions when they responded so readily to Jesus' invitation to follow him. The audience was inclined to crowd in among "those around [Jesus] with the twelve" when he told them that only they had been given "the mystery of the reign of God" (4:10-11). When other characters in the narrative were in the dark, the audience was able to overhear what Jesus told his disciples "in the house," and they were confident of being among "those around him" who were doing the will of God even when Jesus' own family was "standing outside" (3:31-35). When the twelve receive their commission to preach, heal, and cast out demons and to do so successfully (6:7-13), the audience is proud to be counted with them as Jesus' followers. In short, the initially positive portrayal of the disciples in the Markan narrative strongly encourages the audience to identify with them (Tannehill 1979, 70).

The portrayal of the disciples in Mark, however, is not as positive as literary conventions of teacher/disciple relations in antiquity might have led the audience to expect. Greco-Roman audiences were familiar with a pattern of teacher/disciple relations characteristic of the literature about Socrates in which the disciple's questions are necessary for the portrayal of the teacher to be complete. Moreover, it was understood that "the disciple is never completely able to fathom the system of thought and action taught and manifested by the teacher" (Robbins 1992, 168). Nevertheless, even an audience conditioned to expect less than perfection would have become increasingly nervous about identifying with these disciples.

Jesus' disciples can be excused for interrupting his prayer when they have
only recently begun to follow him (1:36). Certainly neither the disciples nor
the audience is prepared to follow all the twists and turns of the parable
chapter (4:1-34). If the disciples ask, "Who then is this?" after Jesus stops the
demonic storm (4:41), the audience might wonder why the disciples know
less than the demons about Jesus' identity. The first time that the disciples
have no idea how to feed a large crowd with meager resources, no one could
fault them (6:37). But when, confronted with a smaller group in the same
situation, they still have no idea what to do (8:4), the audience begins to
grow impatient with them. Before long the disciples are muttering about a
bread shortage, even though they have twice witnessed Jesus' miraculous provision of food (8:16). At this point the audience is ready to join the Markan
Jesus in shouting at them, "Do you still not perceive or understand? Are your
hearts hardened?" (8:17). Finally, at Caesarea Philippi, Peter gives the correct
answer to the question of Jesus' identity: "You are the Messiah" (8:29), only
to ruin everything by arguing with Jesus' redefinition of messiahship (8:32-
33).

The situation continues to deteriorate, as the disciples fail to cast out a
demon (9:18), then try to stop an outsider who is casting out demons successfully (9:38). They argue about which of them is the greatest (9:34). They
try to block the children's access to Jesus right after he has held up a child as
an example of one who must be received with hospitality (10:13; 9:37).
James and John ignore the passion predictions and seek places of honor
(10:37). By the time the supper is over and the disciples are stumbling
toward Gethsemane, the audience has realized that Peter and the others will
not be able to "think the things of God." Instead, they are going to "fall
away," as Jesus predicts in 14:27 (*skandalizomai*), like the people symbolized
by the seeds that fell on rocky soil (4:16-17). They are not the sort of people
with whom the audience wants to identify after all. "The implied criticism of
the disciples threatens to become criticism of the reader" (Tannehill 1979,
79). It is now time for the audience to give up on the disciples; they have
given these characters the benefit of the doubt time and time again, but it
has now become clear that since the disciples are all going to "fall away" from
or "desert" Jesus, the audience will have to take their places. In this frame of
mind the audience is led, along with the disciples, to Gethsemane.

Jesus' Prayer and Arrest on
the Mount of Olives (14:32-52)

The events on the Mount of Olives are arranged into two units: Jesus' struggle and prayer (14:32-42) and Jesus' arrest and the flight of the disciples (14:43-52). The scene of Jesus' struggle with the necessity of his suffering and death is rounded off on both ends by references to the movements of Jesus and the disciples. In 14:32 the evangelist writes, "And they went to a place named Gethsemane"; in 14:42 the evangelist has Jesus say, "Rise—let us be going." Verse 43 begins a new literary unit, as evidenced by the introduction of additional characters: "And immediately, while he was still speaking, Judas came . . ." The same narrative device is used at 5:35 to mark the end of the story of the hemorrhaging woman and the resumption of the narrative about Jairus' daughter: "While he was still speaking, they came from the ruler's house . . ."

The Gethsemane pericope is constructed of three sections. The first and third sections each have three parts, and the central section has four. In the first section, 14:32-36a, there are three reports of movements, each followed by a report of Jesus' speech:

(v. 32) and *they came* to a place called Gethsemane,
    and *he said* to his disciples . . .

(v. 33) and *he took along* Peter and James and John . . .
(v. 34) and *he said* to them . . .

(v. 35) and *going ahead* a little, he fell down . . .
(v. 36) and *he said* . . .

Jesus' prayer is expressed first in indirect discourse ("he prayed that if it were possible, the hour might pass from him" [14:35b]), and then in direct discourse (14:36b):

Address	Abba, Father
Formula of omnipotence	Everything is possible for you.
Petition	Take this cup away from me.
Submission	But not what I want, but what you [want].

In the third section (14:37-42) there are three reports of Jesus' returning from prayer to find the disciples sleeping:

(v. 37) and *he came* and found them *sleeping*
(v. 40) and, *coming again*, he found them *sleeping*
(v. 41) and *he came the third time* and said to them, "*Sleep, then*"

The narrator signals the solemnity of this scene from the beginning by having Jesus take Peter, James, and John out of the larger group of disciples. These were the three who saw Jesus defeat death in the case of Jairus' daughter (5:35-43) and who were present at the epiphanic transfiguration scene (9:2-8). Again they are being called upon to witness a crucial event, but this time they have an important role to play. While Jesus prays, they are to "keep alert," to begin the eschatological watchfulness that he had enjoined upon them and "all" in 13:37. One of the reasons Jesus appointed the disciples was to be "with him" (3:14), and now the three most problematic of the group (except, of course, for Judas, who has slipped off into the night) have an opportunity to do something positive to make up for all their jostling for position (9:38; 10:37) and blurting of inanities (8:32b; 9:5; 10:28).

The verbs used in 14:33b to describe Jesus' emotional state (*ektham-beisthai kai ademonein*) express deep anguish. The Jerusalem Bible translates, "And a sudden fear came over him, and great distress." Phillips has, "He began to be horror-stricken and desperately depressed." Reports of Jesus's emotions are rare in the Markan narrative, and never up to this point has the audience had any indication that Jesus felt distress about his own situation. Previously the Markan Jesus has reacted in anger, compassion, or amazement to the actions or conditions of other characters, but up to this point in the narrative he has talked about his own suffering and death with seriousness but also with detachment. All three of the passion predictions are cast in the third person: "The Son of Man must suffer many things . . ." (8:31; cf. 9:31; 10:32-34). The same device is also employed at 10:45 and 14:21.

Jesus' emotional detachment from the announcements of his impending suffering is the narrative device by means of which the author has avoided a direct collision between the two conflicting roles of Jesus: the victor over sickness and demons and the victim of humiliation and execution. The audience is aware that there is a problem, because they have witnessed the dramatic conflict between Jesus and Peter in 8:31-33, where Peter's attempt to persuade Jesus to choose one role over the other earned him the rebuke that he was siding with Satan rather than with God.

As we have seen, the narrator has influenced the audience to abandon their identification with the hapless disciples and to identify instead with Jesus, who appears to have everything under control. Arriving at Gethsemane, Jesus leaves most of the disciples behind and takes with him Peter, James, John, and the audience. At this point the audience learns, to their shock and horror, that his emotional distress over his impending passion is enough to kill him right there on the spot (14:33b-34). Leaving the three with the admonition to keep alert, Jesus goes on a little further alone—

except for the audience, who have no choice but to follow, dragged along by the omniscient narrator. Now the Markan Jesus throws himself to the ground and begs for a way out of his assignment to suffer and die.

So it turns out that the narrator has betrayed the audience. Jesus has *not* dealt in advance with the tension between God's miracle-working power and the necessity of Jesus' suffering. And unlike the snoring disciples, the audience is forced to watch Jesus' agonized struggle with the God who is at the same moment wielder of unlimited power, trusted *abba*, and the source of Jesus' assignment to experience unspeakable agony "for many."

That struggle takes the form of the four-line prayer that stands at the center of the pericope. The first and fourth lines express trust in the goodness of God. The Markan Jesus addresses God as a parent who can be trusted without reservation. That God is only and always benevolent and trustworthy is the reason that the Markan Jesus can say with confidence that he prefers God's will, however mysterious and frightening, to his own. He entrusts himself to God because he is certain that what God wants will be a better choice for him than any choice he could make for himself.

The issue of possibility changes from a condition in 14:35b to a statement of fact in 14:36: "Everything is possible for you." This, as we have seen, is the position on the God/world relationship that the author of Mark regards as nonnegotiable for the Christian community. The possibility of God's salvific intervention may not be brought into question (9:23) because what is impossible for humans is always possible for God (10:27). To hold to this worldview in the face of alternative philosophical positions and despite its problems for theodicy is, for the author of Mark, to "have faith in God" (11:22).

Since everything is possible for God, those who live in that reality are instructed to ask boldly for God to intervene, even to the extent of moving a mountain (11:23) or changing the timetable of the eschatological events (13:18: "Pray that it may not happen in winter"). The death of Jesus is one of those eschatological events that must take place (8:31) in connection with the final defeat of evil and the liberation of the royal Messiah's captive people (10:45), but, taking his own advice (11:22-24), the Markan Jesus pleads for a change of plans in his prayer in Gethsemane.

According to the narrative logic of the Gospel, such a change is a real possibility. It is that potential for divine rescue that makes the scene in Gethsemane so terrible. The fact that the audience already knows that Jesus will die does not diminish the narrative tension, any more than the familiarity of Greek audiences with the mythological traditions prevented their experiencing the catharsis that the tragedies evoked.

It is important to recognize that, in the final line of the prayer, the Markan Jesus does not reject miraculous rescue and choose to suffer. Rather, he rejects his own will; that is, he "denies himself," as he advocated in 8:34, and chooses the will of God. What the evangelist has Jesus model here is not Stoic resignation but its contrary. The Markan Jesus prays for deliverance from suffering even in the face of overwhelming evidence that God wills *not* to intervene. In addition, he repeats the petition for rescue even after his initial submission to the will of God: "And again, having gone apart, he prayed, saying the same prayer"—14:39). The prayer of submission does not replace the prayer for divine intervention; rather, it accompanies it.

The prayer scene in Gethsemane is the evangelist's last word on the problem of theodicy. In response to the Epicurean conundrum he has firmly established the principle that "everything is possible for God"; God *is* able to eliminate human suffering and often does so in response to believing prayer. This the Epicureans denied, because they denied all divine agency in the material world. The Stoics' solution amounted to the same thing, even though their rhetoric was different. Since everything that happens is the will and the act of the divine, petitionary prayer is irrelevant. The Stoic's god neither wills nor is able to eliminate human suffering. The Markan narrative rejects the notion that God wills to eliminate suffering but is not able to do so. Up to this point in the story God has, in every case, been both able *and* willing to do so. Now, however, God's will is different from the will of the petitioner.

Another possible solution, namely the idea that suffering can be attributed to a lack of faith, is also eliminated by the narrative, as we have seen. Jesus is the exemplar of both faith and righteous obedience to God, and yet his prayer to be spared the cross is not granted by the God who could have granted it. Solutions to the problem of theodicy that amount to blaming the sufferer in order to vindicate God are not acceptable to the evangelist.

The leper had said, "If you *will*, you *are able*." The father had said, "If you *are able* . . ."—and Jesus had quickly corrected him. In his prayer Jesus says, in effect, "You *are able*, if you *will*," and when he meets with nothing but silence he makes the trusting response: "Do, then, what you *will*." This is not a philosophical solution to the problem; it is a way of coping with the tension inherent in living in covenant relationship with a God who is *able* to eliminate suffering, but does not always *will* to do so.

The power of this scene, then, is to be attributed to the evangelist's refusal to compromise the power of God in the face of suffering. The scene is terrible, not because Jesus must suffer, but because his suffering is the will of the God who is powerful enough to prevent it. What makes discipleship in the Markan community so difficult is not that it involves suffering, but that it involves suffering by healers and exorcists who participate in God's power to do the impossible. The God who wills to cleanse the leper and to set free the demon-possessed child does not always will to take away the cup of martyrdom. Those who belong to Jesus' true family do the will of God (3:35), whether it involves miraculous deliverance or unrelieved agony.

To sum up: The disciples and the audience are only too happy to do the will of God when it involves preaching, healing, and exorcism. Just before Gethsemane the audience learns that the disciples are not yet ready to do the will of God when that involves suffering. Jesus predicts that they will all fold under persecution. Then in Gethsemane the disciples fail to watch and pray, which is the proper response to suffering, according to Mark 13. The audience is confronted with the decision whether, like the disciples, they will sleep and finally flee, or whether, like Jesus, they will keep alert, pray, and choose the will of God.

The arrest scene (14:43-52) begins with the entrance of Judas and an armed mob from the religious leaders. It ends with the flight of the disciples, including an anonymous member of the group who leaves his clothes behind in his haste to escape (14:52). A change of location in 14:53 shows that a new unit begins there.

The arresting crowd is not, as in Luke, made up of the leaders of the temple police (*strategous tou heirou*—Luke 22:52, cf. John 18:3). In Mark the mob is the *ochlos* who had once been delighted with Jesus' debating victories against the religious leaders (12:37) and whose support of Jesus had previously been the major obstacle to the plots against him (12:12). Now the crowd, like Judas ("one of the twelve—14:43), has become the tool of Jesus' enemies. In the darkness (Mark's crowd has no torches; cf. John 18:3), they need a way of identifying Jesus, so Judas obliges with an exaggerated gesture of greeting (*katephilēsen auton*). Jesus' prediction of 14:18, 20 has been fulfilled.

In the confusion of the arrest one of the lackies of Jesus' enemies loses an ear to friendly fire (14:47). Unlike the authors of Luke and John, the author of Mark has not armed Jesus' disciples. Moreover, in Mark the wielder of the sword is not, as in Matthew, "one of those with Jesus," but "a bystander." The Markan Jesus does not rebuke the aggressor or heal the victim; this suggests that the writer does not regard it as deliberate retaliation or an attempt to defend Jesus, but as a detail illustrating the disorganized tumult of the scene.

The accident provides the Markan Jesus with an opportunity to clarify again for the audience that these things are happening "in order that the

Scriptures be fulfilled" (14:49). The crowd has brought all these dangerous weapons out in the dark of night instead of merely seizing Jesus by day while he was teaching because Isaiah says of God's servant that "he was counted among the lawless ones" (Isa 53:12 LXX).

Finally, the disciples fulfill Jesus' prediction of 14:27 by fleeing the arrest scene in 14:50-52. The follower who runs away naked in 14:51-52 has provoked widespread scholarly speculation and various symbolic interpretations, all of which are unnecessary. Like the inept sword-slinger in 14:47, the Gethsemane streaker has two functions in the overall flow of the narrative. He serves as a vivid illustration of the cowardice and desperate flight of the disciples as a group, and he provides a fleeting moment of comic relief within the terrible story of the passion of Jesus. The chuckle he evokes is badly needed when the disciples' bravado of 14:31 ("And they all said the same thing") is followed so quickly by their actual performance in 14:50 ("And they all abandoned him and ran away").

Interrogations of Jesus and Peter (14:53-72)

The interrogation of Jesus by the Sanhedrin (14:55-65) is followed by Peter's denial of Jesus (14:66-72). But in order to show that the two events are not sequential, but simultaneous, the author of Mark begins each story before he narrates the Sanhedrin interrogation in detail. First the audience learns that Jesus was taken from Gethsemane to the presence of the high priest, where all the religious leaders were assembled (14:53). Then the audience is told that Peter, after escaping from Gethsemane, had followed "from a distance" and managed to get into the courtyard of the building where Jesus had been taken. There he sat down among the guards, warming himself at the fire (14:54). Thus the text falls into the following pattern:

A—Jesus arrives on the scene (14:53)
B—Peter arrives on the scene (14:54)
A'—Interrogation regarding Jesus' identity (14:55-65)
B'—Interrogation regarding Peter's identity (14:66-72)

In fact, the interrogations are similar. At the risk of their lives, both Jesus and Peter confront questions about their respective identities. Their responses are very different.

The Markan account of the Sanhedrin's examination of Jesus begins with the notice that there was no evidence found on which Jesus could be condemned to death. As the audience has known all along, Jesus does the will of God, always doing good and not evil, saving life rather than taking it (3:35; 3:4).

With respect to the charge that Jesus had threatened to destroy the temple and build another "not made with hands" in three days, the narrator tells us that this charge was brought by false witnesses and that their testimony did not agree, an essential element for a capital conviction (Deut 17:6; 19:15; cf. Susanna and the Elders 52-62). The charge is false because the Markan Jesus has said no such thing in the Gospel. But although the false witnesses are lying about Jesus's words, they are making an accurate statement about the effect of his life, death, and resurrection.

Jesus has already acted in such a way as to cancel the temple cult proleptically by forbidding anyone to carry out its functions (11:15-17). Instead of making it a "house of prayer for all the nations," the religious leadership has transformed the temple into a robber's den. Therefore, upon leaving it, the Markan Jesus predicted its destruction (13:2). At his death God will rip apart the tapestry covering the entrance to the temple, further signifying its coming destruction. But even before the prediction of the temple's destruction can be fulfilled by the Romans, Jesus will create a new temple, "not made with hands," by his resurrection from the dead. That "temple" will be the eschatological Christian community in which the presence of the Risen Christ is manifested, mutual forgiveness is practiced, and the unlimited power of God is available to answer prayers (11:22-25). That "temple" is the Markan community.

Since the testimony of the false witnesses does not agree, the high priest puts the question directly to Jesus as to whether or not he made the threat against the temple as accused. Jesus says nothing. This is not the primary issue in the Gospel of Mark; the identity of Jesus is the question that has driven the narrative from the beginning.

The high priest then asks the right question—the question for which the Markan Jesus is prepared to lose his life in order to save it. Bringing together both of the royal Davidic titles, the high priest asks, "Are you the Messiah, the Son of the Blessed One?" Since "the Blessed One" is a pious circumlocation for the unpronounceable name of God, the question here is whether or not Jesus will identify himself in the same way that the narrator identified him in 1:1: Jesus, the Messiah, the Son of God. He will.

Adding his third Markan designation, Son of Man, Jesus goes on to combine Daniel 7:13 LXX with Psalm 110:1 (109 LXX) to identify himself as the Son of Man who will be seated at God's "right hand" and will "come with the clouds of heaven" (cf. 8:38; 12:35-37). There is no need for secrecy any longer. By claiming and affirming the identity he received from the heavenly voice (1:11; 9:7), the Markan Jesus demonstrates that he has embraced the self-definition over which he agonized in Gethsemane. He has chosen the will of God over his own will. To be the Messiah, Son of God, Son of Man means to suffer and die as he himself has predicted so many times in this narrative. By claiming his God-given identity, the Markan Jesus paradoxically "denies himself," as he had earlier said that all his would-be followers must do (8:34).

This is blasphemy, and for this Jesus will die (14:63-64). It is important to note that it was *not* blasphemy to claim to be the Messiah during the life-time of Jesus or even later. Bar Kokhba made the claim in connection with the Second Revolt in 132–135 and was supported in his claim by important Jewish leaders. But at the time of the writing of Mark it would have been blasphemy, or at least heresy, for a Jew to claim that Jesus, a crucified crimi-nal, was the Messiah. According to the author of Mark, of course, it was precisely Jesus' crucifixion that qualified him as Messiah.

In response to Jesus' clear admission of his God-assigned identity, the entire council agrees that he deserves to die. They humiliate Jesus and mock him as a false prophet by blindfolding him and beating him, all the while taunting, "Prophesy!" Ironically, Jesus' most recent prophecy is, at that very moment, being fulfilled in the courtyard below.

There Peter is also being examined about his identity, not by the high priest, but by one of his female servants. When confronted by the most powerful male in the religious hierarchy, Jesus is unflinching, but Peter's simultaneous confrontation, not with a religious leader, or even a soldier or guard, but a virtually powerless female servant, apparently terrifies him.

After a hard stare, the woman states the simple fact, "You, too, were with Jesus the Nazarene." Peter denies this correct naming of his identity. He was the first of those called "to be with" Jesus (3:14), but instead of denying himself to take up his cross and follow Jesus, he tries to save his life by con-cealing his identity, thus falling into the category of those who "are ashamed" of Jesus (8:38). After the first denial Peter tries to escape further confronta-tion by a change of place (14:68b), but the serving-woman is persistent. Now she brings the bystanders into the conversation (14:69). Peter's second denial is recorded, but not quoted. Finally, the bystanders themselves, recog-nizing Peter's up-country origin, push the issue as a group. This final oppor-tunity to claim his God-assigned identity is met with an oath from Peter that he does "not know the man" about whom the bystanders are speaking.

Of course, Peter is lying. But in the exquisite irony of the passion narra-tive, he is also speaking a terrible truth. He neither knows nor understands what it means to be "with" Jesus, as he has already demonstrated by falling sound asleep when Jesus asked him to keep alert and to pray. He really does not "know" in any real sense the man he himself correctly identified as the Messiah in 8:29. He has never known, never understood. He has eyes, but does not see; he has ears, but does not hear; and, sadly, his heart is hardened beyond his ability to soften it again. Peter, the Rock, has proven to be "rocky ground" (Tolbert 1989, 146). Now that tribulation and persecution have come, he has "fallen away" (4:17), like the other disciples, just as Jesus predicted (14:27, 30). By trying to save his life, Peter has, by every criterion available in this narrative, lost his chance at eschatological life in God's reign.

The crowing of the rooster reminds Peter of Jesus' prediction, but too late. All he can do is weep. The use of the imperfect tense (*eklaien*) gives the audience its last glimpse of Peter, weeping continually. He will not appear again in this story, and his words, "I do not know the man," are the last words heard from any disciple in the Gospel of Mark.

Surrender of Jesus to Pilate (15:1-15)

After the story of Peter's interrogation by the bystanders in the high priest's courtyard and his denial of his true identity as a follower of Jesus, the narrator returns to Jesus himself as the focus of the story in 15:1. His trial before Pilate begins with Jesus' being "handed over" to Pilate (15:1) and ends with his being "handed over" by Pilate to the crucifixion squad (15:15). The unit is held together by the vocabulary of "binding" (15:1, 7) and "releasing" (15:6, 9, 11, 15; Robbins 1992b, 1165-67). The Pilate trial has two scenes with similar organizational patterns:

Accusation Scene (15:1-5)
    Narrative introduction (15:1)
    Dialogue between Pilate and Jesus (15:2-5a)
    Narrative conclusion (15:5b)
Substitution Scene (15:6-15)
    Narrative introduction (15:6-8)
    Dialogue between Pilate and the crowd (15:7-14)
    Narrative conclusion (15:15)

The phrase "King of the Jews" is heard for the first time in the Gospel in Pilate's question, "Are you the King of the Jews?" Jesus' answer, "So *you* say," is ambiguous. Jesus is indeed a royal figure in this story, as previous titles have shown. He is the Davidic monarch, the Son of David who was designated Son of God at his enthronement and anointed (Messiah = anointed one) as God's agent in Israel. But when the human characters in the Gospel use the royal titles, they always betray a failure to understand the true meaning of Jesus' kingship. When Peter acknowledges Jesus as "Messiah" (8:29), he does so from a merely human point of view that puts him on the same side as "Satan" (8:33). Similarly, "King of the Jews/Israel" appears in the story only on the lips of those who misunderstand its meaning and are the opponents of God's reign: Pilate (15:2, 9, 12), the soldiers (15:18), and the religious leaders (15:32).

The Markan Jesus' assertion *su legeis* (literally, "you are saying"), with its emphasis on the second person pronoun *su*, means something like, "*You* say I am 'king,' but the label is true in a very different way from the way you use it." Those who use the word "king" in reference to Jesus do so in an entirely ironic sense in this story. Like those who demanded that he "prophesy" at the very moment that his most recent prophecy was being fulfilled (14:65), they mock him as the most unlikely of kings while they unknowingly participate in his coronation. The king who reigns, not from a throne, but from a gallows, is enthroned and acclaimed, not by his followers, who have fled in panic, but by his executioners.

Jesus' first response to Pilate's question is the last word he has to say to any human being in this narrative. When Pilate demands that he answer the charges against him, he "does not open his mouth" (Isa 53:7 LXX). According to the narrator, Pilate, the representative of the "many [gentile] nations," is "amazed" by Jesus (Isa 52:15 LXX: *thaumasontai*; cf. 15:5: *thaumazein*).

The second scene of the Pilate trial is heavy with irony. Interestingly, a Roman custom of releasing a prisoner at Passover is attested nowhere outside the Gospel passion narratives, though prisoners were sometimes released in connection with other festivals in antiquity (Wilkins 1992, 607). But the passion tradition supplied the author of Mark with the name of a prisoner believed to have been released and replaced by Jesus: Barabbas. The author, in turn, supplied the members of the audience who may have been unfamiliar with Aramaic with the means of interpreting this name: "bar" means "son of" (10:46) and "abba" means "father" (14:36).

Thus, Jesus, the one who saves life (3:4; 4:35–5:43) and is the beloved son (1:11; 9:7) of the One he calls "Abba" (14:36) will die in the place of one who is also "son of Abba," but a murderer. The crowd that had recently appeared to stand between Jesus and his opponents (14:2) now howls for his crucifixion (15:13, 14). They prefer the freedom-fighter who embraces violence in the name of the revolution (15:7) to the more ambiguous warrior-king who destroys only demons and pigs, speaks in riddles, and would rather die than do his own will (14:36)—let alone the will of the mob. Jesus' opponents had feared the crowd for nothing. Like the disciples, they have abandoned Jesus to his enemies (Malbon 1986a, 123).

Mocking and Crucifixion of Jesus (15:16-32)

Continuing the irony so characteristic of the passion narrative, the author of Mark appears to have based the next section (15:16-32) on the general pattern of the Roman triumphal procession (For what follows, see Schmidt 1995). The Roman triumphal procession developed out of Greek and Etruscan cultic rituals in which the king, representing a god (Dionysos or Zeus), was borne in a procession that ended with the sacrifice of a bull and the epiphany of the king as god to the accompaniment of a ritual shout from the people. According to Schmidt, the ceremony temporarily lost its connection both with the divinity and with the king during the period in which the Roman Senate granted triumphs to successful generals. However, "the triumph [became] the exclusive privilege of the emperor from 20 BC onward." and "for the mid-first century tyrants Gaius and Nero, this privilege brought the triumph together with the notion of the imperator's own deification. Thus, the ceremony became reconnected with its roots as a display of the ruler as a god" (4).

On the occasion of a triumph the entire Praetorian guard was called together around dawn as preparation for the procession (Josephus, *War* 7.5.4.123; Dio Cassius 63.4.3; Plutarch, *Aem.* 34.4). According to Mark, after Pilate's decision the soldiers led Jesus into the *praitōrion* and called together "the whole cohort." Markan chronology places this event after "early in the morning" (15:1) and before "the third hour" (15:25; [9 AM]).

The soldiers are portrayed as dressing Jesus like a king and mocking him as "King of the Jews" in 15:17-19. The Markan narrator specifies the color of the cloak as purple (15:17, 20). A color permitted only to the nobility would not have been owned by any soldier such as the ones portrayed in this scene, but it was precisely the color of the cloak worn by the emperor in a triumphal procession, along with a crown (Livy, *Epit.* 10.7.9; 30.15.11; Dio Cassius 62.4.3-6.2; 62.20.2-6; Dionysus of Halicarnassus 5.47.2-3; Suetonius *Tiberius* 17; *Nero* 25; Plutarch *Aem.* 34.4; Josephus, *War* 7.5.4.123-57). In Jesus' case the crown is made of thorns (15:17). The mocking homage of the soldiers corresponds ironically to the usual shouts of approval received by a triumphator. By the time this Gospel was written, Rome had seen Caligula hailed as the god Jupiter himself (Suetonius, *Caligula*, 22.3).

The procession itself, already foreshadowed by 11:7-10, is not described here in detail, except for the remarkable appearance of Simon of Cyrene, identified for the Markan audience as "the father of Alexander and Rufus," (15:21), people who must have been known to the audience. Simon, a resident of Africa, is a conscript, a victim, like Jesus, of the brutality of Roman soldiers (Crowder, 1997). In the imagery of the triumphal procession Simon corresponds to the person depicted in artistic renderings of triumphs who carries the axe that will be used to kill the sacrificial victim.

The Roman triumphal procession ended at the temple of Jupiter on the Capitoline hill, so named because of the legend that a human head had been found there. This led to prophecies that "the place in which you found the head shall be the head of all Italy" (Dionysus of Halicarnassus 4.59-61). The author of Mark translates the place of Jesus' crucifixion, Golgotha, as "the place of the head" (*kranion*, not "skull" as in most English translations). The author of Mark has already alluded in 12:10 to Psalm 118 in which the rejected stone becomes the "head" of the final edifice; this is also a passage about a king's procession up to the temple altar after success in battle (Ps 118:19-27).

A few further allusions to the triumphal procession complete the irony of this motif. The Markan Jesus is offered "wine mixed with myrrh," but he refuses it (15:23). No record can be found that myrrhed wine was understood to dull pain, but Pliny records that it was prized as the finest of delicacies (*Nat Hist* 14.92), enjoyed by royalty, but not affordable for the common people. Again we have a historical improbability that functions as a part of the soldiers' mockery. Some members of the audience might have recalled that at the moment of sacrifice at the end of a triumph, a cup of wine was handed to the one performing the sacrifice; he did not drink it, but poured it out as a libation to the gods. Similarly, signs proclaiming the triumphator's achievements are carried in procession with him, and when at last he stands on the Capitoline hill, raised high above his adoring subjects, loud acclamations attest to their respect for his power. Jesus, by contrast, is mocked by those standing below his cross (15:29-32), and the placard announcing his kingship (15:26) is not an accolade, but a criminal charge. The places of honor on the right and the left that had been coveted by James and John are occupied by two dying criminals.

To sum up: In this play upon the motif of the Roman triumph, the Markan Jesus is both victorious king and sacrificial victim. The soldiers are portrayed as mocking him as a properly attired victor about to begin his procession through the streets; they capture a provincial to play the role of the bearer of the instrument of sacrifice; they lead him to "the hill of the head," where they offer him the traditional libation cup and place his royal title above his head as they elevate him above the bystanders, flanked by his associates. But all of this humiliation reveals to those who "have eyes to see" the truth about Jesus according to Mark's Gospel. He *is* the divine warrior-king, and this *is* the moment of his triumph. Here the king gives his life as a ransom for the welfare of his people. Here he saves others by refusing to save himself.

Allusions to the Psalms, the Wisdom of Solomon, and Deutero-Isaiah begin to sound in the ears of the audience as the allusions to the Roman triumph taper off. This narrator never neglects either his Jewish or his gentile constituency for long. The division of Jesus' clothes by gambling is a clear reference to Psalm 22:18. The mockers at the foot of the cross recall verses 6-7 of the same psalm, along with Wis 2:17-20 and 3:5, where the ordeal of the innocent righteous one is vividly portrayed. By his crucifixion between two bandits, as by his baptism among sinners, Jesus is "numbered among the transgressors" (Isa 53:12).

Death of Jesus (15:33-39)

The only actual quote from Psalm 22 occurs in 15:34, when the Markan Jesus cries out the first words of the Psalm, addressing the one he had called "Abba" now as "My God," and calling on God for an explanation for his utter abandonment and desolation. This should *not* be understood as a mere introduction to the expression of trust that ends the Psalm. This interpretation is ruled out by the way in which the Markan author arranges the references to Psalm 22 in reverse order, placing end stress on the Psalm's opening cry of desolation (Robbins 1992b, 1175-80).

These last words of Jesus are a prayer, but they contrast sharply with his prayer of submission in 14:36. The evangelist apparently believes that there is no contradiction between commitment to doing the will of God and the anger and abandonment one feels when God's will leads to unbearable suffering and Godforsakenness. The Markan Jesus models the expression of honest anguish in prayer to God; this would have been especially important to Christians under persecution who may have found enough strength to confess their faith, but not enough to remain stoically silent during torture.

But like so many other things he has said, these final words of the Markan Jesus meet with misunderstanding. Some of the bystanders think that he is calling on Elijah rather than on God (15:35). In addition, Elijah's role is interpreted in terms of his miracle-working power, whereas the Gospel of Mark understands Elijah/John the baptizer as Jesus' predecessor in rejection and suffering (6:14-29; 9:11-13).

The darkness in 15:33 recalls Isaiah 13:9-10 and 50:3. But a knowledge of the Scripture would not be required for an understanding of the significance of the darkness and the ripping of the temple veil. In the Greco-Roman and Hellenistic Jewish worldview, the births and deaths of important people, especially royalty, were accompanied by portents, often involving astronomical phenomena. The assassination of Julius Caesar was associated with portentous daytime darkness by Pliny (*Natural History* 2.30), Josephus (*Antiquities* 14.12.3) and Plutarch (*Caesar* 69.4).

The darkening of the sun is particularly important in light of the agency of Roman soldiers in Jesus' crucifixion. Throughout the imperial legions the most popular deity was Mithras, "the invincible Sun." Since the Mithras cult was a mystery religion, detailed certainty about Mithraic rites is not possible; nevertheless, examination of the paintings and carvings in excavated worship sites and of the fragmentary literary evidence yields some information.

Mithras was worshipped in natural caves or in temples built to resemble caves, the ceilings of which were decorated to symbolize the vault of heaven. The god's most famous exploit was the killing of a mythological bull, whose death resulted in life and fertility for the world. The sacrifice of a bull, then, became a central feature of Mithraism. The prominence of meals in the cult suggests that "normally the bull's flesh was consumed and its blood drunk," but on some occasions bread and wine were substituted for the flesh and blood. Soldiers who were initiated into the cult became "brothers" of each other and "sons of the Father," or local cult leader. Nero was the first of several Roman emperors whose initiation into the cult of Mithras is recorded, and thereafter, Nero "insisted on being worshipped as the Sun-god" (Vermaseren 1963, 102, 131, 24 and *passim*).

The Markan darkness at midday would have indicated to the audience that the unconquerable Sun worshipped by the soldiers who were executing Jesus had indeed been conquered. The death of the king who was not recognized by any of the onlookers was identified as royalty by the portents that always accompanied the death of a ruler.

The offer of sour wine recalls Ps 69:21: "for my thirst they gave me vinegar to drink" (NRSV). The irony is heightened for those members of the audience who would have been familiar with the next verses of Psalm 69: "Let their eyes be darkened so that they cannot see" (23a). Spiritual blindness, first introduced in 4:12, characterizes the bystanders who see Jesus without understanding and cannot comprehend his words, his actions, or the significance of his passion (Marcus 1992b, 183-84).

Jesus' death is portrayed in such a way as to recall the moment of his baptism. The Spirit went into Jesus then (1:10, *to pneuma . . . eis auton*); now the dying Jesus expels his spirit (15:37, 39—*exepneusen*) with a loud cry. At the same time a portent occurs at the temple inside the city walls. There was an ornate tapestry hanging in front of the outer doors of the temple, on which, according to Josephus, "was portrayed a panorama of the heavens" (*War* 5.5.4.212-14). This tapestry is ripped apart (*eschisthē*) from above by unseen hands (15:38), just as the heavens had been ripped apart (*schizomenous*) at the baptism (1:10) prior to the descent of the Spirit into Jesus (Ulansey 1991).

The tearing of the temple tapestry has at least two functions in Mark. First, it signifies the royal stature of Jesus; a Greco-Roman audience would expect the death of a ruler to be accompanied not only by astronomical portents, but also by supernatural events associated with cultic places or images. According to Suetonius, Tiberius dreamed on his last birthday that a statue of Apollo spoke to him, announcing that he would not be present for its dedication in the temple of Augustus (*Tiberius*, 74). The statue of Jupiter at Olympia laughed aloud before the death of Caligula (*Caligula*, 57.1), and a statue of Jupiter was struck by lightning before the death of Domitian (*Domitian*, 15.2). The Lares fell to the ground before the death of Nero (*Nero*, 46.2). Evil omens connected with sacrifices portended the deaths of Julius Caesar (81.2), Caligula (57.4), Galba (19.1), and Titus (10.2). The tearing of the temple veil at Jesus' death would have meant to the Markan audience that this was indeed the death of a king.

Second, the destruction of the veil is the proleptic destruction of the temple, the cancellation of the cult that had been prophetically enacted by the Markan Jesus in 11:15-16 and explicitly predicted by him in 13:2. No longer is the presence of God to be found in the temple; instead, God will be worshipped in the temple "not made with hands," as the false witness had unwittingly prophesied. The positive aspect of the tearing of the curtain is the release of the divine presence into the world.

The response of the centurion to Jesus' death is a "confession" only in the ears of Mark's audience. On the level of the story it is a sarcastic comment on the lips of a jaded professional executioner who has just watched one more Jewish peasant die calling on his God: "Oh sure—*that's* a son of Zeus all right!" (15:39; Fowler 1991, 205-208). The comment is not a response to the tearing of the temple curtain, since the centurion is portrayed as facing the cross, not the temple. His attitude is the same as that of the others at the foot of the cross: if Jesus had really been anyone special, he would have been translated to heaven before dying such a shameful death (Origen, *CCel* 2.68).

Ironically, however, the centurion represents all the gentiles who will hear the gospel and make a sincere confession as a result of Jesus' death (13:10; cf. Isa 52:15; 2:1-4; 56:6-8). Their inclusion has already been prefigured in the proclamation of the gentile man whom Jesus freed from demonic oppression (5:20) and in the insistence of the gentile woman that Jesus is the "Lord" at whose table even the "dogs" will be satisfied (7:24-30).

Immediately after the remark of the centurion, the narrator introduces the other witnesses to Jesus' death. A group of women disciples who had "followed" and "served" Jesus in Galilee had also followed him to Jerusalem (15:40-41). These two important word groups, "follow/come after" and "serve/servant," are consistently used by the Gospel writer to characterize a faithful disciple of Jesus. The first four disciples "followed/came after" Jesus (1:18, 20), as did Levi and other tax collecters (2:14, 15). In 8:34 Jesus had invited anyone in the group made up of "the crowd with his disciples" to deny self, prepare for martyrdom, and "follow" him. The invitation to "follow" was issued to the rich man in 10:21, but rejected, whereas Bartimaeus, after his sight was miraculously restored, ignored Jesus' dismissive "Go!" and chose instead to "follow" Jesus "on the way" to the cross. As Malbon has pointed out, the crowd also "follows" Jesus (Malbon 1986a, 107-108), so following alone is not enough.

The Markan Jesus has predicted in 9:35 and 10:43 that those among his followers who have been seeking precedence and greatness will, at some point in the future, experience a reversal of their priorities and become "servants." The audience now learns that women followers of Jesus—namely, Mary Magdalene, Mary the mother of James and Joses, and Salome—had been in the habit of "serving" Jesus during his own time of service in Galilee (15:41; note the imperfect *diēkonoun*, suggesting habitual or repeated action).

Like Peter (14:54), these women have kept an eye on events "from afar." They may have buckled under pressure and fled like the rest (14:50-52), but they have slunk back to the scene of the crucifixion and watched Jesus' death at a distance. By naming them here, the author of Mark confirms an impression created through the story as a whole. That impression is that the group of Jesus' disciples was always larger than the traditional "twelve," who were designated "apostles" (3:14; 6:30), named in 3:16-19 and sent out in 6:7-13. What remains to be seen is whether these women disciples may even yet be prepared to deny themselves by claiming their identity as followers of Jesus and act in faithful witness despite the possibility of losing their lives for the sake of the good news (8:34-45).

Burial of Jesus (15:42-47)

Narrative notices of the watching women form a frame around the Markan account of Jesus' burial (*theōrousai*, 15:40; *etheōroun*, 15:47). In order for this account to be understood in its Markan context, it is necessary to distinguish it from the burial accounts of the other Gospels, which are quite different from Mark's.

In all four Gospels Joseph of Arimathea takes responsibility for aquiring Jesus' body from the Romans. The author of Mark describes Joseph as "a respected member of the council, who was also himself looking for the kingdom of God." In Matthew and John this person is described as a disciple of Jesus and the author of Luke explains that Joseph "had not consented to [the Sanhedrin's] purpose and deed." In Mark, however, Joseph is understood as one of those who condemned Jesus to death (14:64, "*All* of them") and handed him over to Pilate for execution (15:1, "the *whole* council"). The fact that Joseph is still "looking for the kingdom of God" shows that he, like so many in this story, has missed the whole point. God's reign began to burst into history before his very eyes, but he condemned the messenger and kept looking for a kingdom more to his liking. He is not a secret disciple, but an opponent, and the author of Mark uses him to draw the contrast between the burial of John the Baptist by his disciples (6:29) and the burial of Jesus by one of his enemies (For what follows, see Brown 1988).

This, in fact, is why Pilate is willing to give Joseph the corpse at all. The author of Mark has portrayed Pilate as perpetuating the mistaken notion that Jesus had attempted violent revolution against Rome by having the charge against him stated as "King of the Jews." Such revolutionaries would not have been handed over to their families or friends for burial, since funerals of freedom fighters, then as now, tended to stir up the masses against the oppressive government. Joseph's initial reluctance, signaled by *tolmēsas* (15:43), portrays him as fearful of being taken for a sympathizer, but he need not have worried; the Markan Pilate has no qualms about turning the corpse over to a collaborator from among the religious elite.

But why would Joseph bother? He is portrayed as caring nothing for Jesus, but caring a great deal about the requirements of Torah. Deut 21:22-23 specifies that a criminal who has been impaled must be buried before sundown, lest the land be defiled. The time is short (15:42), and the next day is a Sabbath, so Joseph has little time to do his pious duty. Fortunately for him, the other victims are not yet dead, so he has only one burial to accomplish before dark. It takes a good deal of discussion before Pilate believes that Jesus is already dead, but the testimony of the centurion convinces him (15:44-45). He gives the corpse to Joseph, who hurriedly wraps it up without either washing or anointing it and tosses it into one of the holes cut into the rock nearby for just such a purpose. According to Mark, the tomb was not one Joseph had made for himself (Matt), or even a new one (Matt, Luke, John); it was merely convenient. Having rolled a stone against the opening, Joseph exits the scene and the story.

Epilogue
The Good News Begins Again

(Mark 16:1-8)

The ending of Mark has been the subject of fierce debate and not a little revision through the centuries. Before engaging the issues it is appropriate to study the ending as it stands in the oldest and most reliable manuscripts of the Gospel: 16:1-8.

The author follows the scene of Jesus' burial with more of the time references that have marked the passion narrative. The introductory narrative sandwiches the action of the women among the time references, creating some suspense:

The sabbath having gone by,
> Mary Magdalene, Mary the mother of James, and Salome brought aromatics so that they might go and anoint him.
Very early, the first of the week
> they came to the tomb,
the sun having risen.

After the tolling of the hours during the crucifixion (15:25, 33) and the previous references to darkness (15:33) and evening (15:42), the audience is no doubt relieved to be in the light again. But they cannot be very encouraged about the women's stated purpose, since the audience knows that Jesus has already been anointed for his burial (14:8) and, according to the passion predictions, the time of the resurrection is getting close.

The women disciples' conversation on the way to the tomb suggests that resurrection is the last thing on their minds. They are worrying about how to move the stone from the entrance to the tomb (16:3). Since Joseph had put it there by himself (15:46), their concern seems a bit disingenuous (van Iersel 1988, 204) and may be intended to emphasize the absence of the male disciples. But they find the stone rolled back from the entrance, so they walk right in to start the anointing.

The final section of Mark is framed by the movements of the women. In 16:5 they go into the tomb; in 16:8 they go out and flee from the tomb. Within this frame only two things are narrated about the women: they *see*, not Jesus, but a young man in a white robe, and they *are astonished*. All the talking, however, is done by the young man, who is dressed in white like the transfigured Jesus (9:3) and has therefore been taken to be a heavenly messenger by many interpreters, including the author of Matthew.

The young man, like the audience, knows that there is no cause for astonishment (16:6). Jesus of Nazareth, the crucified one, is not in the tomb because he has been raised. The women should have known that, but now it has been confirmed. The messenger now conveys their assignment; they are to go and tell.

If amazement is not the appropriate response to the empty tomb, it certainly is the appropriate response to what comes next, because the entire fabric of cause and effect so carefully woven by the narrator thus far is ripped apart by the words of the messenger: "Go tell his disciples—even Peter—that he is going ahead of you into Galilee; there you will see him, just as he said to you." The disciples' cowardice has been forgiven. Even Peter is to be included, despite his having proven to be too rocky to bear fruit, too eager to save his life, too ready to deny his identity as a follower of Jesus, too ashamed of Jesus and his words and therefore one of the adulterous and sinful generation of whom the Son of Man should be ashamed on the day of judgment. The news this Gospel has to tell is much better than Jesus' initial statement that "the reign of God is at hand." The truly astonishing, amazing good news is, "even Peter." Even Peter is to be included in the story about to begin anew in Galilee, the place of service and witness.

This message, though shocking, is thoroughly consistent with the gospel according to Isaiah. In LXX Isaiah 42:16 and 43:8 God had announced:

> I will lead the blind by a way they do not know, I will turn their darkness into light, . . . These deeds I will do, and I will not forsake them . . . I lead out the people who are blind, yet have eyes, who are deaf, yet have ears.

The author of Mark had learned from his reading of Isaiah that the blind and deaf would be led out *despite* their obduracy—not because they have done the best they could, not because others were more stubborn and malevolent than they, not even because they have repented and become enlightened people, but only because they are and always have been the people called by God to belong to God. And so the author of Mark ends his story on the same note: the Markan Jesus goes ahead of the still blind and faithless disciples, even the rock-headed Peter, to the place where they will finally see, just as Isaiah and Jesus had promised (For a detailed defense of this interpretation, see Dowd 1995).

The message given to the women to deliver is related in indirect discourse rather than direct discourse, as all manuscripts except Bezae and one Latin codex confirm. This means that the women disciples are included in the second-person plural pronouns of the message: " . . . that he is going before *you* into Galilee; there *you* will see him, just as he told *you*." If the author had intended otherwise, he would have written either, "tell his disciples, . . .*I* am going before you . . ." (so D, k), or, "tell his disciples . . . that he is going before *them*" (cf. Matt 28:10).

After all the commands to keep silent about things that would seem impossible to conceal, such as the raising of Jairus' daughter, finally a group of disciples is given a straightforward command to go and tell. "And they went out and fled from the tomb, for trembling and amazement had taken hold of them; and they said nothing to anyone, for they were afraid" (16:8).

This ending was regarded as so unsatisfactory by ancient readers that they composed alternatives with more closure, which may be found as the rest of verse 8 ("the shorter ending") and verses 9-20 ("the longer ending") in most translations. Obviously there are four choices for the interpreter: (1) the intended ending was originally 16:8a; (2) another ending was intended, but never completed; (3) the original ending has been lost; or (4) one of the extant additions is original.

Everything that is extant after "they were afraid" (*ephobounto gar*) must be ruled inauthentic on text-critical grounds. The oldest Greek manuscripts lack the shorter and longer endings, and the ending at 16:8 is attested by Clement, Origen, Eusebius, and Jerome. Some manuscripts that have one of the additions have it marked as spurious (Metzger 1994, 102-105).

Choices (2) and (3) cannot be ruled out because they are not arguments. They do not claim to know what the ending was, merely that 16:8a *cannot* plausibly be the intended ending of an ancient document. Advocates of (2) and (3) point out that only in recent times has 16:8a even been considered a plausible ending, and this must be seen as an anachronistic judgment influenced by modern writers who end their works with ellipsis dots.

However, Lee Magness has demonstrated that to read 16:8a as the intended ending of Mark is far from anachronistic, since numerous ancient works, both among Old Testament documents and in the corpus of Greek literature end in similarly inconclusive ways (Magness 1986). In fact, there are critical problems with the endings of both the *Iliad* and the *Odyssey*, which suggest that early readers of those epics were unsatisfied with the unfinished appearance of the works. In addition, Virgil's *Aeneid* ends abruptly on "a note of tension," which provoked a number of more satisfactory sequels (Magness 1986, 28, 31-36; see also Cox 1993).

If the author of Mark intended to close the Gospel at 16:8, why would he have done so? Certainly the fact that he is able to tell the story at all means that somehow someone told another that Jesus had been raised from the dead. The resurrection and the power of the risen Lord in the community of faith is the premise that underlies the entire story from beginning to end. Besides, the Markan Jesus had predicted in 14:28 that he would go before the disciples into Galilee. He had also predicted that those who sought power during his life would eventually become servants of others (9:35; 10:43), that James and John would at some point stop running and face their martyrdom (10:39); that Peter, James, John, and Andrew would have to stand trial for their confession (13:9, 11); and that the good news would be proclaimed to all nations (13:10).

None of these predictions were fulfilled during the story prior to 16:8, but the audience knows that because Jesus is a reliable predictor, all of these promises, like the promise of the baptism in the Holy Spirit (1:8) will certainly be fulfilled. The audience may know that some have been fulfilled between the time of the story and the time of their hearing of the story. So it is obvious that the author did not mean this strange ending to convey the message that word of the resurrection never reached Peter or the other male disciples.

Although it is impossible to be certain of the intentions of a long-dead author, it is possible to speak about the likely effect of such an ending on an ancient audience. For one thing, it must have been disappointing. The women disciples had appeared more or less out of nowhere in 15:40 and offered the audience the expectation of a happy ending involving some response to the demands of discipleship other than fear and flight. That expectation was disappointed in 16:8. On the other hand, the many earlier promises to the disciples and, implicitly to the audience, offer hope (Juel 1994, 107-21). Since the women do not obey the young man's command within the story, the audience is left with the responsibility to pick up the baton that the women seem to have dropped. If anyone is to go and tell about the resurrection, if anyone is to meet Jesus in the various Galilees where people need healing, deliverance, and good news, there would seem to be no one left to do those things except the audience.

Certainly the audience can have had no illusions about their superiority to the disciples in the story, whether male or female, because if they have learned anything it is not to boast of one's faithfulness to Jesus and not to count oneself an insider until the story is over. But they have witnessed God's ability to do "that which is impossible for humans," and they have also been stunned by God's amazing grace in response to cowardice and failure. So there is reason for hope, for even Peter, for even the audience, for even new audiences who hear the story told yet again, and who stand bewildered and frightened at the door of the empty tomb with nothing to do except to go and tell.